# ELEMENTARY STATISTICAL METHODS IN PSYCHOLOGY AND EDUCATION, SECOND EDITION

## Study Manual

Paul J. Blommers
Robert A. Forsyth
The University of Iowa

UNIVERSITY PRESS OF AMERICA

LANHAM • NEW YORK • LONDON

**Study Manual**

# ELEMENTARY STATISTICAL METHODS
## in Psychology and Education

**SECOND EDITION**

# Contents

# Contents

# Preface

This study manual provides a large number of exercises to accompany the material in *Elementary Statistical Methods in Psychology and Education* (2nd edition). The nature and purpose of the text and this manual are described in the Preface to the First Edition and in Chapter 1 of the text. Students using this manual should observe closely the remarks made in Section 1.4 of the text.

While much of the content of the study manual for the first edition of the text has been retained, many new problems have been added. Given the large number of problems in this manual, instructors may wish to exercise some selection in the problems assigned.

The problems are numbered in such a way as to indicate the section of the text which treats the major concept involved. The first two numbers given identify chapter and section within chapter respectively. The last number is simply the number of the problem within the chapter. Of course, many problems are based on concepts treated in more than one section of the text. Only the most directly related section is identified in the above manner. Teachers using these materials with a minimal course (see the Preface to the 2nd edition of the text, p. xvii) will find this numbering scheme particularly convenient in identifying exercises based on omitted sections of the text.

The pages of this manual are perforated and may be torn out of the book, should instructors desire to collect the students' work for checking or evaluation. However, it is essential that any such material so collected be promptly returned to the student, since some of the exercises are based on data presented in the earlier chapters. Also, as a student's grasp of the subject develops, new questions requiring added background and a greater depth of understanding ought properly to be asked about previously presented problem situations; again, this must necessarily lead to frequent reference to earlier exercises. For these reasons—not to mention the fact that a completely worked manual constitutes, to a degree, a second text of the student's own writing—it is imperative that students make provision for preserving in some manner any pages of the manual which they may have to remove.

*Paul J. Blommers*
*Robert A. Forsyth*

**Study Manual**

# ELEMENTARY STATISTICAL METHODS
## in Psychology and Education

SECOND EDITION

# 1

# Introduction

**1.1.1** What is the basic purpose of statistical methods?

........................................................................................................................

........................................................................................................................

**1.1.2** Most of the illustrative examples in the text come from the fields of psychology and education. Why is this not a severe limitation of the text?

........................................................................................................................

........................................................................................................................

........................................................................................................................

**1.1.3** As noted in the text, the following three categories represent one scheme for classifying statistical techniques.

    **1** Descriptive statistics
    **2** Statistical inference
    **3** Prediction and regression

Three hypothetical situations are described below. Each situation raises a specific problem to be solved. For each situation you are asked to specify which of the above categories includes the statistical techniques that would be needed to solve the problem.

**a** The student government organization at a particular university of 25,000 students wants to assess the attitudes of the students toward current political issues and social questions. (For example, should marijuana be legalized?) The organization decides to gather the information by interviewing students. Since it is impossible to interview all 25,000 students, a sample of 200 students is selected and then interviewed. The student government wishes to use the data gathered from the 200 students to make statements about the attitudes of all 25,000 students. To accomplish this purpose, the organization will need to use statistical techniques from which category?

........................................................................

**b** All fifth-grade students in a school have taken a reading comprehension test. A faculty meeting is to be held at which the principal will use the test results to describe the performances of these fifth-grade students. The principal will need to use statistical techniques from which category?

........................................................................

**c** In education, *underachievers* are sometimes defined as students whose predicted achievement is higher than their observed achievement. The predicted achievement is frequently found by using an aptitude measure such as IQ to make the prediction. To identify underachievers in this way, statistical techniques from which category would be used?

.................................................................

**1.2.4** Which of the following aspects of statistics will be emphasized most in the text?

    **a** Mathematical basis of statistics
    **b** Computational procedures
    **c** Interpretation of statistical techniques

.................................................................

**1.2.5** The *correlation coefficient* is a number used to describe the relationship between pairs of scores. The three questions listed below are related to this number. Which of these questions will be answered in greatest detail in the text?

    **1** What computational procedures do I use to compute this number?
    **2** What factors must I consider in interpreting this number?
    **3** What mathematical theory serves as the basis for this number?

.................................................................

**1.2.6** What degree of mathematical sophistication is expected of students reading the text?

.................................................................

.................................................................

**1.3.7** Is the text better classified as a reference text or as an instructional text?

.................................................................

**1.3.8** Although the text does not present a wide variety of topics, it is a rather long book. Why?

.................................................................

.................................................................

.................................................................

**1.3.9** What are the two major purposes of this study manual?

.................................................................

.................................................................

.................................................................

.................................................................

**1.3.10** Which of the following two procedures is recommended by the authors of the text?

>   **1** Do all the study manual problems for a specific chapter after the entire chapter has been read.
>   **2** Do the study manual problems for each section of the chapter after that section has been read.

..............................................................................

**1.4.11** Should you expect to achieve complete comprehension of the material in the text after a first reading?

..............................................................................

**1.4.12** Why do the authors recommend that a student work through the illustrative examples given in the text?

..............................................................................

..............................................................................

..............................................................................

# 2

# Nature of Behavioral Science Data

**2.1.1**[1] Find a recent issue of a journal in your field of interest (clinical psychology, reading, etc.). Look through the journal and note several of the variables that have been identified. Assign two possible values to the variables you have listed.

|   | Variables | Values |
|---|-----------|--------|
| **1** | ................................................ | ............................................ |
| **2** | ................................................ | ............................................ |
| **3** | ................................................ | ............................................ |
| **4** | ................................................ | ............................................ |
| **5** | ................................................ | ............................................ |

**2.2.2** Below are examples of variables that you might encounter in the psychological and educational literature. In the blank provided following each statement, print an O or a U depending on whether the variable is ordered or unordered.

**a** Arithmetic achievement .................................................

**b** Region of country
(Northeast, Southeast, etc.) .................................................

**c** Chronological age .................................................

**d** Parent's occupation .................................................

**e** Intelligence .................................................

**f** Creativity .................................................

**g** Handicapped classification
(cerebral-palsied, blind,
etc.) .................................................

**h** Religious preference .................................................

---

[1] *Remember:* The first two numbers identify the section of the text that treats the major concept involved in the exercise. Thus, the concepts involved in 2.1.1 are contained in Section 2.1. The last number is merely the number of the exercise within the chapter.

**2.2.3** Label the variables you identified in 2.1.1 as either ordered (O) or unordered (U).

**1** ............... **2** ............... **3** ............... **4** ............... **5** ...............

**2.3.4** Assume a researcher wants to measure a student's "enthusiasm for the acquisition of knowledge." Identify two possible ways you might define this conceptual trait in order to measure it in an experimental situation.

.................................................................................................................................

.................................................................................................................................

.................................................................................................................................

.................................................................................................................................

**2.3.5** Assume an instrument has been developed to measure a student's "attitude toward his or her peers." The student is given a list of statements and marks whether each statement is true or untrue for him or her. Two statements might be:

**1** Other children bother me when I'm trying to do my school work.
**2** Other children often get me into trouble at school.

One characteristic of an instrument of this type that would be of concern to the researcher is the consistency of the responses over a period of time. For example, are the scores obtained on Monday consistent with the scores obtained on Friday (assuming students do not remember their responses from Monday)? Given the nature of the attribute under study, why would the researcher have this concern?

.................................................................................................................................

.................................................................................................................................

.................................................................................................................................

**2.3.6** An essay entitled "Of Imaginary Numbers" that appeared in the August 2, 1971 issue of *Time* magazine supplied the following data.

Statement: It has been estimated that heroin addicts in New York steal $2 billion to $5 billion worth of goods each year. How was this figure estimated? The following procedure was reported.

**1** Estimated number of addicts = 100,000
**2** Estimated average habit cost per day = $30
**3** According to appropriate arithmetic based on the data in steps 1 and 2, estimated need for a year = $1.1 billion
**4** Since a thief generally sells stolen property to a fence for about one-fourth of its value, total worth of the stolen goods = (4)($1.1 billion) = $4.4 billion

However, as *Time* reported, ". . . the value of all the stolen goods in New York does not amount to nearly that much."

How does the above example illustrate the phrase, "Garbage in, garbage out"?

...............................................................................................................

...............................................................................................................

...............................................................................................................

**2.3.7** Assume you are interested in studying the factors that are related to reading achievement. You have found two articles dealing with the relationship between students' creativity and reading achievement. In the first study a high relationship was reported between creativity test scores (as measured by the XYZ test) and scores on the Stanford Reading Achievement Test. In the second article only a moderate relationship was reported between creativity (as measured by the ABC test) and the Metropolitan Reading Achievement Test.

Using the concepts discussed in Section 2.3, provide one possible explanation of why the relationship reported was high in one article but only moderate in the other.

...............................................................................................................

...............................................................................................................

**2.4.8** Below are examples of numerical data that might be collected. In the blanks following each statement, print a C or a D depending on whether the data described ought properly to be interpreted as continuous or discrete.

**a** Numbers of word meanings correctly identified on a high-school-level vocabulary test            ...........................................

**b** Salaries of U.S. government employees            ...........................................

**c** Acreages of Iowa farms            ...........................................

**d** Ages of students in high schools with enrollments of less than 100            ...........................................

**e** Numbers of words read per minute on a test of reading rate            ...........................................

**f** Percentages of males enrolled in junior colleges located in Pacific Coast states            ...........................................

**g** Incidences of diagnosed
poliomyelitis in U.S. cities
of over 10,000 during a
certain time period ..................................................................

**h** Tonnages of ships in
U.S. merchant marine ..................................................................

**i** Numbers of nonsense
syllables recalled one day
after being learned on a
test of memory ..................................................................

**j** Depth of hypnosis as
indicated by each subject's
responses to seven
hypnotic suggestions ..................................................................

**k** Amenability to extinction
of a conditioned eye-
blink response as indicated
by the number of blinks
during 10 extinction trials
administered to each of 50
conditioned subjects ..................................................................

**2.4.9** Label the variables you identified in 2.1.1 as either continuous (C)
or discrete (D).

**1** ................    **2** ................    **3** ................    **4** ................    **5** ................

# 3

# The Frequency Distribution

**3.2.1a** What information is in part lost when numerical data are organized into a grouped frequency distribution?

..................................................................................................................................

**b** To what aspect of the grouped frequency distribution is the amount of this loss related?

..................................................................................................................................

**c** What information may be gained (at least in certain situations) as a result of organizing numerical data into a grouped frequency distribution?

..................................................................................................................................

..................................................................................................................................

..................................................................................................................................

**3.2.2** In general terms, what are the two most important things to take into consideration in defining the classes of a frequency distribution?

..................................................................................................................................

..................................................................................................................................

..................................................................................................................................

**3.3.3** The questions listed below are items selected from a questionnaire addressed to high school teachers. Different teachers filled out the questionnaire at different times during the school year. The numbers in parentheses are the answers provided by one of the teachers. For each of these numbers, if the data are continuous, write the real limits of the *unit* interval that contains the number. If the data are discrete, simply copy the number. For example, does the number 11 (item **a**) fall in the unit interval extending from 10.5 to 11.5, or from 11 to 11.99, or from 10.01 to 11; or does it fall at the discrete point 11? In each case, give the reason for your selection.

**a** How many years of teaching experience have you had?

(11) ..........................................Reason: ...........................................

..................................................................................................................................

**b** What is your age in years? (35) ..................................................

Reason: ................................................................................

...................................................................................

**c** How many brothers and sisters do you have?

(6) ......................................Reason: .........................................

...................................................................................

**d** On the average, how many hours do you spend per week (outside of school hours) in study and preparation for teaching?

(15) ....................................Reason: ..........................................

...................................................................................

**e** How many years did your father attend school? (Answer by writing in the blank the last grade he attended. Consider the freshman year in college as grade 13, the sophomore year as grade 14, etc.)

(7) ......................................Reason: ___*(0.01 - 7*___

___*MEASUREMENT TO THE NEXT UNIT*___

**f** In how many professional organizations do you hold membership?

(2) ......................................Reason: .........................................

...................................................................................

**3.4.4** In the space allowed for the figure for 3.4.4, draw a histogram for the data of Table 3.1 (p. 20) of the text.

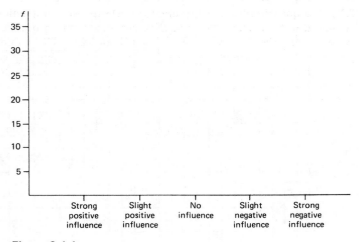

Figure 3.4.4

**3.4.5a** In the squared space below, construct a histogram for the data of Distribution C of Table 3.4 (p. 23) of the text. (*Note:* It will be convenient in drawing this histogram to turn the grid on its side.)

**b** Superimpose on the histogram constructed in **a** the frequency polygon for the same data.

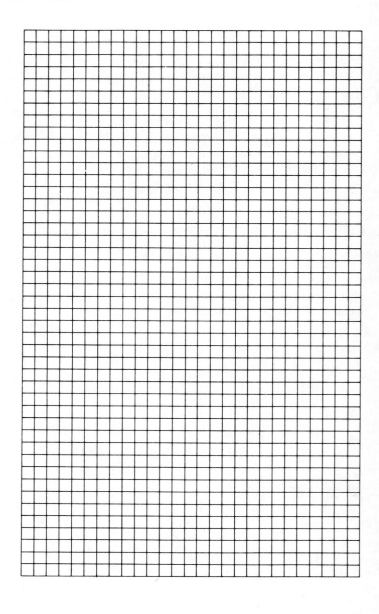

**3.4.6a** How does the histogram imply that the scores are *evenly* distributed within each interval?

...........................................................................................................

...........................................................................................................

...........................................................................................................

...........................................................................................................

**b** How does the polygon imply that there is a *gradual* change in frequency *within* each interval?

...........................................................................................................

...........................................................................................................

...........................................................................................................

**c** Which type of graphical representation would you use if you wished to emphasize the continuity of the scores involved?

...........................................................................................................

**3.4.7** In which type of figure, histogram or polygon, is it easier to compare differences in frequency in pairs of adjacent intervals?

...........................................................................................................

**3.4.8a** In constructing polygons (or histograms), why is it usually not desirable to extend the score scale to the zero point?

...........................................................................................................

...........................................................................................................

**b** Show by drawing a polygon for an imaginary set of data that beginning the frequency scale at some point above zero is equivalent to showing only a portion cut off from the top of the complete polygon. (For your polygon, use the space provided for the figure for 3.4.8.) Shade that portion of the complete polygon that would *not* appear.

Figure 3.4.8

**c** Why must the frequency scale of a polygon (or histogram) always start at the zero point?

.............................................................................................................

.............................................................................................................

.............................................................................................................

.............................................................................................................

.............................................................................................................

.............................................................................................................

**3.4.9** Why is it generally more difficult to read frequencies from a polygon than from a histogram?

.............................................................................................................

.............................................................................................................

.............................................................................................................

.............................................................................................................

.............................................................................................................

.............................................................................................................

**3.4.10** For purpose of comparison it is desired to superimpose the graphical pictures of two frequency distributions involving the same class size on the same axes. Which type of graphical representation (histogram or polygon) is better suited to use in this situation? Explain.

.............................................................................................................

.............................................................................................................

.............................................................................................................

.............................................................................................................

.............................................................................................................

**3.6.11** Using the sets of axes provided in the figure for 3.6.11, sketch smooth polygons for distributions that are roughly:

    **a** Unimodal, moderately skewed to left
    **b** Bimodal, symmetrical
    **c** J-shaped, markedly skewed to right
    **d** Rectangular

**3.6.12** The counselor of a large high school has developed an instrument that she feels measures "attitude toward teachers." She wishes to assess the attitude of the current student body but cannot justify having all students respond to her questionnaire. However, there are 100 students

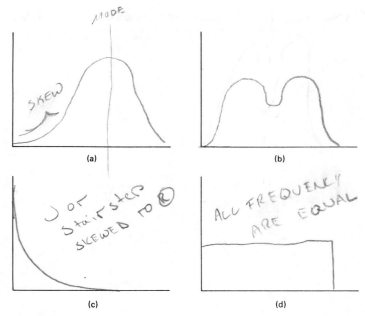

**Figure 3.6.11**

available in a particular study hall who, the counselor feels, are representative of the students in the school. She decides to administer the instrument to this group. On the basis of the results she obtains, she will make generalizations about the entire student body. The scores for the 100 students are shown in Table 3.A.

**a** Enter in Table 3.B the tally marks indicating the frequency of each score for the first three columns of scores. These tally marks provide a crude graphical representation of the frequency distribution.

**Table 3.A**   Counselor's Sample of 100 Scores

| | | | | | | | | | |
|---|---|---|---|---|---|---|---|---|---|
| 24 | 27 | 22 | 30 | 23 | 25 | 30 | 32 | 28 | 30 |
| 26 | 31 | 29 | 33 | 26 | 25 | 28 | 21 | 23 | 21 |
| 31 | 23 | 24 | 33 | 29 | 28 | 20 | 30 | 21 | 31 |
| 22 | 27 | 25 | 19 | 31 | 20 | 22 | 28 | 27 | 31 |
| 24 | 30 | 24 | 32 | 25 | 23 | 28 | 19 | 20 | 26 |
| 21 | 21 | 33 | 19 | 21 | 19 | 22 | 27 | 21 | 32 |
| 23 | 32 | 30 | 22 | 32 | 30 | 25 | 22 | 22 | 30 |
| 22 | 30 | 23 | 32 | 26 | 20 | 29 | 33 | 21 | 27 |
| 23 | 31 | 29 | 22 | 24 | 32 | 28 | 31 | 33 | 32 |
| 25 | 20 | 24 | 29 | 23 | 31 | 24 | 22 | 29 | 31 |

**Table 3.B**   Frequency Distribution of Scores of Table 3.A

| Scores | Tallies for First 30 Scores | Tallies for All 100 Scores |
|---|---|---|
| 33 | | |
| 32 | | |
| 31 | | |
| 30 | | |
| 29 | | |
| 28 | | |
| 27 | | |
| 26 | | |
| 25 | | |
| 24 | | |
| 23 | | |
| 22 | | |
| 21 | | |
| 20 | | |
| 19 | | |

**b** Assume that the distribution of scores for all students (the population distribution) is actually bimodal and symmetrical. The counselor, of course, does not know this. Had her sample consisted of just the 30 scores tallied in **a**, how would she probably have erred in describing the form of the population distribution?

..................................................................................................................................

..................................................................................................................................

..................................................................................................................................

..................................................................................................................................

..................................................................................................................................

**c** Enter in Table 3.B the tally marks indicating the frequency of each class for all 100 scores.

**d** Considering these 100 scores as a sample, how would the investigator probably describe the form of the population distribution?

................................................................................................................................

**e** Why did the first set of tally marks provide a less accurate picture of the form of the population distribution than the second set?

*too small of a sample & too*

*many classes*

................................................................................................................................

**3.6.13** Consider the data in Table 3.C as being derived from a sample of individuals selected in a random manner to represent a larger group.

**a** In the squared space on page 16, construct the frequency polygon that portrays graphically the frequency distribution of these data for an interval of size 5. Let the lowest interval be 9.5–14.5. (Use ruler to connect points with *solid* lines.)

**b** Superimpose on the polygon constructed in **a** a polygon picturing the frequency distribution of these data for an interval of size 10. (Use ruler to connect points with *dashed* lines.)

**c** What accounts for the greater irregularity in the form of the first of these polygons?

*smaller interval size*

................................................................................................................................

................................................................................................................................

................................................................................................................................

**Table 3.C**  Vocabulary Test Scores for 50 Individuals Selected at Random from a Fifth-Grade Population

| | | | | |
|---|---|---|---|---|
| 12 | 66 | 59 | 53 | 57 |
| 54 | 56 | 49 | 56 | 52 |
| 48 | 56 | 31 | 44 | 49 |
| 35 | 45 | 57 | 35 | 56 |
| 61 | 36 | 54 | 50 | 46 |
| 39 | 38 | 53 | 56 | 55 |
| 39 | 52 | 69 | 67 | 40 |
| 50 | 53 | 21 | 53 | 54 |
| 65 | 28 | 41 | 49 | 53 |
| 25 | 46 | 47 | 55 | 43 |

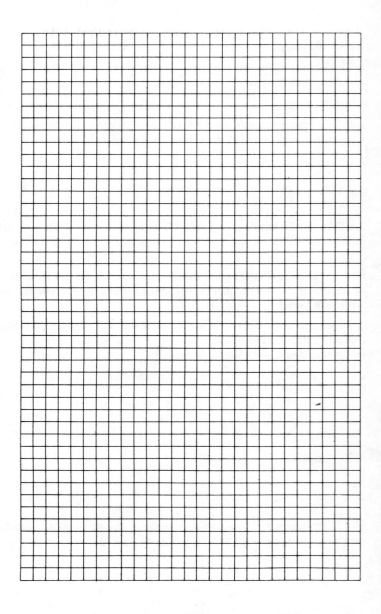

**d** Under what condition might the form of the first of these polygons have become almost as smooth as that of the second?

larger SAMPLE SIZE

_irregularities_

**e** In plotting a polygon in this type of situation, why should one ordinarily use a relatively coarse interval?

_a course interval will smooth irregularities_

**f** Is it possible in this type of situation to use an interval size that is too large? Explain.

_Yes you could smooth out important representation_

**g** If there is any doubt as to whether a particular observed irregularity in the form of a polygon is due to chance, how should this doubt be resolved?

_increase sample size_

**h** Superimpose on the polygon constructed in **a** a smooth curve picturing the probable form of the population distribution.

**i** How is the form of this ideal population distribution described verbally in statistical terminology?

_unimodel skewed to the left or negatively skewed_

**3.6.14a** In general, how does increasing or decreasing the size of the interval affect the smoothness or regularity of the polygon or histogram?

_↑ smooth_
_↓ more irregular_

**b** What in general is the effect of increasing the number of cases?

_smooth_

**3.6.15** Suppose that you wish to prepare a frequency distribution of the population of villages, towns, and cities in Illinois. Assume the range is from 25 to 4,000,000.

**a** If 20 equal-sized intervals were used, why would you be unable to differentiate among the frequencies with which various-sized villages or smaller towns occur?

**b** If it is desired to make discriminations of the type specified in **a**, approximately what size interval would be needed at the lower end of the scale?

...............................................................

**c** If this size interval were used throughout, approximately how many intervals would there be?

...............................................................

**d** How could you construct a frequency distribution of these data that would not have more than 25 intervals and would still permit discriminations of the type specified in **a**?

...................................................................................................................................

...................................................................................................................................

...................................................................................................................................

...................................................................................................................................

**3.6.16** The first two columns of Table 3.D show the frequency distribution of the years of service of 361 classroom teachers in a city of approximately 85,000 people. (For the moment ignore the last two columns of Table 3.D.) The years of service were reported as of the last full year completed. Hence, depending on when the service first began and on the time a particular report is made, it is possible for a teacher reporting, say, 5 years to have served actually anywhere from 5 to 5.99 years.

**Table 3.D**  Frequency Distribution of Number of Years of Service of 361 Teachers of a City School System

| Years of Service (X) | f | Size of Interval (Base of Rectangle) (i) | Height of Rectangle in Histogram (f/i) |
|---|---|---|---|
| 35–44.99 | 10 | 10 | 1 |
| 30–34.99 | 10 | 5 | 2 |
| 25–29.99 | 15 | 5 | 3 |
| 20–24.99 | 20 | 5 | 4 |
| 15–19.99 | 35 | 5 | 7 |
| 12–14.99 | 27 | 3 | 9 |
| 10–11.99 | 20 | 2 | 10 |
| 8– 9.99 | 22 | 2 | 11 |
| 6– 7.99 | 24 | 2 | 12 |
| 5– 5.99 | 13 | 1 | 13 |
| 4– 4.99 | 15 | 1 | 15 |
| 3– 3.99 | 19 | 1 | 19 |
| 2– 2.99 | 24 | 1 | 24 |
| 1– 1.99 | 35 | 1 | 35 |
| 0– .99 | 72 | 1 | 72 |
|  | 361 |  |  |

Intervals of different sizes were used in the construction of the frequency distribution presented in Table 3.D. Small intervals were used at the lower end of the distribution and relatively large intervals at the upper end. The primary purpose of this exercise is to consider the distortion introduced as a result of varying the interval size.

**a** What do the data in the first two columns of Table 3.D suggest about the shape of the distribution?

...............................................................................................................................

...............................................................................................................................

**b** If your answer in **a** was that the distribution is bimodal, you have been deceived by the distortion introduced as a result of the varying sizes of the intervals. Such a conclusion results from failure to note that the frequency 35 in the upper part of the distribution represents the total number of teachers reporting either 15, or 16, or 17, or 18, or 19 years of service, while the frequency 35 toward the bottom of the distribution represents the total number of teachers reporting only 1 year of service. The illusion created in this table, which makes large distances along the score scale appear to be the same as small distances, may be removed by representing the data in the form of a histogram.

However, it is not reasonable to plot the histogram in the manner described in Section 3.4. Recall that the bases of the rectangles of a histogram extend from the lower to the upper real limits of each interval. The rectangles of the histogram of this distribution will, therefore, have bases varying in length. This being the case, it will not be possible, as before, to make the areas of the rectangles proportional to the class frequencies simply by making their heights equal to their frequencies. In a situation of this type, the simplest way to make the areas of the rectangles proportional to their respective class frequencies is to demand that these areas be equal to the corresponding frequencies. If this is done, the heights of the rectangles can be obtained by dividing their areas (that is, their frequencies) by the lengths of their respective bases. The appropriate heights of the rectangles representing each class are shown in the last column of Table 3.D. On the axes provided for the figure for 3.6.16, construct the appropriate histogram for the data in Table 3.D.

**c** Describe the form of the histogram constructed in **b**.

...............................................................................................................................

...............................................................................................................................

...............................................................................................................................

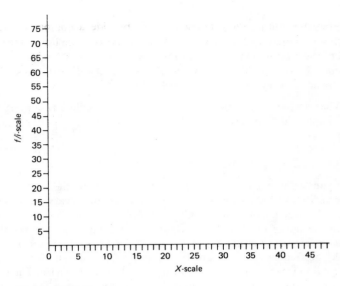

**Figure 3.6.16**

**d** The histogram you drew in **b** was a fairly smooth J-shaped distribution. Did the use of differing interval sizes contribute to the degree of smoothness shown by this histogram? Explain.

.......................................................................................................................

.......................................................................................................................

.......................................................................................................................

.......................................................................................................................

**3.7.17a** Two frequency polygons representing distributions of reading comprehension scores are superimposed on the same axes, the scales being marked off in terms of number correct on the test and frequency counts. Both sets of scores are for representative samples of fifth-grade boys. One set involves the scores for 50 boys from School A and the other the scores for 200 boys from School B. Which figure will create the impression of greater variability in test scores? That is, which will appear relatively low and flat in relation to its width? Explain.

.......................................................................................................................

.......................................................................................................................

.......................................................................................................................

.......................................................................................................................

.......................................................................................................................

**b** If the purpose of these polygons is to provide a comparison of the relative variability of these two sets of scores, what revision should be made in their construction?

.................................................................................................................

.................................................................................................................

**3.7.18** The actual experiment that we described only partially on p. 40 of the text investigated "cheating" under six different conditions. The cheating scores for the 106 sixth-grade students on two of the four conditions not treated in the text are shown in Figure 3.7.18 in the form of frequency polygons.

Compare these distributions on the following characteristics:

Shape .................................................................................................................

Location .............................................................................................................

Spread (or variability) ......................................................................................

.................................................................................................................

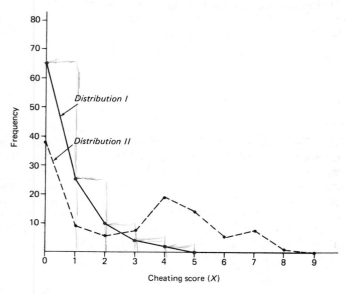

**Figure 3.7.18**

**3.7.19** During the fall of the 1974–1975 school year, 300 students at a certain university were selected to participate in an evaluation of the campus transportation system. Each student was given a list of items dealing with such factors as the number of buses in service, hours of operation, and areas of service. A sample item is shown below.

The hours during which the campus transportation system operates are sufficient for student needs.

................    ................    ................    ................    ................

$\mathcal{L}_{I}KERT$
$\mathcal{S}CALE$

| Strongly | Disagree | Neutral | Agree | Strongly |
| disagree |          | opinion |       | agree    |

On the basis of the results of this survey, the officials of the transportation system modified the system. After the new procedures had been in effect for several months, the officials decided to conduct a new survey. A new sample of 100 students was selected and asked to respond to the same items the group of 300 students had answered earlier. As part of the data analysis, the officials gave each student (in both the old and new groups) a total score based on the sum of the individual item scores. This total score was assumed to represent overall satisfaction (or dissatisfaction) with the system. The smoothed relative frequency distributions for the two sets of total scores are shown in the figure for 3.7.19.

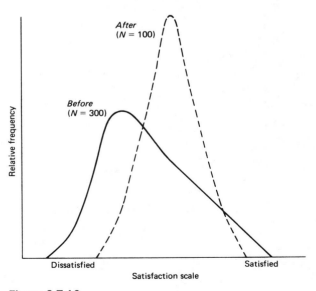

**Figure 3.7.19**

**a** Why were relative frequency distributions plotted?

*DIFFERENT SAMPLE SIZES*

**b** Why were smoothed frequency distributions presented?

*REMOVE CHANCE CHARACTERISTICS REPRESENT LARGER POP.*

**c** Compare these distributions in terms of the following characteristics:

Shape *UNIMODEL SLIGHTLY SKEWED / UM SYM*

Location *DISATISFIED / SATISTIFIED*

Variability *BEFORE IS MORE VARIABLE / COMPRESSED*

**d** What conclusion(s) can be reached on the basis of these data?

*MOST OF THE STUDENTS ARE MODERATELY SATISFIED / DEGREE OF SATISFACTION HAS GONE UP*

**3.7.20** An elementary school principal felt that the difficulty her third-grade students had had in using a machine-scoreable answer sheet was part of the reason for their low scores. She decided to perform an experiment to investigate this possibility. Of the 100 current third-grade students she assigned 50 to take part in a practice session related to the use of the answer sheet. The other 50 students were to serve as a control group. After the practice session both groups took a standardized reading test. The results shown in the accompanying table were obtained.

| No-Practice Group ($N = 50$) | | Practice Group ($N = 50$) | |
|---|---|---|---|
| Score ($X$) | $f$ | Score ($X$) | $f$ |
| 55–56 | 0 | 55–56 | 2 |
| 53–54 | 1 | 53–54 | 3 |
| 51–52 | 2 | 51–52 | 3 |
| 49–50 | 3 | 49–50 | 2 |
| 47–48 | 5 | 47–48 | 7 |
| 45–46 | 7 | 45–46 | 11 |
| 43–44 | 6 | 43–44 | 7 |
| 41–42 | 8 | 41–42 | 5 |
| 39–40 | 7 | 39–40 | 4 |
| 37–38 | 4 | 37–38 | 4 |
| 35–36 | 5 | 35–36 | 2 |
| 33–34 | 2 | 33–34 | 0 |

**a** On the axes provided for the figure for 3.7.20, sketch smoothed frequency polygons for these two sets of results. (A crude sketch will be sufficient.)

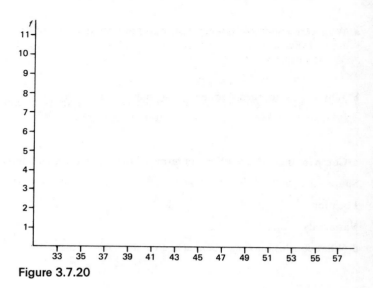

Figure 3.7.20

**b** Compare these two distributions in terms of shape, location, and variability.

Shape ...............................................................................................................

........................................................................................................................

Location ........................................................................................................

........................................................................................................................

Variability ......................................................................................................

........................................................................................................................

**c** What conclusion(s) can be drawn on the basis of these data?

........................................................................................................................

........................................................................................................................

........................................................................................................................

**3.8.21a** Suppose it is desired to plot a polygon (or histogram) of a distribution of IQs for a given class of pupils in such a way as to convey the impression of great individual differences in intelligence—that is, in such a way as to emphasize the variability of the distribution and the heterogeneity of the class. Which scale (frequency or score) should be elongated more than otherwise?

*SCORE*

**b** How might the selection of scale units be revised so as to create an impression exactly the opposite of that desired in **a**?

*SHORTEN SCORE SCALE OR ELONGATE FREQUENCY*

**c** Distinguish between "score scale units" in the sense of **b** and class (interval) size.

*SSU — PHYSICAL UNIT OF MEASUREMENT*

**d** How might someone use a polygon (or histogram) to misrepresent data deliberately without resorting to actual falsification of fact?

*ADJUST SCALE UNITS*

**3.8.22** Cite two reasons why it is unwise to base one's impression of the variability of a distribution on the width or apparent flatness of a polygon (or histogram).

*GROUP SIZE ; RESOLUTION RF*
*H+W due to scales of UNITS*

**3.8.23** The histogram shown as Figure 3.8.23 was part of a report on the quality of the five high schools in a large city. The vertical axis represents the percentage of students that dropped out of school. The definition of a dropout was the same for all five schools.

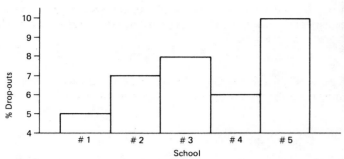

Figure 3.8.23

**a** The drop-out rate in School 5 is approximately how many times as great as the drop-out rate in School 1?

...................................................................

**b** Consider the comparison of drop-out rates in part **a**. If this comparison were made using only visual impressions from the histogram, what conclusion would be reached?

...................................................................................................................

...................................................................................................................

**c** Why do the answers given in **a** and **b** differ?

...Vertical....does...not....START AT ZERO.............................................

...................................................................................................................

...................................................................................................................

# 4

# Percentile Ranks and Percentiles

*Percentage of correct answers* →

*percent of scores below score*

**4.2.1** Explain the difference between a percentile rank and the ordinary percentage grade sometimes used in scoring examinations.

*There is no relationship a percentile ranks could be higher or lower than the percentage grade.*

**4.2.2** Five scores in a collection of 25 have values less than 50. Four scores have the value 50. What is the approximate percentile rank of the score point 50?

**4.2.3** Pupil A's score on an arithmetic test had a *PR*-value of 45 in an eighth-grade class. Pupil B's score on the same test had a *PR*-value of 40 in a seventh-grade class. Assume the test to be a valid measure of achievement in arithmetic. Why does it not necessarily follow that Pupil A is superior in arithmetic to Pupil B?

**4.2.4** The classes in a certain school are divided into sections on the basis of ability. Student A is in a "fast" section and Student B in a "slow" section. The same test is given to both sections. Student A's score has a *PR* of 70 in his section and Student B's score a *PR* of 80 in hers. Why can't we tell from this information whether A or B made the higher score on this test?

..................................................................................................................

..................................................................................................................

..................................................................................................................

..................................................................................................................

..................................................................................................................

**4.3.5a** Strictly speaking, why is it incorrect to say "Pupil A is *in* the 40th percentile"?

..................................................................................................................

..................................................................................................................

**b** Pupil B's score is among the lowest 25 percent of the scores in a collection. Strictly speaking, should one say "Pupil B is *in* the lower quartile" or "Pupil B is *in* the lowest one-fourth"? Why?

..................................................................................................................

..................................................................................................................

**4.4.6a** In the squared space on page 29, construct the unsmoothed relative cumulative frequency ogive for the data of Table 4.A. Use a ruler to connect the points.

**Table 4.A**    Distribution of Scores on a Statistics Examination

| X | f | cf | rcf | |
|---|---|----|-----|---|
| 37 | 1 | 40 | 1.000 | $cf/n = rcf$ |
| 30 | 2 | 39 | .975 | |
| 29 | 1 | 37 | .925 | |
| 28 | 1 | 36 | .900 | |
| 27 | 1 | 35 | .875 | |
| 26 | 2 | 34 | .850 | |
| 25 | 2 | 32 | .800 | |
| 22 | 4 | 30 | .750 | |
| 21 | 3 | 26 | .650 | |
| 20 | 4 | 23 | .575 | |
| 19 | 3 | 19 | .475 | |
| 18 | 2 | 16 | .400 | |
| 16 | 2 | 14 | .350 | |
| 15 | 4 | 12 | .300 | |
| 14 | 2 | 8 | .200 | |
| 13 | 4 | 6 | .150 | |
| 11 | 1 | 2 | .050 | |
| 5 | 1 | 1 | .025 | |
| | 40 | | | |

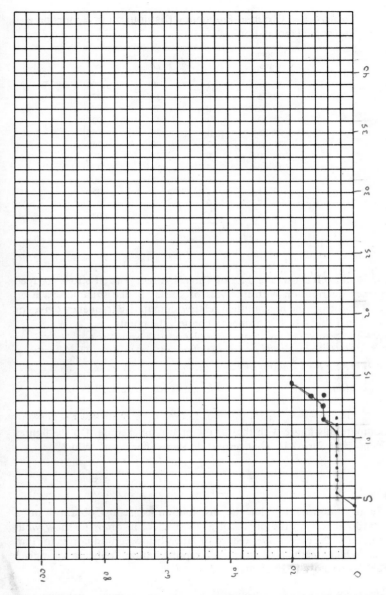

**b** Show by drawing direction lines how this figure can be used to read the following statistics. What numerical values do you obtain?

**1** The *PR* of a score of 15 .........................................................

**2** *Mdn* .........................................................

**3** $Q_3$ .........................................................

**Table 4.B**    Grouped Frequency Distribution of Scores on a
Statistics Examination

| Integral Units | f | cf | rcf |
|---|---|---|---|
| 36–38 | 1 | 40 | 1.000 |
| 33–35 | 0 | 39 | .975 |
| 30–32 | 2 | 39 | .975 |
| 27–29 | 3 | 37 | .925 |
| 24–26 | 4 | 34 | .850 |
| 21–23 | 7 | 30 | .750 |
| 18–20 | 9 | 23 | .575 |
| 15–17 | 6 | 14 | .350 |
| 12–14 | 6 | 8 | .200 |
| 9–11 | 1 | 2 | .050 |
| 6– 8 | 0 | 1 | .025 |
| 3– 5 | 1 | 1 | .025 |
|  | N = 40 |  |  |

**4.4.7a**  Table 4.B shows the data of Table 4.A reorganized into a grouped frequency distribution with intervals of size 3. In the squared space on page 31 construct the unsmoothed relative cumulative frequency ogive for the data in Table 4.B. Use a ruler to connect the points.

**b**  Use this figure to estimate:

    **1** The *PR* of a score of 15   ...............................................................

    **2** *Mdn*   ...............................................................

    **3** $Q_3$   ...............................................................

**c**  Compare this figure with that of the preceding exercise. Do the figures differ much in form? In what respect do they differ most? Why?

...........................................................................................................................

...........................................................................................................................

**4.4.8a**  It is desired to plot the distribution of scores obtained on a standardized test by the pupils of a given class, in order to show what *proportion* of the class had exceeded or fallen below certain norms for that grade. Which method of graphical representation (polygon or ogive) should be employed? Explain.

...........................................................................................................................

...........................................................................................................................

...........................................................................................................................

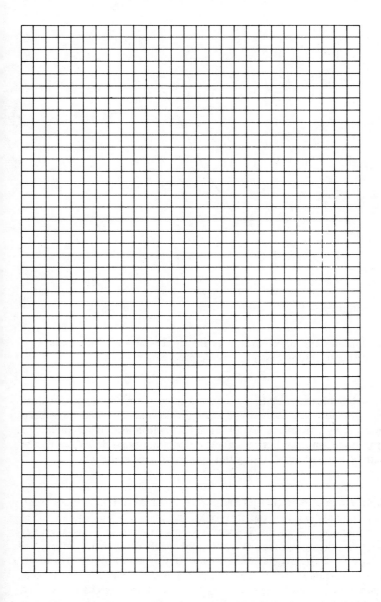

**b** Which type of graph would be most effective for picturing the variability in achievement? Why?

..........................................................................................................................................................

..........................................................................................................................................................

..........................................................................................................................................................

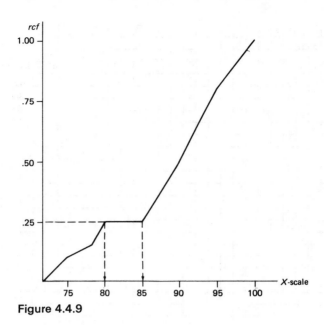

Figure 4.4.9

**4.4.9a** Consider the ogive shown as the figure for 4.4.9. Estimate $P_{25}$. (*Note:* Estimate this as best you can before going on to **b**.)

.................................................

**b** It was difficult to estimate $P_{25}$ because there are many possible values for $P_{25}$. In fact, any score value between 80 and 85 could have been identified as $P_{25}$. In such situations, the convention usually adopted is to take the point midway between the two extreme possible values as the estimate of the percentile. Using this convention, estimate $P_{25}$.

.................................................

**4.4.10** In estimating percentiles and percentile ranks in the previous study manual exercises (and in the textbook), we assumed that the variables were continuous. When this is true, it seems reasonable to assume that the scores within a given interval are spaced evenly throughout the interval (see Section 4.2 for a detailed rationale of this assumption). However, when the variables are discrete, such an assumption does not seem reasonable. Can the concepts of percentile rank and percentile be used with discrete data? Yes, if we modify the procedures somewhat. We shall illustrate this modification with an example.

Table 4.C shows the results for part of a survey undertaken to provide officials of a particular city with information related to characteristics of families living in the city. The variable of interest to us is the number of children living at home.

**Table 4.C** Distribution of Families with Respect to Number of Children

| X | f | cf (Below) | cf (At and Below) |
|---|---|---|---|
| 7 or more | 1 | 99 | 100 |
| 6 | 1 | 98 | 99 |
| 5 | 4 | 94 | 98 |
| 4 | 6 | 88 | 94 |
| 3 | 30 | 58 | 88 |
| 2 | 30 | 28 | 58 |
| 1 | 18 | 10 | 28 |
| 0 | 10 | 0 | 10 |
|   | N = 100 |   |   |

With discrete data such as these, it seems reasonable to give additional meaning to a particular score value by computing the percentage at and below that value, or the percentage below it. (Of course, you could just as easily compute the percentage at and above or simply above.)

**a** What percentage of the families reported in Table 4.C have fewer than three children living at home?

..............................................................................

**b** What percentage of the families have three or fewer children living at home?

..............................................................................

Although the percentages you calculated in **a** and **b** cannot be labeled percentile ranks under our definition, these statistics obviously are conveying a similar type of information.

**c** Why is it unreasonable to assume that the six families with four children living at home are evenly spread over the interval 3.5–4.5?

..........................................................................................................

..........................................................................................................

..........................................................................................................

(*Note:* Mathematically, it is possible to use the procedures developed for continuous data with discrete data such as those in Table 4.C. In fact, you may have seen data such as the following: "The median family size is 2.2 children." This median value probably was estimated according to procedures similar to those used in 4.4.6 and 4.4.7 for estimating medians.)

**4.4.11** A group of 100 parents was asked to indicate their opinion regarding the degree of influence that participation in athletics has on the moral character of children. The parents were asked to indicate their opinion on the scale shown below.

Athletics has

   (30)
........... a great positive influence on moral character.

   (25)
........... a slight positive influence on moral character.

   (20)
........... no influence on moral character.

   (15)
........... a slight negative influence on moral character.

   (10)
........... a great negative influence on moral character.

The numbers in parentheses represent the number of parents checking the indicated statement. (These data were presented previously in Table 3.1 of the text.)

The concepts of $PR$ and $P_x$ as defined in the text cannot be used with these data. In this instance, the variable of interest is a continuous but *unscaled* variable (i.e., the "scores" are not numerical values). Therefore, it is meaningful to compute the percentage below a given statement or the percentage at or below a given statement. This is the same procedure as we employed in 4.4.10. What percentage of parents indicated a negative opinion?

........................................................................

**4.5.12** Suppose that the figure of 4.4.6a is to be used to establish a table of $PR$-values corresponding to each score point for the statistics examination in question, and that this table will then be used to determine the percentile ranks of students taking this examination in the future. How should this figure be revised so as to improve the accuracy of $PR$-values established for this purpose?

........................................................................

........................................................................

**4.5.13** A large sample of eighth-grade pupils in Illinois is tested in arithmetic, and a table of percentile norms is established. A similar table is also established for the same test for a large sample of Iowa eighth-grade pupils. Pupil A from Illinois achieved the same $PR$ with reference to the Illinois sample as Pupil B from Iowa achieved with reference to the Iowa sample. Assume the test provides a valid measure of achievement in arithmetic, and assume both samples are representative of their respective populations. What would have to be true of the two sample score distributions before it could be said that Pupils A and B are equal in arithmetic achievement?

.................................................................................................................

.................................................................................................................

.................................................................................................................

**4.6.14a** In the distribution of Table 4.A (see page 28), how does the distance from $P_{40}$ to $P_{50}$ compare with the distance from $P_{80}$ to $P_{90}$? (*Note:* These percentile values can be found using the ogive constructed for 4.4.6a.)

.................................................................................................................

.................................................................................................................

**b** What determines the distance in score units between successive deciles or successive percentiles in a frequency distribution?

.................................................................................................................

.................................................................................................................

**c** An "intercentile distance" is the distance in score units between two successive centiles—for example, the distance between $P_9$ and $P_{10}$ or between $P_{27}$ and $P_{28}$. In general terms, in what part of the distribution will these intercentile distances be the smallest?

.................................................................................................................

**d** In what part will they be the largest?

.................................................................................................................

**e** If the intercentile distances are relatively constant over a *portion* of the score scale, what would have to be true of the *f*-values over this portion of the scale?

.................................................................................................................

**4.6.15a** On a given test Pupil A scores at the 40th percentile and Pupil B at the 20th. Why may A not be said to have done twice as well as B?

.................................................................................................................

.................................................................................................................

.................................................................................................................

**b** Pupil C scored at the 30th percentile on the same test. Why may it not be inferred that his score is midway between the scores of pupils A and B?

.................................................................................................................

.................................................................................................................

**4.6.16a** Heights for a large group of boys of about the same age tend to fall into a unimodal symmetrical distribution. In such a distribution, Boy A's height has a $PR$-value of 90 and Boy B's height has a $PR$-value of 70. Boy C's height is midway between those of A and B. Would you expect C's height to be at, above, or below the 80th percentile? Explain.

..............................................................................................................................

..............................................................................................................................

..............................................................................................................................

..............................................................................................................................

..............................................................................................................................

..............................................................................................................................

**b** The average of the $PR$-values for the heights of A and B is 80. Would the percentile rank of the average of their heights be the same as the average of their $PR$-values? (That is, would the $PR$ of the average of their heights be 80?) Why?

..............................................................................................................................

..............................................................................................................................

..............................................................................................................................

**4.6.17a** In a distribution of annual incomes for the adults in a given city, $Q_1$ is \$4,800, $Q_2$ is \$9,600, $Q_3$ is \$19,200, and $P_{95}$ is \$40,000. Describe the form of the distribution.

..............................................................................................................................

**b** Explain in general how the form of a distribution may be inferred from information about selected percentile points.

..............................................................................................................................

..............................................................................................................................

..............................................................................................................................

**4.6.18** Given the following series of percentile points, describe the form of the distribution involved.

$$
\begin{array}{lll}
P_{99} = 68 & D_6 = 45 & D_2 = 18 \\
D_9 = 57 & D_5 = 37 & D_1 = 12 \\
D_8 = 53 & D_4 = 25 & P_1 = 1 \\
D_7 = 49 & D_3 = 21 &
\end{array}
$$

..............................................................................................................................

..............................................................................................................................

..............................................................................................................................

**4.6.19** Describe the modality and form of the score distribution giving rise to the ogives shown in the figure for 4.6.19. (*Hint:* Estimate the distances between $P_1$, $P_{25}$, $P_{50}$, $P_{75}$, $P_{99}$.)

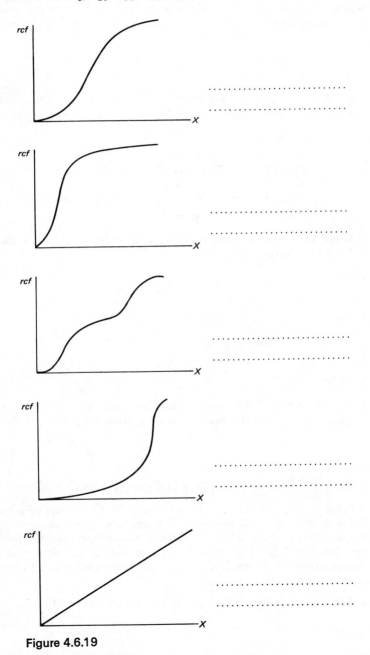

**Figure 4.6.19**

**4.7.20** In the distribution of annual incomes for people holding full-time jobs in a certain city, $Q_1$ is \$4,000 and $Q_3$ is \$24,000. In which city, this one or the one referred to in 4.6.17, is there the greater variation in incomes? Why?

..........................................................................................................................

..........................................................................................................................

..........................................................................................................................

**4.8.21** Consider the situation described in 3.7.19. Assume the following summary data were supplied for the Before and After groups.

| Before ($N = 300$) | After ($N = 100$) |
|---|---|
| $P_1 = 25$ | $P_1 = 38$ |
| $P_{25} = 30$ | $P_{25} = 45$ |
| $P_{50} = 35$ | $P_{50} = 50$ |
| $P_{75} = 50$ | $P_{75} = 55$ |
| $P_{99} = 70$ | $P_{99} = 62$ |

**a** Using these selected percentiles compare the two distributions on the following characteristics:

Shape ..........................................................................................................

..........................................................................................................................

Location ......................................................................................................

..........................................................................................................................

Variability ...................................................................................................

..........................................................................................................................

**b** For which one of these comparisons is it obviously better to use the frequency polygons rather than the selected percentile points?

..........................................................................................................................

..........................................................................................................................

**c** Compare your answers in part **a** with the answers to 3.7.19c.

**4.8.22** The graph for 4.8.22 shows the ogives for two groups of subjects. Ogive A is a smoothed graphical representation of the scores of 3,035 subjects who participated in the norming of the Quantitative subtest of the Graduate Record Examination. Ogive B is a smoothed graphical representation of the scores of 1,096 subjects who enrolled in the graduate school of a particular university.

**a** Compare these distributions on the following characteristics:

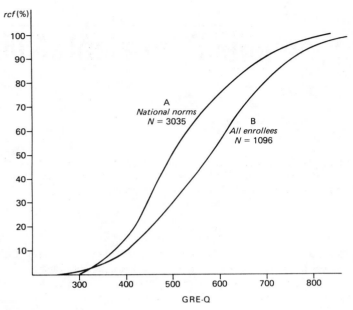

Figure 4.8.22

Shape. (*Note:* You should try to make this comparison without computing selected percentile points. See the ogives in 4.6.19 for additional help.)

.........................................................................................................................

.........................................................................................................................

Location. (*Hint:* Either estimate $P_{50}$ for each group or just note the shift.)

.........................................................................................................................

.........................................................................................................................

Variability. (*Hint:* Estimate $P_{75}$ and $P_{25}$ for each group.)

.........................................................................................................................

.........................................................................................................................

.........................................................................................................................

**b** What type of graphical representation is better (ogives or relative frequency polygons) for making comparisons between the shapes of distributions?

.........................................................................................................................

**c** Approximately what percentage of the Enrollee group (Ogive B) were above the median of the Norm group (Ogive A)?

.........................................................................................................

# 5

# Symbolic Representation of Data

**5.2.1** If $W_t$ represents the magnitude of a score for the individual designated as $t$ in a collection of such scores for $k$ individuals, indicate two ways in which the entire collection might be represented.

...................................................................

...................................................................

**5.2.2** Given the set of 15 scores shown in Table 5.A. Assume that the five scores in the first row were made by individuals identified by the numbers 1, 2, ..., 5, that the scores in the second row were made by individuals 6, 7, ..., 10, and so on. Fill in the following blanks.

    **a** $X_{13} =$ ...................................................................

    **b** $X_{15} - X_5 =$ ...................................................................

    **c** $X_1 + X_6 + X_{11} =$ ...................................................................

    **d** $(X_3)(X_8) =$ ...................................................................

    **e** $X_{14}/X_2 =$ ...................................................................

    **f** If $i = 11$, $X_i =$ ...................................................................

    **g** If $s = 4$, $X_s + X_{s+3} =$ ...................................................................

    **h** $X_3 + X_4 + \cdots + X_8 =$ ...................................................................

### Table 5.A

| | | | | |
|---|---|---|---|---|
| 4 | 3 | 3 | 0 | 15 |
| 8 | 4 | 7 | 3 | 3 |
| 9 | 6 | 0 | 15 | 10 |

**5.3.3** Using the data of Table 5.A, evaluate the following.

   **a** $\sum X_i$    $(i = 1, 2, \ldots, 15)$ ...............................................

   **b** $\displaystyle\sum_{i=6}^{10} X_i$       .................................

   **c** $\displaystyle\sum_{i=1}^{5} X_i - \sum_{i=11}^{15} X_i$     .................................

   **d** $\displaystyle\sum_{i=1}^{5} X_i^2$       .................................

   **e** $\displaystyle\left(\sum_{i=1}^{5} X_i\right)^2$     .................................

   **f** $\displaystyle\sum X_i^2 - \frac{(\sum X_i)^2}{N}$    .................................

**5.3.4** Use the summation operator to represent the following.

   **a** $W_1 + W_2 + \cdots + W_{20}$    .................................

   **b** $Y_1 + Y_2 + \cdots$
          $+ Y_{10} + Y_{20}$
          $+ Y_{21} + \cdots + Y_{25}$   .................................

   **c** $Z_1 + Z_2 + \cdots$
          $+ Z_5 - X_1$
          $- X_2 - \cdots - X_{10}$   .................................

   **d** $(T_1 + T_2 + \cdots + T_N)^2$    .................................

   **e** $(T_1^2 + T_2^2 + \cdots + T_N^2)$   .................................

**5.4.5** Given a collection of $N$ values of $R$. These $R$-values are organized into a frequency distribution involving $k$ classes. The class frequencies are designated by $n$'s with the class identification numbers affixed as subscripts.

**a** Express $N$ in terms of the values of $n$.

.................................

## Table 5.B

| Class Midpoints | $f$ |
|---|---|
|  |  |
|  |  |
|  |  |
|  |  |
|  |  |
|  |  |
|  |  |

**b** In the space provided in Table 5.B, represent this frequency distribution in tabular form.

**5.5.6a** Given the situation of 5.4.5, express the approximate sum and sum of squares of the $n_1$ values of $R$ belonging to class 1 in terms of the frequency distribution notation.

.................................................................

.................................................................

**b** Express the approximate sum and sum of squares of the $N$ values of $R$ in terms of the frequency distribution notation.

.................................................................

.................................................................

**c** Explain why the expressions called for in **a** and **b** represent only approximations of the corresponding sums and sums of squares of the actual $R$-values involved.

.................................................................................................................

.................................................................................................................

.................................................................................................................

.................................................................................................................

.................................................................................................................

.................................................................................................................

**Table 5.C**

| X | f |
|---|---|
| 5 | 1 |
| 4 | 0 |
| 3 | 3 |
| 2 | 4 |
| 1 | 2 |

**5.5.7** Use the unit-interval frequency distribution shown in Table 5.C to demonstrate numerically the fact that the following pairs of expressions are not in general equivalent.

**a** $\displaystyle\sum_{j=1}^{5} f_j X_j$ and $\displaystyle\left(\sum_{j=1}^{5} f_j\right)\left(\sum_{j=1}^{5} X_j\right)$

......................................................................................................

......................................................................................................

**b** $\displaystyle\sum_{j=1}^{5} f_j X_j^2$ and $\displaystyle\left(\sum_{j=1}^{5} f_j\right)\left(\sum_{j=1}^{5} X_j^2\right)$

......................................................................................................

......................................................................................................

**c** $\displaystyle\sum_{j=1}^{5} f_j X_j^2$ and $\displaystyle\left(\sum_{j=1}^{5} f_j X_j\right)^2$

......................................................................................................

......................................................................................................

**5.6.8** Use the frequency distribution of Table 5.C to demonstrate numerically that

$$\sum_{j=1}^{5} p_j = 1$$

where $p$ represents a relative frequency.

......................................................................................................

**5.7.9** Use the frequency distribution of Table 5.C to demonstrate numerically that if $p$ represents a relative frequency, then

**a** $\displaystyle\sum_{j=1}^{5} f_j X_j = N \sum_{j=1}^{5} p_j X_j$

.......................................................................................

.......................................................................................

**b** $\displaystyle\sum_{j=1}^{5} f_j X_j{}^2 = N \sum_{j=1}^{5} p_j X_j{}^2$

.......................................................................................

.......................................................................................

*Note:* The remaining problems in this chapter are related to optional Section 5.8 in the text.

**5.8.10** Using the collection of scores given in Table 5.A, demonstrate numerically that

$$2 \sum_{i=1}^{5} X_i = \sum_{i=1}^{5} 2X_i$$

.......................................................................................

.......................................................................................

**5.8.11** Consider the first row of the scores given in Table 5.A as $X$-values and consider the score below each such $X$ in the second row as a corresponding $Y$-value (that is, as a value paired with the $X$ above it) so that $X_1 = 4$ and $Y_1 = 8$; $X_2 = 3$ and $Y_2 = 4$; and so on. Demonstrate numerically that

**a** $\displaystyle\sum_{i=1}^{5} (Y_i - X_i) = \sum_{i=1}^{5} Y_i - \sum_{i=1}^{5} X_i$

.......................................................................................

.......................................................................................

**b** $\displaystyle\sum_{i=1}^{5} (X_i + 2Y_i) = \sum_{i=1}^{5} X_i + 2 \sum_{i=1}^{5} Y_i$

.............................................................................................................

.............................................................................................................

**5.8.12** Organize your solutions to the following in the same way as those of the examples given on p. 78 of the text.

**a** For a collection of $N$ pairs of values of $X$ and $Y$, show that

$$\sum_{i=1}^{N} (X_i - Y_i)^2 = \sum_{i=1}^{N} X_i^2 + \sum_{i=1}^{N} Y_i^2 - 2 \sum_{i=1}^{N} X_i Y_i$$

.............................................................................................................

.............................................................................................................

.............................................................................................................

**b** For a collection of $c$ values of $Z$, show that

$$\sum_{i=1}^{c} (Z_i - A)^2 = \sum_{i=1}^{c} Z_i^2 - 2A \sum_{i=1}^{c} Z_i + cA^2$$

.............................................................................................................

.............................................................................................................

.............................................................................................................

# 6
# Indexes of Location or Central Tendency

**6.2.1** Consider the following collection of 20 scores on a ten-point science quiz:

> 0, 0, 1, 1, 2, 2, 2, 3, 4, 4,
> 5, 5, 5, 6, 6, 7, 7, 8, 8, 8

**a** What is the median of this collection?

..............................................................................

**b** Assume that one of the score values of 4 was changed to a 5. Why is it difficult to estimate the median of this new set by finding a score value that has an equal number of scores above and below it?

..............................................................................

..............................................................................

..............................................................................

**c** Consider the original set of 20 scores. Assume that the three individuals with scores of 8 actually had scores of 10. What is the median of this set of scores?

..............................................................................

How does this value compare to the value you found in part **a**?

..............................................................................

Why are these two values the same even though the distribution of scores has changed?

..............................................................................

..............................................................................

..............................................................................

**6.2.2** Using equation (6.1), estimate the median of the distribution of Table 4.A (see p. 28).

..............................................................................

**6.2.3** Using equation (6.1), estimate the median of the distribution shown in Table 4.B (see p. 30).

**6.2.4** In a recent year, there were 40,000 public school teachers in a particular state. Of these teachers, 19,800 were receiving annual salaries of $8,000 or less. Another 400 were receiving salaries between $8,001 and $8,200. Approximately, what was the median salary for these teachers?

**6.3.5a** What is the mode of the distribution of Table 6.2 (p. 84) of the text?

**b** What is (are) the mode(s) of the frequency distribution given in Figure 3.1 (p. 28) of the text?

**6.3.6** The figure for 6.3.6 shows the smoothed polygons of two score distributions superimposed on the same axes (i.e., drawn to the same scale). Which distribution, A or B, has the greater mode? Explain.

**6.3.7** What is the mode of the frequency distribution of Table 3.D (see exercise 3.6.16)?

**6.4.8** Consider the relative frequency distribution of the arithmetic quiz scores given in Table 5.2B (p. 73) of the text. Compute the mean of these 50 scores using (6.3a).

**6.5.9a** From which index of location or central tendency can the sum of the scores involved be determined if the number of scores is known?

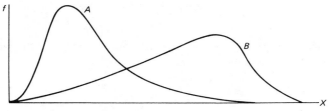

Figure 6.3.6

**b** Which index of location may be described as "proportional to the total of the scores" for collections of the same size?

.......................................................................

**6.5.10a** Does the numerical value of the mean depend directly on the value of *each* score in a collection?

.......................................................................

**b** Does the value of the median?

.......................................................................

**c** Of the mode?

.......................................................................

**d** Which index or indexes of location would you characterize as "rigidly and arithmetically defined" in the sense of being dependent on the value of *each* of the scores in a collection?

.......................................................................

**6.5.11a** A group of 25 students earned a mean score of 30 on a certain test. A second group of 25 students earned a mean score of 40 on this same test. What was the mean score of the 50 students?

.......................................................................

**b** A third group of 150 students earned a mean score of 50 on this same test. What was the mean score of the 200 students in all three groups?

.......................................................................

**6.5.12a** For each student in a statistics class, a composite measure of achievement was secured by adding the scores obtained on the mid-term and final examinations. The class means on these examinations were 20 and 24, respectively. What was the class mean of the composite scores?

.......................................................................

**b** Could problems similar to **a** above and to **a** and **b** of exercise 6.5.11 be solved for medians? for modes? Explain.

.......................................................................

.......................................................................

.......................................................................

.......................................................................

**c** Which index(es) of location would you describe as "amenable to arithmetic manipulation"?

.......................................................................

**6.5.13** A group of 11 persons was involved in a three-day workshop designed to increase the participants' understanding of the problems faced by minority groups. As part of the evaluation of the workshop, an instrument that purportedly measured "empathy for minority groups" was given before and after the workshop. The results from these two testings are shown below (high score = more empathy).

| Subject | Score Before | Score After | Difference (After — Before) |
|---------|--------------|-------------|------------------------------|
| 1 | 105 | 109 | |
| 2 | 100 | 104 | |
| 3 | 95 | 99 | |
| 4 | 90 | 94 | |
| 5 | 85 | 80 | |
| 6 | 80 | 84 | |
| 7 | 75 | 79 | |
| 8 | 70 | 74 | |
| 9 | 65 | 69 | |
| 10 | 60 | 64 | |
| 11 | 55 | 59 | |
| | $\overline{X}_B = 80$ | $\overline{X}_A = 83.2$ | |

**a** What are the medians for the two distributions?

Before = .......................................... After = ............................................

**b** Compute the difference score for each subject. What is the mean of the difference scores?

..................................................................

**c** How does the mean of the difference scores compare to the difference between $\overline{X}_B$ and $\overline{X}_A$?

..................................................................

**d** For practical purposes, we can assume the median of the difference scores is 4. How does this compare to the difference between the Before and After medians?

..................................................................

**e** Briefly explain why the mean of the difference scores is equal to the difference between means, and the median of the difference scores is not equal to the difference between medians.

.................................................................................................................................................

.................................................................................................................................................

.................................................................................................................................................

**6.5.14** For a set of test scores, $\sum_{i=1}^{N} (X_i - 7) = 0$. What is the value of $\overline{X}$?

.................................................................................

**6.6.15** Fifteen families live in separate houses on a straight street 1,000 yards long. The houses are on the same side of the street, but they are *not* equally spaced; vacant lots lie between some of them. The families wish to take their old newspapers to a central location for collection by the local Boy Scout troop. They want to select as a collection point the spot that will require the least total amount of walking by all 15 families. What location would meet the requirement? Why?

.................................................................................................................................................

.................................................................................................................................................

.................................................................................................................................................

**6.7.16** When we speak of the "average" size of families, do we usually imply the mean, median, or mode? Explain.

.................................................................................................................................................

.................................................................................................................................................

.................................................................................................................................................

.................................................................................................................................................

**6.7.17** Which statistical index is usually implied when we speak of the "average American," the "average personality," the "average school"? Explain.

.................................................................................................................................................

.................................................................................................................................................

**Table 6.A** Distribution of Communities in the United States

| Population | f |
|---|---|
| 1,000,000 or more | 5 |
| 500,000–999,999 | 13 |
| 250,000–499,999 | 23 |
| 100,000–249,999 | 66 |
| 50,000–99,999 | 128 |
| 25,000–49,999 | 271 |
| 10,000–24,999 | 814 |
| 5,000–9,999 | 1,133 |
| 2,500–4,999 | 1,570 |
| 1,000–2,499 | 3,408 |
| Less than 1,000 | 9,827 |
| | 17,258 |

**6.7.18a** The distribution in Table 6.A shows the number of communities in the United States at each of 11 population intervals for a particular year. How do the mean and median compare? Explain. [*Notes:* (1) It should be possible to answer this question without computing the approximate value of either index. (2) The *extreme* skew of this distribution is partially hidden by the fact that a constant interval size is not used (see 3.6.16).]

..........................................................................................................................................

..........................................................................................................................................

..........................................................................................................................................

..........................................................................................................................................

..........................................................................................................................................

**b** Which index—mean, median, or mode—would best describe the population of the typical community? Why?

..........................................................................................................................................

..........................................................................................................................................

**c** The *PR* of the approximate mean of this distribution is 87. What characteristic of the mean accounts for the fact that only about 13 percent of the communities have populations larger than the mean?

..........................................................................................................................................

..........................................................................................................................................

**6.7.19a** Suppose the mean annual income is much larger in one community than in another. Assuming the cost of living is roughly the same in each community, can you conclude that the "average" ability to "live well" is much greater in the first community? Why?

..............................................................................................................

..............................................................................................................

..............................................................................................................

..............................................................................................................

..............................................................................................................

..............................................................................................................

**b** Which index of location would provide the most appropriate indication of the annual income of the "typical" adult in a given community?

..............................................................................................................

**c** Why are per capita figures often seriously misleading in discussions of the status of typical individuals?

..............................................................................................................

..............................................................................................................

..............................................................................................................

**6.7.20** In exercise 3.6.16 we gave the frequency distribution for the years of service of 361 teachers in a certain city. For this distribution the following facts obtain.

1 Modal value = .5
2 Median value = 6.2
3 Mean value = 9.7
4 Approximately 90% of the scores exceed the modal value
5 Approximately 61% of the scores are below the mean value

**a** Approximately what percentage of the scores are above the median value?

..............................................................................................................

**b** If the local teacher's association wanted to describe the typical teacher (in terms of years of service), which index would best serve this purpose? Explain.

..............................................................................................................

..............................................................................................................

..............................................................................................................

..............................................................................................................

**6.7.21** The situation described below, while somewhat outdated, illustrates very clearly the potential danger in using an inappropriate index as a basis for making a decision.

The distribution of time spent in college and university programs by the rural school teachers in a certain state was markedly skewed. The mean of this distribution was about 32 weeks, the median about 8 weeks. The legislators of this state decided to raise the requirements for certification to teach in the state's rural schools. They legislated that within a two-year period each rural school teacher must have attended college for a minimum of 32 weeks to qualify for recertification. They reasoned that since the "average" teacher could already meet this requirement, and since two years were allowed for acquiring the additional training, a serious hardship would be worked on very few teachers if any at all. What was the fallacy in this reasoning?

............................................................................................................................

............................................................................................................................

............................................................................................................................

............................................................................................................................

............................................................................................................................

............................................................................................................................

............................................................................................................................

............................................................................................................................

**6.8.22** The student newspaper at a certain Midwestern university reported salary data for its university and also for the highest-paying university in a surrounding ten-state area. The "average" salaries for assistant professors were reported as:

|  |  |
|---|---|
| Local "average" | $12,850 |
| Highest-paying "average" | $13,890 |

The particular "average" being used was not specified.

**a** If the purpose for presenting these data was to indicate the typical salary of the assistant professors at each university, what index should have been used?

............................................................

**b** If the purpose for presenting these data was to indicate to the board of regents of the local university (the group in control of the budget) the amount of money allocated for salaries (per assistant professor) at each university, what index should have been used?

............................................................

**6.8.23** Consider the situation described in 3.7.20. Assume the principal computed the mean and median for both the Practice and No-Practice groups and found the following results. (*Note:* These results are not consistent with the data given on p. 23.)

|  | Mean | Median |
|---|---|---|
| Practice | 47 | 44 |
| No-Practice | 44 | 44 |

**a** If only the median values for each distribution had been computed, what conclusion might have been reached?

........................................................................................................................

........................................................................................................................

**b** Would a different conclusion have been reached on the basis of the mean values?

........................................................................................

**c** Assume someone examining these results says that an error must have been made. Explain how it would be possible for this set of results to occur. (*Hint:* Consider the possibility that the practice session was most helpful to students who would normally score very low on the reading test.)

........................................................................................................................

........................................................................................................................

........................................................................................................................

........................................................................................................................

**d** In the space provided for the figure for 6.8.23, sketch smoothed frequency polygons for these two distributions that would yield the mean and median values given above. (A crude sketch is sufficient.)

**6.8.24** A principal administered a standardized arithmetic test to all seventh-grade classes in her school. Finding that the *median* score of the pupils in one of the classes was seriously below the norm, she mentioned this fact to the teacher of that class. The teacher resolved to raise the median on the next test to be given by the principal. He reasoned correctly that his best chance of success lay in concentrating his instructional efforts on just a certain few of his pupils.

**a** On which pupils did he concentrate his efforts?

..................................................................................................................

..................................................................................................................

**b** What characteristics of the median did he recognize?

..................................................................................................................

..................................................................................................................

**c** Why would the use of the mean discourage this practice?

..................................................................................................................

..................................................................................................................

**6.8.25** Which best indicates the value of a piece of farm land—mean yield per acre, median yield per acre, or modal yield per acre? Explain.

..................................................................................................................

..................................................................................................................

..................................................................................................................

**6.8.26** A large trucking concern kept track for several years of the miles of service received from two makes of tires. It found that the *median* length of life was 50,000 miles for Tire A and 52,000 for Tire B, but that the *mean* length of life was 52,000 miles for Tire A and 50,000 for Tire B. Assuming that both makes sell for the same price, which make of tire should the concern buy in the future? Explain.

..................................................................................................................

..................................................................................................................

..................................................................................................................

..................................................................................................................

**6.9.27** As part of a Gallup poll of public attitudes toward education,[1] a representative sample of parents was asked the following question.

> How much time would you say your child spends in reading not connected with homework on a typical school day in the hours when he or she is not in school?

The responses to this question made by a group of parents who had previously indicated that their child was at the "top" of her or his class were summarized as follows.

**1** 11 percent responded that their child spent 0 minutes on this activity.

**2** The median number of minutes spent on this activity was 35.

**3** The mean number of minutes spent on this activity was 53.

**a** Considering the nature of the variable being measured and the information supplied above, explain why it is reasonable to believe that the distribution of reading time scores is multimodal (or at least bimodal). (*Hint:* For this question, what would be the most common responses? Would 23 be a common response? Would it be reasonable to assume that 0, 15, 30, 45, and 60 are common responses?)

..................................................................................................................

..................................................................................................................

..................................................................................................................

..................................................................................................................

**b** Suppose that the distribution really had three modes: 0, 30, and 60 (are these reasonable values?). Why would it have been useful to supply such information as part of the summary data? Would it have been reasonable to indicate also the percentage of parents responding at each modal value?

..................................................................................................................

..................................................................................................................

..................................................................................................................

..................................................................................................................

[1] This exercise is based on information given in the "Sixth Annual Gallup Poll of Public Attitudes toward Education," *Phi Delta Kappan*, September 1974, pp. 20–32.

**6.11.28** Suppose you operate a single truck and need to buy a single tire. Given the information in 6.8.26 about the length of life of tires of makes A and B, which make would you buy? Explain. (*Hint:* Consider the forms of the distributions of the lengths of life in miles of the two makes of tires. The life of the typical tire is not markedly different for the two makes. Furthermore, far from being assured of getting a typical tire, you run a chance of getting one of the poorer as well as one of the better tires of whichever make you buy. For each make, therefore, consider the likelihood of getting a very good tire, as well as of getting a very poor one.)

..................................................................................................................

..................................................................................................................

..................................................................................................................

..................................................................................................................

..................................................................................................................

..................................................................................................................

..................................................................................................................

**6.11.29** The mean enrollment in Iowa high schools in a certain year was about 204 pupils. The median enrollment was about 113. Individual A is in possession of the first fact only; B knows only the second fact; C knows both. What characteristic of the distribution is known to C that is not known to either B or A?

..................................................................................................................

..................................................................................................................

**6.11.30** Consider the situation described in 6.8.22. Why would it be useful for the newspaper to supply both the median and mean values for these salaries?

..................................................................................................................

..................................................................................................................

..................................................................................................................

# 7
# Measures of Variability

**7.1.1a** Indexes of variability provide some indication of the spread of scores along the score scale. Consider Figure 7.1 in the text (p. 105). Any index of variability that is devised should be greater for which of the distributions in Figure 7.1—School A or School B?

..................................................................

**b** For which distribution in Figure 7.2 of the text (p. 105)—seniors or freshmen—should an index of variability be greater?

..................................................................

**7.2.2** Table 7.A gives the number of trials required by the subjects of Groups A and B to learn a list of eight paired associates (nonsense syllables) to a criterion of seven out of eight correct. The task differed for the two groups in that the exposure time for Group A was two seconds, whereas that for Group B was three seconds. It is important to note that the smaller the number of trials required to achieve this criterion, the better the performance, and vice versa. This inversion in the meaning of a score value (large = poor, small = good) is fairly common to psychological data. While this inversion must, of course, be heeded in the interpretation of statistical indexes, it does not usually complicate their computation. Thus the means of the two groups of scores are still found by

**Table 7.A**  Numbers of Trials to Criterion

| Group A (Two Seconds) | | | | Group B (Three Seconds) | | | | |
|---|---|---|---|---|---|---|---|---|
| 41 | 17 | 25 | 34 | 18 | 6 | 20 | 18 | 36 |
| 14 | 40 | 27 | 19 | 16 | 40 | 23 | 27 | 17 |
| 50 | 39 | 26 | 22 | 28 | 18 | 15 | 18 | 18 |
| 28 | 18 | 42 | 33 | 22 | 27 | 15 | 8 | 16 |
| 25 | 28 | 27 | 33 | 18 | 24 | 16 | 24 | 17 |
| 34 | 7 | 12 | 36 | 31 | 27 | 25 | 21 | 15 |
| 34 | 40 | 19 | 40 | 16 | 12 | 21 | 18 | 5 |
| 16 | 26 | 30 | 48 | 34 | 24 | 25 | 27 | 6 |
| 28 | 33 | 25 | 50 | 27 | 39 | 19 | 24 | 9 |
| 33 | 29 | 26 | 30 | 25 | 17 | 23 | 25 | 5 |

| | | | |
|---|---|---|---|
| $N = 40$ | $Mdn = 28.5$ | $N = 50$ | $Mdn = 19.5$ |
| $\Sigma X = 1{,}184$ | $P_{75} = 35.0$ | $\Sigma X = 1{,}025$ | $P_{75} = 25.1$ |
| $\Sigma X^2 = 39{,}008$ | $P_{25} = 24.8$ | $\Sigma X^2 = 24{,}197$ | $P_{25} = 16.1$ |
| $\Sigma x^2 = 3{,}961.6$ | $H = 50$ | $\Sigma x^2 = \ldots\ldots$ | $H = 40$ |
| $\overline{X} = 29.6$ | $L = 7$ | $\overline{X} = 20.5$ | $L = 5$ |

dividing the sum by the number of scores. In using these means as an index of group performance, however, it is important to recognize that the performance of the group having the smaller mean was actually superior to that of the group having the larger mean.

One possibility of ambiguity and confusion with data involving an inversion in meaning arises in connection with the determination of percentiles and percentile ranks. If the scores are ranked from large to small, the $P_x$- or $PR$-values simply refer to the scores themselves; $P_x$ is simply a point on the score scale below which $x$ percent of the score values fall. But these scores below $P_x$ represent better performances than the $(100 - x)$ percent of the scores above it. Hence, if quality of performance rather than score magnitude is to be indicated, $P_x$ as obtained above must be interpreted as $P_{100-x}$. Of course, quality-of-performance percentiles and percentile ranks may be obtained directly by ranking the scores from small to large or by simply redefining $PR$- and $P_x$-values as referring to percentages of larger rather than smaller score values.

Although the researcher who is reporting percentile ranks or percentiles should make clear to the reader whether they pertain to quality of performance or simply to the magnitude of the score values, it is easy to tell from inspection which course has been followed. Obviously, if the $P_x$-values decrease with increases in $x$, quality of performance is the criterion; if they do not, they have been reported simply with reference to the magnitudes of the score values themselves.

**a** The highest score value in Group A is 50 and the lowest is 7. In using the range as an index of variability, does the fact that these values are inversely related to quality of performance need to be taken into account? Explain.

...................................................................................................................................

...................................................................................................................................

...................................................................................................................................

**b** Values of $P_{75}$ and $P_{25}$ for Group A are given in Table 7.A. Do the values reported for these points pertain to quality of performance on the task or to the magnitude of the score values? Why?

...................................................................................................................................

...................................................................................................................................

**c** What is the semi-interquartile range for the scores of Group B?

...................................................................................................................

**d** Using quality of performance as a criterion, what are the values of $P_{75}$ and $P_{25}$ for Group B?

$$P_{75} = \text{...............................................}$$

$$P_{25} = \text{...............................................}$$

**e** Using quality of performance as a criterion, what is the semi-interquartile range for Group B? (*Hint:* Range indexes are based on distances between score points. Does the direction in which the distance is measured contribute information regarding the degree of variation?)

...........................................................................................................

**f** Using either $R$ or $Q$ as indexes, in which group, A or B, was performance the more variable?

...........................................................................................................

**7.3.3** Consider this set of five scores:

     5, 4, 3, 2, 1

**a** Using formula (7.3), compute the $MD$ of this set of scores.

...........................................................................................................

**b** Using formula (7.4), compute the variance of this set of scores.

...........................................................................................................

**c** What is the standard deviation of this set of scores?

...........................................................................................................

**d** Assume an additional score of 9 is added to the original five scores. What is the $MD$ of the new set of six scores?

...........................................................................................................

**e** What is the variance of the new set of scores?

...........................................................................................................

**f** What is the $S$ of the new set of scores?

...........................................................................................................

**g** The ratio of the $MD$ of the six scores to the $MD$ of the five scores is $2.0/1.2 \approx 1.65$. The $S$ of the original five scores is $\sqrt{2} \approx 1.414$. The $S$ of the six scores is $\sqrt{6.6667} \approx 2.582$. The ratio of the two standard deviations is $2.582/1.414 \approx 1.83$. If the results of this one example can be generalized, what conclusion can be reached concerning the effect of extreme scores on the $S$ as compared to the $MD$?

...........................................................................................................

...........................................................................................................

...........................................................................................................

...........................................................................................................

**7.3.4a** Consider the two smoothed relative frequency polygons shown in Figure 7.1 of the text (p. 105). How do the indexes of variability ($R$, $Q$, $MD$, and $S$) of A compare with those of B?

..............................................................................................................................

..............................................................................................................................

**b** Consider the two smoothed relative frequency polygons shown in Figure 7.2 of the text (p. 105). How do the indexes of variability ($R$, $Q$, $MD$, and $S$) for the freshman distribution compare with those of the senior distribution?

..............................................................................................................................

..............................................................................................................................

**7.3.5** In a particular medical research study, only individuals above $P_{67}$ and below $P_{33}$ on a given variable were selected as experimental subjects. Assume the frequency distribution for all subjects is unimodal and symmetrical. Let E refer to the experimental subjects and T refer to the total group.

The two smoothed relative frequency polygons of the figure for 7.3.5 may help you answer the questions given below.

**a** How does the mean of the T group compare to the mean of the E group?

..............................................................................................................................

..............................................................................................................................

**b** Why is the $MD$ of the T group much less than the $MD$ of the E group? (*Hint:* Remember, the $MD$ is the mean of all absolute deviations from the mean.)

..............................................................................................................................

..............................................................................................................................

..............................................................................................................................

**c** How does $S_T$ compare with $S_E$?

..............................................................................................................................

..............................................................................................................................

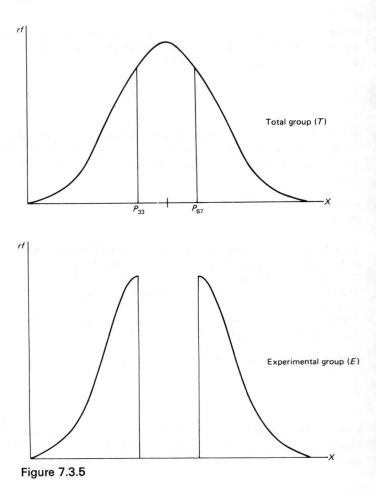

Figure 7.3.5

**7.3.6** It should be obvious that if $R$, $Q$, $MD$, and $S$ are to be computed, the variables involved must be scaled (i.e., the "scores" must be numerical values). This does not mean, however, that the concept of spread or variability cannot be applied to unscaled data. Consider, for example, the accompanying table, which shows the overall rating of four different statistics instructors by their students.

| Overall Rating | Instructor | | | |
| --- | --- | --- | --- | --- |
| | I | II | III | IV |
| Excellent | 0 | 25 | 10 | 25 |
| Good | 15 | 40 | 20 | 25 |
| Fair | 35 | 30 | 40 | 25 |
| Poor | 50 | 5 | 30 | 25 |
| Total $N$ | 100 | 100 | 100 | 100 |

**a** For which instructor did the students show the most disagreement (i.e., for which were the ratings most variable)?

...................................................................

**b** For which instructor did the students show the most agreement?

...................................................................

**7.4.7a** Using (7.8), obtain the variance of the scores of Group A in Table 7.A (exercise 7.2.2).

$$S^2 = \text{.....................................................}$$

What is the standard deviation?

$$S = \text{.....................................................}$$

**b** Does the fact that the scores involved are inversely related to quality of performance affect the computation of the variance or standard deviation? Explain.

...................................................................

...................................................................

...................................................................

...................................................................

...................................................................

**c** Does the fact that the scores involved are inversely related to quality of performance need to be taken into account in interpreting the variance or standard deviation as an index of variability? Explain.

...................................................................

...................................................................

...................................................................

**7.4.8a** In Table 7.A (exercise 7.2.2) what is the sum of squares of the deviations of the group B scores from their mean [use (7.6)]?

...................................................................

**b** Given the result you obtained for **a**, compute the variance of the Group B scores using equation (7.4).

...................................................................

**c** What is their standard deviation?

...................................................................

**7.4.9** Consider the relative frequency distribution of 50 arithmetic quiz scores given in Table 5.2B (p. 00) of the text. Compute the variance of these scores using (7.10a). (*Note:* The mean of these 50 scores is 5.44.)

...................................................................

**7.5.10** Using the results of a first scoring, the $Q$ of the scores on a given test was computed for a group of 200 students. A rescoring showed that each of the 10 highest original scores was from one to three points too high.

**a** Why would the value of $Q$ of the corrected score distribution almost certainly be the same as that previously obtained?

..................................................................................................................................

..................................................................................................................................

..................................................................................................................................

..................................................................................................................................

**b** Why would the value of $S$ certainly be changed?

..................................................................................................................................

..................................................................................................................................

..................................................................................................................................

**c** How would the value of $S$ be changed? Would it be larger or smaller?

.........................................................................

**d** Which index of variability—$Q$ or $S$—is the more sensitive to the presence of extreme scores?

.........................................................................

**7.5.11** Suppose that A knows only that the $Q$ of a given distribution is 20, while B knows that $P_{75}$ is 30 units from the median and that $P_{25}$ is 10 units from the median.

**a** What can B tell about the distribution that A cannot?

..................................................................................................................................

**b** Are the scores much more variable in one part of this distribution than in another?

.........................................................................

**c** For what type of distribution is it better to describe variability in terms of $P_{25}$, $P_{50}$, and $P_{75}$ than in terms of $Q$ alone? Why?

..................................................................................................................................

..................................................................................................................................

..................................................................................................................................

..................................................................................................................................

**7.5.12** Given the following three facts or sets of facts about the distribution of community populations given in Table 6.A (exercise 6.7.18).

**1** $Q \approx 970$
**2** $S \approx 58{,}200$
**3** $P_{99} \approx 74{,}400$
  $D_9 \approx 8{,}210$
  $Q_3 \approx 2{,}370$
  $Mdn \approx 880$
  $Q_1 \approx 440$
  $D_1 \approx 180$
  $P_1 \approx 20$

**a** Why does neither fact 1 nor fact 2, when used alone, adequately describe the variability of community populations?

..................................................................................................................

..................................................................................................................

..................................................................................................................

..................................................................................................................

..................................................................................................................

**b** What do the facts of set 3 indicate about *just the variability* of this distribution that neither 1 nor 2 indicates?

..................................................................................................................

..................................................................................................................

..................................................................................................................

..................................................................................................................

**c** What information about the distribution other than its variability can be gained from set 3 but not from either 1 or 2?

..................................................................................................................

..................................................................................................................

**7.5.13** In 3.6.16 we gave the frequency distribution of the years of service for 361 teachers. The following facts are also true for this distribution.

**1** Mean = 9.7 years
  $Q$ = 6.7 years
  $S$ = 10.0 years
  $P_{95} = 31.0$ years, $P_{75} = 15.0$ years, $P_{50} = 6.2$ years, $P_{25} = 1.5$ years, $P_5 = .3$ years
**2** Percentage of teachers with scores between a point 1 $Q$-distance below the mean (3.0) and a point 1 $Q$-distance above the mean (16.4) is approximately 48.

**3** Percentage of teachers with scores between a point 1 $S$-distance below the mean (0 in this instance) and a point 1 $S$-distance above the mean (19.7) is approximately 84.

**4** Approximately 61 percent of the scores are less than the mean.

**a** Assume a superintendent wants to provide the school board with certain information about this group of teachers. For one thing, he wants to give the board some summary data regarding years of service. He decides to provide the board with a location index and an index of variability. Should he provide the mean and $S$ or the median and $Q$? Explain.

........................................................................................................................

........................................................................................................................

........................................................................................................................

**b** With data of this type, why are the summary indexes referred to in **a** inadequate?

........................................................................................................................

........................................................................................................................

........................................................................................................................

**7.5.14a** In distributions that are approximately unimodal and symmetrical, about what percentage of the scores deviate from the "average" (mean, median, or mode) by more than 1 $Q$-distance?

........................................................................................................................

**b** In a markedly positively skewed distribution, will the proportion of score values within 1 $Q$ of the *median* be one-half, less than one-half, or more than one-half? Explain.

........................................................................................................................

........................................................................................................................

........................................................................................................................

........................................................................................................................

........................................................................................................................

........................................................................................................................

........................................................................................................................

........................................................................................................................

**7.5.15** In a certain unimodal symmetrical frequency distribution, two-thirds of the score values were within 1 $S$ of the mean. Six scores were added to the distribution, three of which were *extremely* larger and three *extremely* smaller than any scores in the original distribution.

**a** How would the $S$ of the augmented distribution compare with that of the original? (*Hint:* Refer to your answers to 7.3.3.)

.............................................................................................................................

**b** In the augmented distribution would two-thirds of the score values still fall within 1 $S$ of $\overline{X}$? If not, would the proportion be larger or smaller than two-thirds?

.............................................................................................................................

**c** What would be characteristic of the form of a unimodal symmetrical distribution in which more than two-thirds of the score values fall within 1 $S$ of $\overline{X}$?

.............................................................................................................................

**7.5.16** From what part of a distribution would you remove a score so as to:

**a** Increase the value of $S$?

.............................................................................................................................

**b** Increase the value of $\overline{X}$?

.............................................................................................................................

**c** Decrease $S$ and increase $\overline{X}$?

.............................................................................................................................

**7.5.17** To what part of a distribution would you add a score so as to:

**a** Increase the value of $S$?

.............................................................................................................................

**b** Increase the value of $\overline{X}$?

.............................................................................................................................

**c** Increase $S$ and decrease $\overline{X}$?

.............................................................................................................................

**7.6.18** The $S$ of IQs is 6 for one class of seventh-grade pupils and 12 for another. The mean IQ for both classes is 105. What is the significance of this difference from the point of view of the teacher?

.............................................................................................................................

.............................................................................................................................

.............................................................................................................................

**7.6.19** The $S$ of the number of trials to criterion for Group B, Table 7.A (exercise 7.2.2), is roughly 8. As part of this same investigation, the researcher measured the subjects' ability to recall after 48 hours by having them relearn the list to the seven-out-of-eight correct criterion used with the original learning. Instead of using number of trials as a score, the researcher kept a record of the total number of correct responses given by subjects from their first through their last relearning trial. The $S$ of the number of correct response scores for the Group B subjects was approximately 10. May the researcher conclude from these data that, for *these particular subjects*, recall performance is somewhat more variable than learning performance? Explain.

..................................................................................................................................

..................................................................................................................................

..................................................................................................................................

**7.6.20** Students at a particular school were required, as part of their physical education class, to do as many pushups as possible at the beginning of each class. After ten classes the following statistics were computed for a sample of four students:

> *Student 1:* $\overline{X} = 10, S = 3$
> *Student 2:* $\overline{X} = 20, S = 6$
> *Student 3:* $\overline{X} = 30, S = 8$
> *Student 4:* $\overline{X} = 40, S = 4$

On the basis of these data, what conclusion about the relationship between level of performance and variability of performance seems reasonable?

..................................................................................................................................

..................................................................................................................................

..................................................................................................................................

**7.6.21** Consider the two relative frequency polygons for 3.7.19. For which distribution (Before or After) are $Q$, $S$, and $MD$ greater?

..................................................................................................................................

**7.7.22** In a psychological investigation of pitch discrimination, a series of tuning forks is set up behind a screen. The experimenter strikes these forks at random, and after each tone is sounded, the subject records his estimate of its pitch in double vibrations per second. This is continued until a certain one of the forks has been sounded 50 times. Only the estimates for this one fork are retained.

**a** Without knowing its true pitch, how could one derive from these data a quantitative measure of this subject's accuracy in recognizing the pitch of this fork? (Assume that the subject's errors are not systematic; that is, assume that his estimates differ from the true pitch by being too high by a given amount as often as they are too low by this amount.)

........................................................................................................................

........................................................................................................................

........................................................................................................................

**b** Suppose that two subjects, A and B, are to be compared in terms of ability to recognize pitch. Suppose further that A's estimates are quite accurate, but that a small proportion of them are extremely bad due to wavering attention. Suppose also that B attends closely during the test and makes no extremely bad estimates, but that most of her estimates are not as good as A's. Would you prefer to use the value of the $S$ or the $Q$ of the estimates of each of these subjects in comparing their abilities? Explain.

........................................................................................................................

........................................................................................................................

........................................................................................................................

........................................................................................................................

**7.7.23** In an investigation of the reliability (in the sense of agreement) of judges' ratings of a theme, a number of judges are asked to read and then rate a given theme on a ten-point scale. Explain how one could provide a quantitative index of the reliability of such ratings.

........................................................................................................................

........................................................................................................................

........................................................................................................................

........................................................................................................................

........................................................................................................................

**7.7.24** The head of the freshman English program at a large university became concerned about the inconsistencies in the grading of essay questions. She decided to investigate the usefulness of a one-hour mini-course on the grading of essay questions that was offered periodically by the examination service at her university. She asked 20 of her instructors to attend this mini-course. About a week after the course was over, she asked these 20 instructors and a control group of 20 instructors who had not participated in the course to grade (on a scale of 1 to 10) a particular essay paper. What statistical index (or indexes) should be used to check on the effectiveness of the mini-course for achieving a more consistent grading system?

........................................................................................................................

........................................................................................................................

# 8

# Linear Transformations

**8.2.1a** Suppose you are informed that a certain college freshman's score on a vocabulary test is 65. On the basis of this information alone, what can you conclude about the quality of his performance on this test?

.................................................................................................................

**b** Now suppose you are told that the score in **a** is a standard score in a system that for college freshmen in general involves the standard values of 50 and 10 for the mean and standard deviation, respectively. Now what can you conclude about the quality of this individual's test performance?

.................................................................................................................

.................................................................................................................

**8.3.2** Consider the linear transformation $Y_i = 3X_i + 2$, where $i = 1, 2, \ldots, 50$.

**a** Let $X_1 = 10$ and $X_2 = 20$. What are the values of $Y_1$ and $Y_2$?

$Y_1 = $ .............................................  $Y_2 = $ .............................................

**b** Compare $X_2 - X_1$ with $Y_2 - Y_1$. How many times greater than $X_2 - X_1$ is $Y_2 - Y_1$?

.................................................................................

**c** Let $X_3 = 5$ and $X_4 = 7$. What are the values of $Y_3$ and $Y_4$?

$Y_3 = $ .............................................  $Y_4 = $ .............................................

**d** Compare $X_4 - X_3$ with $Y_4 - Y_3$. How many times greater than $X_4 - X_3$ is $Y_4 - Y_3$?

.................................................................................

**e** Given the results of **b** and **d**, what is characteristic of the differences between corresponding pairs of values of two linearly related variables?

.................................................................................................................

.................................................................................................................

**8.4.3** Consider the following set of five $X$-scores:

5, 4, 3, 2, 1

For these scores $\bar{X} = 3$, $S^2 = 2$, and $S = \sqrt{2} \approx 1.4$.

**a** Assume the following linear transformation is performed: $Y_i = X_i + 10$. What is $\bar{Y}$?

.................................................

What is $S_Y^2$?

.................................................

What is $S_Y$?

.................................................

**b** If $Y_i = 3X_i$, what is $\bar{Y}$?

.................................................

What is $S_Y$?

.................................................

**c** If $Y_i = 3X_i + 10$, what is $\bar{Y}$?

.................................................

What is $S_Y$?

.................................................

**d** Show that your values in **c** are correct by actually calculating the new $Y$-scores and using them to compute $\bar{Y}$, $S_Y^2$, and $S_Y$.
**e** If $Y_i = -3X_i$, what is $\bar{Y}$?

.................................................

What is $S_Y$?

.................................................

**f** If $Y_i = 3X_i - 10$, what is $\bar{Y}$?

.................................................

**g** If $Y_i = -3X_i - 10$, what is $\bar{Y}$?

.................................................

What is $S_Y$?

.................................................

**8.4.4a** Assume a teacher wishes to find the mean score on a scholastic aptitude test for her 30 students. The scores range from 101 to 143. The teacher decides to subtract 100 from every score before computing the mean. If the original score values are represented by $X$, write the linear transformation she is using.

$Y_i = $ .................................................

**b** If the actual mean of the aptitude scores is 112, what will be the mean of the transformed scores?

.................................................

**c** If the teacher calculates the mean of the $Y$-scores, what must she do to change this mean to the mean of the aptitude scores?

.................................................................................................................................

.................................................................................................................................

**d** Transformations of the type used in **a** are particularly useful if the score values are large. This is true even if some type of electronic calculating equipment is used, since such equipment frequently has limited storage capacity. Consider the following illustrative data.

For 1,000 scores ranging between 9,001 and 9,099 the actual mean is 9,050.5 and the actual variance is 833.25. These 1,000 scores served as input into a computer. The mean was calculated by (6.2) [i.e., $\overline{X} = \sum X_i/N$], and the variance was calculated by (7.7) [i.e., $S^2 = \sum X_i^2/N - (\sum X_i/N)^2$]. The output from the computer indicated that the mean was 9,050.5 and the variance was 452.00. The mean value determined by the computer was accurate; however, the computed variance differed rather markedly from the actual value of 833.25.[1]

In this example, 1,000 scores with values between 9,001 and 9,099 were used. With such a large number of scores and with values this great, the particular computer being used to perform the calculations did not accurately store the quantity $\sum X^2$. (Even if all 1,000 individuals had had the lowest possible score of 9,001, the value of $\sum X^2$ would have been 81,018,001,000.) While sample sizes of 1,000 and score values that range from 9,001 to 9,099 probably are not very common, a general computing formula should be developed to minimize the inaccuracy that could occur in computations involving large numbers. One possible procedure for computing the mean and variance is the following.

**1** Use the first score value as a constant to be subtracted from each score in the collection. In other words, form the quantity $Y_i = X_i - X_1$ for each individual in the collection. For the collection of scores given above, if the first score was 9,050, the $Y$-scores would range from $-49$ to $+49$.

**2** Find $\overline{Y}$ and $S_Y^2$ for the transformed scores. For our example,

$$\overline{Y} = \frac{\sum Y_i}{1,000} \approx .5 \quad \text{and} \quad S_Y^2 = \frac{\sum Y_i^2}{1,000} - \left(\frac{\sum Y_i}{1,000}\right)^2 \approx 833.25$$

**3** Use these values involving $Y$ to compute directly the corresponding values for the original collection of scores. What is the value of $\overline{X}$?..............................................................................................

What is the value of $S_X^2$?..............................................................................

**Table 8.A**  Grouped Frequency Distribution for Scores for Group B in Table 7.A

| Class | X (midpoint) | f | d | fd | fd² |
|-------|--------------|---|---|-----|------|
| 39–41 | 40 | 2 | +6 | +12 | +72 |
| 36–38 | 37 | 1 | +5 | + 5 | +25 |
| 33–35 | 34 | 1 | +4 | + 4 | +16 |
| 30–32 | 31 | 1 | +3 | + 3 | + 9 |
| 27–29 | 28 | 6 | +2 | +12 | +24 |
| 24–26 | 25 | 8 | +1 | + 8 | + 8 |
| 21–23 | 22 | 5 | 0 | 0 | 0 |
| 18–20 | 19 | 9 | −1 | − 9 | + 9 |
| 15–17 | 16 | 10 | −2 | −20 | +40 |
| 12–14 | 13 | 1 | −3 | − 3 | + 9 |
| 9–11 | 10 | 1 | −4 | − 4 | +16 |
| 6–8 | 7 | 3 | −5 | −15 | +75 |
| 3–5 | 4 | 2 | −6 | −12 | +72 |
| | | 50 | | −19 | +375 |

$$d = -.38 \qquad S_d^2 = 7.36$$

**8.4.5*** Consider the data in Table 8.A. The first three columns of this table were obtained by forming a grouped frequency distribution with an interval size of 3 for the data for Group B in Table 7.A (see exercise 7.2.2).

Before the widespread availability of computing machinery, descriptive indexes for a given set of data were often computed from such grouped frequency distributions to relieve some of the computational burden. The computation of the mean was done using formula (6.3) [i.e., $\bar{X} \approx \sum f_j X_j / N$, where $X_j$ is the midpoint of interval $j$.] The variance was computed using either formula (7.9) or (7.10) [i.e., $S^2 \approx \sum f_j X_j^2 / N - (\sum f_j X_j / N)^2$].

To relieve the computational burden even more, a linear transformation of the $X$-values was often employed. For example, in Table 8.A consider the $d$-column. The $d$-values are obtained from a linear transformation of the $X$-values:

$$d_j = \frac{1}{3} X_j - \frac{22}{3} \qquad \text{or} \qquad d_j = \frac{1}{3}(X_j - 22)$$

The computations were then performed on the $d$-values. For example,

$$\text{Mean} = \frac{\sum f_j d_j}{N} = \frac{-19}{50} = -.38$$

$$\text{Variance} = \frac{\sum f_j d_j^2}{N} - \left(\frac{\sum f_j d_j}{N}\right)^2$$

$$= \frac{7.5}{50} - \left(\frac{-19}{50}\right)^2$$

$$= 7.5 - (.38)^2 \approx 7.36$$

\* Optional exercise.

The mean and variance of the $X$-values were then found by noting that if $d_j = \frac{1}{3}(X_j - 22)$, then

$$X_j = 3d_j + 22$$

That is, $X$ can be considered a linear transformation of the $d$-values with $b = 3$ and $c = 22$. Thus, the mean and the variance of the $X$-scores can be found using formulas (8.8) and (8.9).

**a** Using (8.8), calculate the mean of the $X$-scores.

..................................................................

**b** Using (8.9), calculate the variance of the $X$-scores.

..................................................................

**c** The mean of the actual $X$-scores is 20.5 (see Table 7.A). You found a value of 20.86 for the mean called for in part **a**. Why do these mean values differ?

..................................................................

..................................................................

**d** The variance of the actual $X$-scores is approximately 63.69 (see exercise 7.4.8b). You should have estimated this variance to be 66.24 in part **b** above. Why do these values differ?

..................................................................

..................................................................

**8.5.6** The teacher of a particular seventh-grade class gives the pupils an arithmetic test and converts the raw test scores into $z$-scores.

**a** Pupil A's $z$-score is $+1.8$. What does this indicate about the quality of A's performance?

..................................................................

..................................................................

**b** Pupil B's score is $-.7$. What does this indicate about B's performance?

..................................................................

..................................................................

**c** Pupil C's score is .0. What does this indicate about C's performance?

..................................................................

**d** Can you determine Pupil A's percentile rank from the information given?

..................................................................

**e** From the information given may one conclude that Pupil C's score is at the median? Explain.

.........................................................................................................

.........................................................................................................

.........................................................................................................

**8.5.7** For the purpose of describing to a college freshman his relative performance on an entrance examination, would you prefer to use a percentile rank or a z-score? Why?

.........................................................................................................

.........................................................................................................

**8.5.8a** Many standardized tests use standard scores ($Z$) with a mean of 50 and a standard deviation of 10. In such a system of $Z$-scores, what $Z$-score corresponds to a $z$-score of $-2.0$?

.........................................................

**b** To a $z$-score of $+.5$?    .........................................................

**8.5.9a** A professor tells her class that the final grades for the course will be based on a midterm exam and a final exam. Furthermore, she says, each exam will contribute equally to the final grade. She administers the two exams (each has a maximum score of 100 points) and finds the following results.

|  | Midterm | Final |
|---|---|---|
| Mean | 50 | 60 |
| $S$ | 3 | 6 |

Assume the professor decides that since both tests are based on 100 items, the grade will be based on a composite score distribution formed by adding the two raw scores for each student. Consider the following sets of scores computed for two students.

|  | Midterm | Final | Composite |
|---|---|---|---|
| Student A | 53 | 54 | 107 |
| Student B | 47 | 66 | 113 |

Obviously, if the grades are based on these composite scores, Student B might receive a higher grade than Student A. However, notice that Student A's scores were 1 $S$ above the mean on the midterm and 1 $S$ below the mean on the final. Likewise, Student B's scores were 1 $S$ below the mean on the midterm and 1 $S$ above the mean on the final. When the scores are examined in this fashion, it seems reasonable to expect that Student A and Student B have the same chance of receiving a given grade —in other words, have *equal* composite scores!

You may have realized that this problem occurs because the standard deviations for the two tests differ. One solution to this problem is to convert each set of scores into a given set of standard scores before forming the composite. For example, the professor could decide to convert each distribution into a standard score distribution with mean = 50 and standard deviation = 10. Assume this is done. Fill in the following table with the appropriate standard scores and composites for Students A and B.

| | Midterm | Final | Composite |
|---|---|---|---|
| Student A | | | |
| Student B | | | |

**b** Are the composite scores now assigned to Students A and B more appropriate? Why?

.....................................................................................................................................

.....................................................................................................................................

.....................................................................................................................................

**8.6.10** A distribution of raw scores ($X$'s) is skewed to the left.

**a** Describe the form of the distribution of $z$-scores.

.....................................................................................................................................

**b** Describe the form of a set of $Z$-scores with $M_Z = 500$ and $S_Z = 100$ obtained by a linear transformation of the $X$-scores.

.....................................................................................................................................

# 9

# Introduction to Some Probability Concepts

**9.1.1** The student government association at a large university wanted to assess student opinion concerning various aspects of the current grading practices. They developed a comprehensive survey instrument, on which one of the questions was:

> Should courses with grades F or U be deleted from a student's transcript?

**a** A random sample[1] of students was asked this question and 52 percent responded "Yes." If all students had been asked this question, would the percentage responding "Yes" equal 52? Explain.

..................................................................................................................

..................................................................................................................

..................................................................................................................

**b** What do we label the difference between the 52 percent found for the representative sample and the true percentage for the entire population of students?

..................................................................................................

**9.1.2** An authoritarian instrument was administered to representative samples of men and women students at a particular university.[2] The following results were obtained.

| Men | Women |
|-----|-------|
| $\overline{X}_M = 53$ | $\overline{X}_W = 48$ |
| $S_M = 8$ | $S_W = 10$ |

[1] In a later chapter we will discuss how random samples can be obtained.
[2] As stated in Section 7.1, authoritarian instruments presumably measure degrees of dependency on clearly delineated hierarchies of authority.

**a** If all students enrolled had been given the authoritarian instrument, would the difference between the mean for men and the mean for women equal 5? Explain.

...............................................................................................................

...............................................................................................................

...............................................................................................................

Would the difference between the two standard deviations be 2? Explain.

...............................................................................................................

...............................................................................................................

...............................................................................................................

**b** The observed difference between the means of the two groups was 5 units. Assume that all students had been given the instrument and that the difference between the means of men and women was 4 units. What was the amount of the sampling error in the observed difference?

...............................................................................

**9.2.3** Consider the information presented in Table 9.A.

**a** For each act or concurrence of circumstances, identify the set of all possible observations.

**b** Briefly describe how each of these acts could be repeated.

**1** ...............................................................................................................

...............................................................................................................

**2** ...............................................................................................................

...............................................................................................................

**3** ...............................................................................................................

...............................................................................................................

**4** ...............................................................................................................

...............................................................................................................

**5** ...............................................................................................................

...............................................................................................................

**c** Which, if any, of these situations can be labeled experiments?

...............................................................................

### Table 9.A

| Act or Concurrence of Circumstances | Nature of Observations | Set of All Possible Observations |
|---|---|---|
| 1 Spinning a pointer on a pivot located at the center of a circle divided into 4 equal sectors of different colors (red, blue, green, yellow) | Color of sector in which pointer stops | |
| 2 Roll of a pair of dice | Number of dots facing up | |
| 3 10 students assembled in the student health clinic | Number with Type A blood | |
| 4 100 freshmen are asked the following question: "Did the orientation program adequately meet your needs?" | Percentage of students responding "Yes" | |
| 5 20 students taking a vocabulary test consisting of 25 items | Mean ($\overline{X}$) of their scores | |

**9.3.4** Identify the sample space for the situations described in Table 9.A.

1 $\mathscr{S} =$ ................................................................................................

2 $\mathscr{S} =$ ................................................................................................

3 $\mathscr{S} =$ ................................................................................................

4 $\mathscr{S} =$ ................................................................................................

5 $\mathscr{S} =$ ................................................................................................

**9.3.5a** For situation 2 in Table 9.A, assume the outcome of interest is whether the number of dots facing up is odd or even. What are the sample points?

................................................................................................................

**b** For situation 5 in Table 9.A, assume the outcome of interest is merely whether the mean is greater than or equal to 13 or less than 13. What are the sample points?

................................................................................................................

**9.3.6** Several of the situations described in Table 9.A are identified below. After each situation is identified, several events are defined. Indicate whether these events should be classified as compound (C) or simple (S).

**Situation 2**
$E_1$ = 7 or 11 .....................................................................

$E_2$ = 2 .....................................................................

$E_3$ = 7 .....................................................................

$E_4$ = 2, 4, 6, 8, 10, or 12 .....................................................

**Situation 3**
$E_1$ = 0 .....................................................................

$E_2$ = 7, 8, 9, or 10 .....................................................

**Situation 4**
$E_1$ = 0% .....................................................................

$E_2$ = 50%, 51%, ..., 100% .....................................................

$E_3$ = 75% .....................................................................

$E_4$ = 0% or 100% .....................................................

**9.3.7a** Consider situation 1 in Table 9.A. Assume we assign the following numbers to each sample point.

Red     = 1/4
Blue    = 1/4
Green   = 1/4
Yellow  = 1/4

Do these numbers represent probabilities? Explain.

....................................................................................................

....................................................................................................

....................................................................................................

**b** Assume the following numbers are assigned to each sample point.

Red     = 1/4
Blue    = 2/4
Green   = 1/4
Yellow  = 0

Do these numbers represent probabilities? Explain.

....................................................................................................

....................................................................................................

....................................................................................................

c You should have answered "Yes" to both **a** and **b**. However, the numbers assigned in part **a** may seem more reasonable to you. If they do, what assumption are you making?

....................................................................................................

....................................................................................................

**9.3.8** Consider situation 4 in Table 9.A. Assume the following sample space is of interest.

$$\mathscr{S} = \{\text{less than } 50\%, 50\%, \text{more than } 50\%\}$$

Further, assume the following values are assigned to the sample points.

$s_1$ (less than 50%) = .50
$s_2$ (50%) = .10
$s_3$ (more than 50%) = .50

Do these values represent probabilities? Explain.

....................................................................................................

**9.3.9a** In Table 9.A, why is it more difficult to justify situations 3, 4, and 5 as random experiments than situations 1 and 2?

....................................................................................................

....................................................................................................

**b** Assume the situations described in Table 9.A are instances of random experiments. Identify the random variable for each situation.

1 ..............................................................................................

2 ..............................................................................................

3 ..............................................................................................

4 ..............................................................................................

5 ..............................................................................................

**9.4.10** In each of the eight situations **a–h** described below, a probability value is given. Indicate for each situation which of the following three statements best expresses the interpretation of the given probability value.

1 A relative frequency interpretation obtained via Monte Carlo–type procedures.

2 A relative frequency interpretation obtained via a theoretical model.

3 A personalistic interpretation obtained via a consideration of one's degree of belief.

**a** The probability that Mary will pass her driver's test on the first try is .90.

....................................................................................

b John has a score of 600 on a particular college entrance examination. One thousand students from John's high school have attended the local university over the last 5 years. Of these 1,000 students, 200 had test scores very close to 600. Approximately 90 percent of these 200 students had grade-point averages above 2.0 (above a C). The counselor tells John that the probability of his earning a GPA greater than 2.0 is .90.

.......................................................................

c The probability that Bill's marriage will end in divorce is .70.

.......................................................................

d The probability that the date of your birth will be drawn first in a draft lottery is 1/366.

.......................................................................

e A labor union official states, "There is an 80 percent chance of a strike" (probability = .80).

.......................................................................

f The publishers of a popular magazine are conducting a sweepstakes. Twenty thousand prizes are to be awarded. Twenty million numbers have been distributed to 20 million people. The company makes the following statement in their advertisement: "Check your number now! You may be one of the lucky one in a thousand people who have won a fabulous prize!" (probability = .001).

.......................................................................

g The probability that the faculty will beat the students in their coming basketball game is .10.

.......................................................................

h A particular paper and pencil instrument is used as a mental health screening device. An examinee scoring above 60 on this instrument is referred for a more intensive analysis by a psychiatrist. When the test was administered to a large group of college students, 100 of these students scored above 60 and were referred to a psychiatrist. Of these 100, 90 were classified as needing psychiatric help. The investigator stated: "Given a person whose score is above 60 on this screening device, the probability of this person's needing psychiatric help is .90."

.......................................................................

9.4.11 In some of the situations of the preceding exercise it may have been somewhat difficult to justify a single interpretation. Some of the situations may, in fact, be viewed as a combination of the relative frequency and personalistic interpretations. Consider part c. Current census data may indicate that 50 percent of all marriages end in divorce. While this statistic (a relative frequency value arrived at from many observations) applies to marriages in general and not to a specific marriage, this fact might be combined with information about a specific marriage to arrive at the probability value given (.70). For part **a** of 9.4.10, briefly identify a piece of relative frequency information that may have been used to help arrive at the probability value of .90.

...........................................................................................................

...........................................................................................................

...........................................................................................................

**9.4.12** Briefly explain why the Monte Carlo method for assigning probability values is less desirable than the theoretical method.

...........................................................................................................

...........................................................................................................

...........................................................................................................

...........................................................................................................

**9.5.13** Consider the experiment that consists of casting a die twice. Suppose we are interested in the sequence of the number of dots on the two casts. Then, the sample space is:

$$\mathscr{S} = \{(1, 1), (1, 2), (1, 3), (1, 4), (1, 5), (1, 6),$$
$$(2, 1), (2, 2), (2, 3), (2, 4), (2, 5), (2, 6),$$
$$(3, 1), (3, 2), (3, 3), (3, 4), (3, 5), (3, 6),$$
$$(4, 1), (4, 2), (4, 3), (4, 4), (4, 5), (4, 6),$$
$$(5, 1), (5, 2), (5, 3), (5, 4), (5, 5), (5, 6),$$
$$(6, 1), (6, 2), (6, 3), (6, 4), (6, 5), (6, 6)\}$$

where in each pair the first number given is the outcome of the first cast. Assuming the die is fair, it seems reasonable to use the equally likely model to assign probability values to each outcome.

**a** If the equally likely model is used, what probability value should be assigned to each sample point?

...........................................................................................................

**b** Now assume the outcome of interest is not the sequence of the number of dots on the two casts, but the total number of dots facing up on the two casts. In this case the sample space of interest becomes

$$\mathscr{S} = \{2, 3, 4, 5, 6, 7, 8, 9, 10, 11, 12\}$$

In Table 9.B fill in the probability value for each of these sample points. [*Hint:* Find the number of sequences that lead to a particular outcome. For example, (1, 3), (3, 1), and (2, 2) each total 4 dots. Therefore, $P(s_j = 4) = 3/36$ (see DN 9.6).]

**Table 9.B**    The Probability Distribution of the Experiment
Described in 9.5.13b

| Sample Point ($s_j$) | $P(s_j)$ |
|:---:|:---:|
| 2 | |
| 3 | |
| 4 | |
| 5 | |
| 6 | |
| 7 | |
| 8 | |
| 9 | |
| 10 | |
| 11 | |
| 12 | |

c Use the scales provided for the figure for 9.5.13c to draw a histogram
showing the probability distribution of Table 9.B.

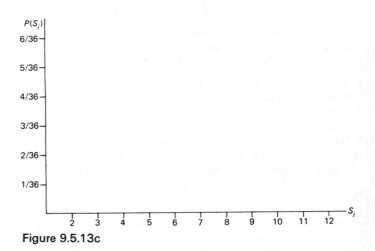

Figure 9.5.13c

**9.6.14** Probability distributions are hypothetical constructs. Why is it nonetheless reasonable to describe such distributions in terms of indexes such as means, medians, variances, and semi-interquartile ranges?

..........................................................................................................................................

..........................................................................................................................................

..........................................................................................................................................

..........................................................................................................................................

..........................................................................................................................................

**9.6.15** Forty-nine one-dollar bills, 2 two-dollar bills, 48 five-dollar bills, and 1 thousand-dollar bill are placed in a bag and mixed thoroughly. For a certain price, you are offered the privilege of drawing and keeping one bill.

**a** The outcome of interest in this experiment (game) is the value of the bill drawn. What is the sample space of this experiment?

$\mathscr{S} =$ ..............................................................................................

**b** If the equally likely model is valid for this experiment, what is the probability distribution for the random variable $X$, where $X$ is the value of the bill drawn?

| $X_j$ | $P(X_j)$ |
|-------|----------|
| \$1 | |
| \$2 | |
| \$5 | |
| \$1,000 | |

**c** What is the mean value of the bills in the bag?

..................................................................

**d** What is the expected value, $E(X)$, of a single draw?

..................................................................

**e** What is the median value of the bills in the bag?

..................................................................

**f** What is the median of the probability distribution of $X$?

..................................................................

**g** Suppose that you made a large number of draws, and each time put the bill drawn back into the bag (keeping track, of course, of how much the experimenter owes you). In the long run, you would break even if you paid how much for each draw?

..................................................................

At this price, what are the odds against your winning on any single draw?

..................................................................

**h** Why should you be willing to pay the expected value for a single draw even though you are "almost certain" to lose on any given occasion?

.................................................................................................................

.................................................................................................................

.................................................................................................................

.................................................................................................................

**9.6.16** Find the variance $(\sigma^2)$ of the probability distribution you constructed in 9.6.15b. Use DN 9.12.

.................................................................................................................

**9.7.17** Using Table 9.5 (p. 169) in the text, find the following probability values.

    **a** $P(r = 5 \mid n = 8, \phi = .30)$   .................................................

    **b** $P(r \geq 5 \mid n = 8, \phi = .30)$   .................................................

    **c** $P(r > 5 \mid n = 8, \phi = .30)$   .................................................

    **d** $P(r \leq 5 \mid n = 8, \phi = .30)$   .................................................

    **e** $P(r < 5 \mid n = 8, \phi = .30)$   .................................................

    **f** $P(r > 8 \mid n = 10, \phi = 1/3)$   .................................................

    **g** $P(r < 3 \mid n = 5, \phi = .25)$   

    **h** $P(3 \leq r \leq 6 \mid n = 10,$

                           $\phi = .50)$   .................................................

    **i** $P(r \geq 8$   or

          $r \leq 2 \mid n = 10, \phi = .40)$   .................................................

**9.7.18a** Consider the situation described in exercise 9.1.1. Assume the universe of students can be identified as $A$ types (people favoring deletion) and $\bar{A}$ types (people not favoring deletion). Assume further that only 40 percent of the students favor deletion. If a binomial experiment is to be performed with $n = 10$, what is $P(r \geq 8 \mid n = 10, \phi = .40)$?

.................................................................................................................

**b** Assume that 75 percent of the students favor deletion. It is not possible to use Table 9.5 directly to find $P(r \geq 8 \mid n = 10, \phi = .75)$. However, we can use Table 9.5 if we make two minor modifications. First, we need to redefine the $A$- and $\bar{A}$-type objects classified. Instead of defining an $A$ type as an individual who favors deletion (responds "Yes" to the question), we define an $A$ type as an individual who opposes deletion (responds "No"). Now, if 75 percent favor deletion, 25 percent oppose deletion and $P(A) = .25$. Second, note that the outcomes 8, 9, or 10 students responding "Yes" are respectively identical to the outcomes 2, 1, or 0 responding "No." Hence,

$$P(r^* \leq 2 \mid n = 10, \phi^* = .25) = P(r \geq 8 \mid n = 10, \phi = .75)$$

where

$r^*$ = the number of "No" responses
$\phi^*$ = the probability of a "No" response
$r$ = the number of "Yes" responses
$\phi$ = the probability of a "Yes" response

The probability value on the left can now be determined from Table 9.5.

Find $P(r \leq 2 \mid n = 10, \phi = .25)$. .................................................

Find $P(r \geq 5 \mid n = 8, \phi = .80)$. .................................................

**9.7.19** Consider a universe of 50,000 eligible voters in a large city. Assume the universe consists of two types of voters: those who favor the passage of a particular bond issue ($A$ type), and those who oppose the bond issue ($\bar{A}$ type). A voter is selected from this universe by a chance procedure and asked if she or he favors the bond issue. This voter is returned to the universe and a second selection is made and the question is asked of this second person. This process is repeated ten times. The outcome of interest is the number of the ten voters interviewed who respond "Yes" to the question.

**a** For this situation to be considered a binomial experiment, the five criteria identified on pp. 164–165 of the text must be met. Answer the following questions by applying these criteria to this situation.

*Criterion 1:* What is the value of $N$? .................................................
Are the $N$ objects of two kinds? .................................................
*Criterion 2:* Is a chance selection procedure used? .................................................

What is the value of $n$? .................................................
*Criteria 3 and 4:* Assume $P(A) = \phi = .50$. Does this probability remain the same for all draws? .................................................
*Criterion 5:* Is the outcome of interest (the random variable) the number of $A$-type objects selected? .................................................

Is this experiment a binomial experiment?

.................................................

**b** If this is a binomial experiment with $\phi = .50$, what is the probability that $r = 10$?

.................................................

**c** What is the probability that $r \geq 7$? That is, find $P(r \geq 7 \mid n = 10,$ $\phi = .50)$.

.................................................................

Three aspects of the above situation are not very reasonable. We will first identify each of these aspects and then consider their ramifications. First, we indicated that after a voter was selected and asked whether he or she favored the bond issue, that voter was returned to the universe before the next one was selected. Such a procedure would permit the same person to be chosen again at a later draw (although the probability of such an occurrence would be very low in this situation). Although there is nothing inherently wrong with this procedure, it is not the one normally used; subjects selected are not usually returned to the universe.

If the more usual procedure is followed, is the binomial probability distribution still valid for assigning probability values to outcomes of the experiment? Let us investigate this question.

**d** Recall that the replacement requirement was necessary to maintain a constant $P(A)$ for all draws. That is, if we assume $P(A) = .50$ (i.e., 50 percent of voters favor the issue), then $P(A)$ must equal .50 for all draws if the binomial $PD$ is to be valid. If replacement does not occur, the $P(A)$-values differ from draw to draw. For example, if $P(A) = 25,000/50,000 = .50$ for the first draw, and if an $A$ type is drawn but not returned, $P(A)$ on the second draw is not exactly .50. What is $P(A)$ on this second draw?

.................................................................

**e** If an $\bar{A}$ type is drawn on the first draw and not returned, what is the $P(A)$ on the second draw?

.................................................................

**f** Your answers to **d** and **e** should have been $24,999/49,999 \approx .49999$ and $25,000/49,999 \approx .50001$, respectively. These values do not differ from .50 sufficiently to invalidate the binomial model.

What is the maximum deviation from .50 that can occur in this experiment? Assume that an $A$-type object was selected on each of the first nine draws. What is $P(A)$ on the tenth and final draw?

.................................................................

**g** If $\bar{A}$-type objects were selected on each of the first nine draws, what is $P(A)$ on the tenth draw?

.................................................................

*Remark:* Your answers to **f** and **g** should have been $24,991/49,991 \approx .49991$ and $25,000/49,991 \approx .50009$, respectively. Thus, for this experiment the $P(A)$-values do not differ from .50 by enough to invalidate the use of the binomial probability distribution for assigning probability values.

This will be true whenever $N$ is large relative to $n$ (see footnote 13, text page 164).

A second unrealistic aspect of this example is the sample size or number of draws ($n = 10$). Ten was used merely for convenience of illustration. Larger $n$-values would be used in any real-life investigation of this nature.

The third unrealistic feature of this example is that a $\phi$-value had to be assumed before the binomial rule could be used. Actually, in experiments of this type the proportion of $A$'s in the population is not known. In fact, the purpose of performing such experiments is usually to make some inference about the value of $\phi$. One type of inferential procedure requires the experimenter to postulate a value for $\phi$, gather data, and then assess the reasonableness of the postulated value. (This idea is mentioned in Section 9.4 of the text.)

**h** Assume that the experimenter postulates $P(A) = \phi = .50$, and that ten voters are selected by a chance procedure. Assume also that no voters respond "Yes" (none of the voters selected favors passage of the bond issue). What is the probability of $r = 0$ if $n = 10$ and $\phi = .50$?

......................................................................

**i** Such probability values can be thought of as relative frequencies of the outcomes of an experiment when the experiment is repeated indefinitely. If, given an outcome of $r = 0$, the experimenter is to retain .50 as a reasonable value for $\phi$, what must he or she be willing to assume?

......................................................................

......................................................................

......................................................................

......................................................................

**9.7.20** An investigator was interested in the incidence of cheating under various test conditions.[3] "Cheating" was determined by pupils' scores on a multiple-choice vocabulary test that contained 20 nonsense syllables ("mock" items) and 25 legitimate vocabulary words. The test materials included the answer key to the test, which, the students were told, had been included only to facilitate later scoring and was not to be looked at until after the test had been completed. Since the mock items had no real meaning, a pupil who "correctly" answered many of these items—whose answers matched the "correct" answer in the key—was identified as having cheated by using the prohibited answer key (Vitro, p. 1, abstract). Obviously, the investigator needed a criterion that could be used to decide whether or not a student should be classified as a "cheater."

---

[3] The situation described in this exercise is based on a doctoral dissertation by F. T. Vitro ("The Effects of Probability of Test Success, Opportunity to Cheat, and Test Importance on the Incidence of Cheating," Ph.D. dissertation, University of Iowa, 1969).

As a first step in the process of identifying cheaters, the investigator must estimate how many of the mock items a student might be expected to answer correctly even had the answer key not been available. Since there were five alternatives to each mock item, it is reasonable to assume that the probability of answering an item correctly is 1/5 (see footnote 16 on p. 169 of the text). Thus, if a student is given 20 such items, the probability of getting 0, or 1, or 2, or anywhere up to 20 correct is of interest. The investigator decided to use the binomial probability distribution as a basis for assigning these probability values.

**a** What is the universe of objects? (*Hint:* Consider what is being selected or drawn. Is it a person or is it an item?)

..................................................................................................

**b** What is the value of $N$? (*Hint:* How many mock items can be formed?)

..................................................................................

**c** What is the value of $n$?

..................................................................

**d** What is the value of $P(A)$ or $\phi$?

..................................................................

**e** Is $\phi$ the same for all selected items?

..................................................................

**f** Using (9.1) with $\phi = .20$ and $n = 20$, the probability of a score of 0, or 1, or 2, or ..., or 20, is as shown in the accompanying table. What is $P(r \geq 8 \mid n = 20, \phi = .20)$?

..................................................................

| $r$ | Probability | $r$ | Probability |
|-----|-------------|-----|-------------|
| 0 | .0115 | 11 | .0005 |
| 1 | .0576 | 12 | .0001 |
| 2 | .1369 | 13 | .0000 |
| 3 | .2054 | 14 | .0000 |
| 4 | .2182 | 15 | .0000 |
| 5 | .1746 | 16 | .0000 |
| 6 | .1091 | 17 | .0000 |
| 7 | .0545 | 18 | .0000 |
| 8 | .0222 | 19 | .0000 |
| 9 | .0074 | 20 | .0000 |
| 10 | .0020 | | |

**g** If students with mock item scores of eight or greater are classified as cheaters, what is the probability that a student has been classified as a cheater when, in fact, he or she should have been labeled a noncheater?

..................................................................

**h** If 100 students responded to the 20 mock items without using the answer sheet, approximately how many of these students would be classified erroneously as cheaters? (Assume that the criterion for classification as a cheater is eight or more "correct" on the mock items.)

.................................................................

**i** What (to the nearest ten-thousandth) is the probability of obtaining a score of 15 on the 20 mock items purely as a result of chance?

.................................................................

**9.9.21** Consider the experiment described in exercise 9.7.20. The probability distribution of this experiment was assumed to be a binomial *PD* with $n = 20$ and $\phi = .20$.

**a** What is the mean of this binomial probability distribution? Use (9.2).

.................................................................

**b** What is the variance? Use (9.3).

.................................................................

**c** What is the standard deviation?

.................................................................

**9.9.22** Consider the situation described in exercise 9.7.19. A binomial *PD* with $n = 10$ and $\phi = .50$ was involved. What is the expected value of the random variable $r$ (the number of "Yes" responses) for this experiment?

.................................................................

**9.9.23a** The expected value of the random variable $r$ (number of $A$-type objects) when the binomial probability distribution is used to assign probability values is $n\phi$. Assume that the random variable of interest is the proportion of $A$-type objects in the sample. What is the expected value of the proportion of $A$-type objects? (*Hint:* Remember $p = (1/n)(r)$. Thus, $p$ can be viewed as a linear transformation of $r$. We noted in Chapter 8 [see equation (8.5), p. 133] that the mean of a new set of scores formed by multiplying the original set by a constant is merely the original mean times the constant. In this situation, the constant is $1/n$ and the mean of the original "scores"—that is, the values of the random variable $r$—is $n\phi$.)

.................................................................

**b** What is the variance of the probability distribution of the proportion of $A$-type objects? [*Hint:* Use the ideas embodied in equation (8.6), p. 134.]

.................................................................

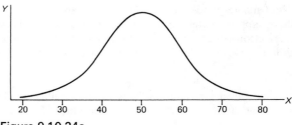

Figure 9.10.24a

**9.10.24a** Consider the graph shown as the figure for 9.10.24a. If this is the graph of the probability distribution of a continuous random variable (say $X$), what is the total area between the graph and the $X$-scale?

.................................................................

**b** Assume the graph of part **a** represents the probability distribution of the random variable $X$. The graph is shown as the figure for 9.10.24b with selected areas of the curve shaded. If the area of the curve directly over the interval 50–60 is .34, what is the probability that $X$ is between 50 and 60?

.................................................................

The area of the curve directly over the interval 30–40 is .28. What is $P(30 < X < 40)$?

.................................................................

What is the probability that $X = 30$?

.................................................................

**c** Indicate whether the following statements are true or false.

    **1** The vertical axis of the graph in part **a** is a scale of probability values.

            True.............    False.............

    **2** The vertical axis of the graph in part **a** is a scale of height values (ordinates) of the curve that correspond to given $X$-values.

            True.............    False.............

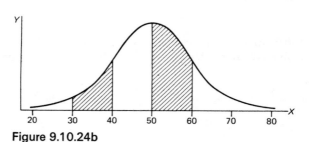

Figure 9.10.24b

# 10
# The Normal Probability Distribution

**10.1.1** The department of public instruction of a certain state has developed a paper and pencil instrument that purportedly measures high school students' "attitude toward school." The possible scores on this instrument range from 0 to 100. In a pilot study, it is found that high school students obtain scores ranging over the full length of the scale, from 0 to 100.

A statewide survey is to be undertaken to estimate the means of scores on this instrument for ninth-, tenth-, eleventh-, and twelfth-grade students. Assume that the method of sampling to be used ensures that the choice of students to take the instrument is strictly a matter of chance.

**a** As indicated above, the possible scores on this instrument range from 0 to 100. Therefore, the outcomes of this experiment (i.e., the means of samples of students in ninth through twelfth grade) must be between what values?

..................................................

**b** Consider the ninth-grade students only. Assume a sample of 400 ninth-grade students was selected and the instrument administered to all these students. Assume further that the outcome of this experiment (the mean of the 400 scores) was equal to 47.4. The purpose of the experiment was to estimate the mean score on this instrument for all ninth-grade students in the state. Is the true mean for all ninth-grade students likely to be equal to 47.4?

..................................................

**c** Assume the experiment is repeated with a new sample of 400 ninth-grade students. Is it likely that the outcome (mean) of this repetition will be equal to 47.4?

..................................................

**d** Imagine that the ninth-grade experiment is repeated a very large number of times. Many new samples, each consisting of 400 ninth-grade students, are selected and given the instrument, and then a mean is computed for each sample. Around what value do you think these means would cluster? (Answer with a verbal statement. We are not asking for a numerical value.)

........................................................................................................................

........................................................................................................................

**e** Consider the four histograms shown as Figure 10.1.1e. Which of these seems most plausible as a picture of the relative frequency distribution of the outcomes of the many repeated runs of the experiment described in **d**?

**f** In the space provided for the figure for 10.1.1f, draw the idealized smoothed relative frequency polygon picturing the distribution of outcomes of repeated runs of the experiment described in **d**.

**g** What is the value of the mean of the distribution you drew in **f**? (We are not asking for a numerical value.)

........................................................................................................................

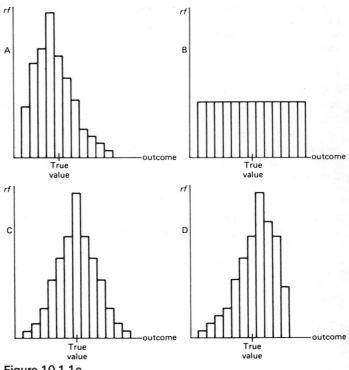

**Figure 10.1.1e**

—————————————————————————————————————————outcome

Figure 10.1.1f

**10.1.2** Performance on a three-minute cancellation test that involves crossing out—canceling—all $c$'s and $v$'s in a given series of letters does not reveal much "practice effect" (systematic improvement) after two or three initial practice trials. Of course, owing to fluctuations in such factors as mental alertness, physical tone, and emotional state, variations occur in a subject's performance from trial to trial, particularly when the trials are separated by a substantial time interval. A *large* number of such perform-ance scores for a given subject tend to fall into a unimodal symmetrical distribution.[1] (Theoretically, the distribution should involve an *unlimited* number of performance scores for the given subject.) It is customary to regard the mean of such a distribution as the subject's "true" score. The difference between any single score ($X$) a subject makes and this subject's true score ($\mu_X$) is the error of measurement involved in this particular single score. That is, if $E$ represents error, then

$$E = X - \mu_X$$

**a** If the normal distribution can be used as a model for the distribution of $X$-values, what is the form of the distribution of $E$-values? Explain. (*Note:* $E$ is a linear transformation of $X$.)

........................................................................................................................

........................................................................................................................

........................................................................................................................

........................................................................................................................

**b** How would the standard deviation of the distribution of $E$-values for this subject compare with that of his $X$-values? Explain.

........................................................................................................................

........................................................................................................................

........................................................................................................................

........................................................................................................................

[1] Assume the various series of letters involved in the various repetitions contain the same number of characters to be canceled, and that each score represents the number of correct cancellations.

**c** What would be the mean of the *E*-distribution? Explain.

.................................................................................................................

.................................................................................................................

.................................................................................................................

**10.2.3** Consider the smoothed relative frequency distribution called for in 10.1.1f. Suppose the true model for these outcomes is a normal distribution with $\mu = 40$ and $\sigma = 5$.

**a** Write the formula for the normal curve that provides a model of this relative frequency distribution of outcomes.

.................................................................................................................

**b** In this experiment $\mu = 40$ is the mean of a hypothetical collection of outcomes. Also, $\sigma = 5$ is the standard deviation of this hypothetical collection of outcomes. Describe the distribution of these outcomes.

Shape .................................................................................................................

Mean .................................................................................................................

Standard deviation .................................................................................................................

**10.3.4** In 10.2.3, we assumed that the outcomes of repeated runs of a particular experiment (see 10.1.1d) were normally distributed with $\mu = 40$ and $\sigma = 5$. Assume that a new definition of the outcome of the experiment is used. This new definition is

$$\text{New outcome} = \frac{\text{old outcome} - \mu}{\sigma}$$

**a** What symbol have we used previously for representing values defined as the new outcome is defined here?

.................................................................................................................

**b** What is the mean of this distribution of new outcomes?

.................................................................................................................

**c** What is the standard deviation of this distribution of new outcomes?

.................................................................................................................

**d** Can the new outcome be thought of as a linear transformation of the old outcome?

.................................................................................................................

**e** If the true model for representing the relative frequency distribution of the old outcomes is a normal curve, what is the shape of the model for representing the relative frequency distribution of the new outcomes?

..................................................................................................................................

**10.4.5** Explain the basis for the often made statement that in approximately normal distributions about two-thirds of the score values are within one standard deviation of the mean.

..................................................................................................................................

..................................................................................................................................

..................................................................................................................................

..................................................................................................................................

**10.4.6a** What *proportion* of the total area under a normal curve is disregarded when it is "cut off" *below and above* three standard deviations from the mean?

..................................................................................................................................

**b** For practical purposes the range of a normal distribution is often arbitrarily considered to be $6\sigma$. What is the basis for this practice?

..................................................................................................................................

..................................................................................................................................

..................................................................................................................................

**10.4.7** A normal distribution may be thought of as a bell-shaped distribution with a certain degree of "peakedness" or "flatness" (i.e., a certain degree of *kurtosis*). A bell-shaped distribution with a narrower hump and longer tails is said to be "peaked" (*leptokurtic*), while one with a broader hump is said to be "flat-topped" (*platykurtic*). Why is it difficult to tell by inspection whether or not a smoothed polygon for a given distribution has the right degree of peakedness to constitute a close approximation to a normal curve? (Consider Figure 10.4 of the text and also 3.8.21.)

..................................................................................................................................

..................................................................................................................................

..................................................................................................................................

..................................................................................................................................

**10.4.8** Distribution A is normal with $\mu = 5$ and $\sigma = 2$. Distribution B is normal with $\mu = 50$ and $\sigma = 10$. How does the proportion of outcomes falling between $\pm 1.48$ standard deviations from $\mu$ in Distribution A compare with the proportion of outcomes falling between $\pm 1.48$ standard deviations from $\mu$ in Distribution B?

..................................................................................................................

..................................................................................................................

**10.5.9** Consider the normal curve model of the hypothetical relative frequency distribution discussed in 10.2.3. (In 10.2.3, a normal distribution with $\mu = 40$ and $\sigma = 5$ was assumed.)

**a** What percentage of the center height is the height of the normal curve at 45?

..................................................................................................................

**b** What is the height (ordinate) of the normal curve at 45? [*Hint:* Use equation (10.5).]

..................................................................................................................

**c** What is the height (ordinate) of the normal curve at 40?

..................................................................................................................

**10.6.10** Evaluate each of the following probabilities to four decimal places.

    **a** $P(X \geq 50 \mid ND: \mu = 40, \sigma = 8)$ ....................................................

    **b** $P(X \leq 34 \mid ND: \mu = 40, \sigma = 8)$ ....................................................

    **c** $P(30 \leq X \leq 42 \mid ND: \mu = 35, \sigma = 10)$ ....................................

    **d** $P(25 \leq X \leq 31 \mid ND: \mu = 35, \sigma = 10)$ ....................................

    **e** $P(39.5 \leq X \leq 40.5 \mid ND: \mu = 36, \sigma = 5)$ ....................................

    **f** $P(X \leq 41 \text{ or } 49 \leq X \mid ND: \mu = 45, \sigma = 2)$ ................................

**10.6.11** Given a normal distribution with mean 50 and standard deviation 5.

    **a** What, to the nearest tenth, is the *PR* of 63?

..................................................................................................................

    **b** What, to the nearest tenth, is the *PR* of 46?

..................................................................................................................

**10.6.12** In each of the following probability statements, find the value of $X_1$, $x_1$ or $z_1$. (Work with the nearest tabled values; do not interpolate.)

    **a** $P(X \geq X_1 \mid ND: \mu = 75, \sigma = 25) = .2$ .........................................

    **b** $P(X \leq X_1 \mid ND: \mu = 75, \sigma = 25) = .2$ .........................................

    **c** $P(|x| \leq x_1 \mid ND: \mu = 0, \sigma = 15) = .99$ .....................................

    **d** $P(|x| \geq x_1 \mid ND: \mu = 0, \sigma = 15) = .2$ .....................................

    **e** $P(|z| \geq z_1 \mid ND: \mu = 0, \sigma = 1) = .001$ .....................................

    **f** $P(|z| \geq z_1 \mid ND: \mu = 0, \sigma = 1) = .05$ .....................................

**10.6.13** Consider the normal curve model of the assumed relative frequency distribution of 10.2.3 ($\mu = 40$; $\sigma = 5$). Let $X$ represent any outcome.

    **a** Find $P(X \leq 33)$.

    **b** Find $P(35 \leq X \leq 45)$.

    **c** Find $X_1$ such that $P(X \leq X_1) = .05$.

    **d** Find $X_1$ such that $P(X \geq X_1) = .05$.

**10.6.14** Given a distribution of 2,000 scores having a mean of 80 and a standard deviation of 16, estimate the following (without interpolating) to the nearest tenth.

    **a** $D_9$

    **b** $Q_1$

    **c** The number of scores between 88 and 92

**10.6.15a** What assumption must be made about the distribution of 10.6.14 before any meaningful degree of accuracy can be attributed to the estimates called for in that exercise?

**b** Table II of Appendix C of the text should be used in the fashion of 10.6.14 only for distributions that are known to have what form?

**10.6.16a** For a large city school system, scores on a reading test designed to identify third-grade students who need remedial reading services have been found to be approximately normally distributed with mean equal to 100 and standard deviation equal to 16. Assume students with scores below 80 are to be assigned to the remedial reading program. The special services director needs to estimate how many students will be involved in this program next year. If the projected enrollment for next year's third grade is 400, about how many students will be involved?

...............................................................................

**b** Assume that instead of using a cutoff score of 80 the director decided that any student whose score was at least 2 *S*-units below the mean would be assigned to the remedial program. Approximately what percentage of the third-grade class will be assigned?

...............................................................................

**10.6.17** The length of the metal rods produced by a particular machine is a normally distributed variable with a mean of 240 centimeters and a standard deviation of 2 centimeters.

**a** A construction company buying metal rods from the manufacturer would not accept rods that deviated more than 4 centimeters from 240 centimeters. About what proportion of rods produced by this machine would *not* be acceptable to the construction company?

...............................................................................

**b** At the end of each day the shortest 5 percent of the rods were removed from the day's production. These rods were then sold to a special customer at a reduced rate. Describe this set of rods.

...............................................................................

...............................................................................

...............................................................................

**10.7.18** Assume that a binomial *PD* with $n = 10$ and $\phi = .40$ is valid for assigning probability values to the random variable *r*. Table 9.5 (p. 169) gives the following probability values.

    **1** $P(r \geq 7 \mid BD$: $n = 10$; $\phi = .40) = .0425 + .0106 + .0016 + .0001 = .0548$

    **2** $P(r \leq 2 \mid BD$: $n = 10$; $\phi = .40) = .1209 + .0403 + .0060 = .1672$

    **3** $P(4 \leq r \leq 6 \mid BD$: $n = 10$; $\phi = .40) = .2508 + .2007 + .1115 = .5630$

**a** If the normal curve approximation is used to approximate these probabilities, what are the mean and the standard deviation of the appropriate normal curve? (Leave the standard deviation in square root notation.)

Mean $= \mu =$ ...............................................................................

Standard deviation $= \sigma =$ ...........................................................

**b** Estimate probabilities 1–3 above using the normal *PD* approximations. (*Note:* $\mu = n\phi = 4$; $\sigma \approx \sqrt{n(\phi)(1 - \phi)} \approx 1.55$.)

**1** ...............................................................................................

**2** ...............................................................................................

**3** ...............................................................................................

**10.8.19** What would you expect to be the general form of the distribution of chronological ages for each of the populations described below? (Answer in such terms as "markedly skewed to the left," "moderately skewed to the right," "unimodal and symmetrical." In this and similar questions that follow, you are expected to base your answer only on general observation and logical considerations. You are not expected to try to look up any actual data.)

**a** All persons now living in California (see Figure 10.17 in the text)

...............................................................................................

**b** All pupils enrolled in the eighth grade of the public schools of California. Explain.

...............................................................................................

...............................................................................................

**10.8.20** How would you expect the distribution of heights to differ in *form* for all persons below the age of 20 in the United States (consider this portion of the age distribution for the U.S. total population as shown in Figure 10.17 in the text) and for all 12-year-old boys in Iowa?

...............................................................................................

...............................................................................................

...............................................................................................

**10.8.21** Mental-age (MA) distributions are approximately normal for large groups of individuals of the same chronological age (CA). (The MA mean is the CA for the given group.) Given MA scores for a large group of children of a CA of 8 years and 6 months, and also for a similar-sized group of children of a CA of 12 years and 6 months, describe the form of the MA distribution for these two groups combined.

...............................................................................................

...............................................................................................

...............................................................................................

**10.8.22** Roughly, what would you suppose to be the form of the distribution of each of the following? (Follow the instructions given in parentheses in 10.8.19.)

    **a** Sizes of families in the United States

    ...............................................................................................................

    **b** Years of experience of all teachers in Iowa high schools enrolling fewer than 150 pupils

    ...............................................................................................................

    **c** Years of schooling of all Ohioans over 40 years old

    ...............................................................................................................

    **d** Ages of all college freshmen in the United States

    ...............................................................................................................

**10.8.23a** Is it likely that many of the distributions of actual data that are roughly bell-shaped are either too flat or too peaked to be normal distributions? (See 10.4.7.)

...............................................................................................................

**b** How might the difficulty referred to in 10.4.7 have contributed to the misconception of a "universal law of normality"?

...............................................................................................................

...............................................................................................................

...............................................................................................................

...............................................................................................................

**10.8.24** For a given group of pupils the scores on a certain arithmetic problems test are markedly skewed to the right.

**a** Explain how, by replacing some of the problems with others of different difficulty, you could revise the test so as to get a distribution of scores for these same pupils that is skewed in the opposite direction.

...............................................................................................................

**b** Could you, by repeated trial replacement of problems, finally devise a test that would yield an approximately normal distribution of scores for the given group?

...............................................................................................................

# 11
# Introduction to Sampling Theory

**11.2.1** In an article describing an experimental comparison of the effectiveness of practice with nonsense words versus practice with meaningful words in learning the typewriter keyboard, the investigator opens with a discussion of introductory typing textbooks. Apparently, he was interested in developing such a book for use by any beginning typist and wanted to know which of these two kinds of materials provides the more effective medium of instruction. The experiment described involved comparing the typing speed and accuracy of two groups of subjects after a period of instruction and practice. One of the groups practiced with nonsense and the other with meaningful material. The latter group was reported as being superior in both speed and accuracy.

The subjects were described as consisting of all of the 500 airmen stationed at a certain United States Air Force base at the time of the experiment who had had no previous typing instruction. Half of the subjects were randomly assigned to one group and the other half to the other group.

**a** Describe the experimentally accessible population from which these subjects might be presumed to have been sampled.

.................................................................................................

.................................................................................................

**b** Describe the target population to which the experimenter apparently wishes to generalize his findings.

.................................................................................................

.................................................................................................

**c** Do you think the findings of this experiment may be generalized to this latter population with a reasonable degree of safety? Why?

.................................................................................................

.................................................................................................

.................................................................................................

.................................................................................................

**11.2.2a** Consider the speed reading experiment described in Section 9.1 of the text. What is the experimentally accessible population for this experiment?

..................................................................................................................

..................................................................................................................

..................................................................................................................

..................................................................................................................

**b** What is a target population for this experiment? (Select a target population that goes beyond the experimentally accessible population.)

..................................................................................................................

..................................................................................................................

..................................................................................................................

**c** The experimenter wishes to generalize the findings to freshmen at other colleges in the state. The college entrance examination scores for the freshman class at the university where the study was conducted are higher "on the average" than the scores for the other freshman classes. How might this fact affect the validity of any generalizations of the results of this study to these other "populations" of undergraduates?

..................................................................................................................

..................................................................................................................

..................................................................................................................

**11.2.3** Two investigators were interested in the effect of different test instructions on the scores students made on an instrument that purportedly measured intelligence.[1] They decided to investigate this issue with seventh-grade students in a particular junior high school. Of the 80 seventh-grade students enrolled, 40 were randomly selected to take the test with instructions as follows:

> The test you are going to take today is a test of intelligence. As you know, a test of intelligence will give us your IQ, which tells us how capable you are. Your IQ also tells us how bright you are compared to other students. Listen to the directions I am going to give and do your best to get a high IQ, OK?

[1] The situation described in this exercise is based on an article by K. Yamamato and H. Dizney, "Effects of Three Sets of Test Instructions on Scores on an Intelligence Scale," *Educational and Psychological Measurement*, 25 (1965), 87–110.

The other group of 40 students took the test under the following instructions:

> This is a routine testing on how well you understand words, their meanings and uses, and how well you can answer questions involving numbers and figures. Listen carefully to the directions I am going to give and do your best to get a high score, OK?

**a** What is the experimentally accessible population in this study?

................................................................................................................

................................................................................................................

**b** Assume the results of this study indicated that the group receiving the first directions made higher scores. Why would it be important to have information on the socioeconomic status of these students before generalizing the findings to a target population of seventh-grade students in general?

................................................................................................................

................................................................................................................

................................................................................................................

**11.2.4a** Consider the situation described in 3.7.20. What is the experimentally accessible population for this experiment?

................................................................................................................

................................................................................................................

................................................................................................................

**b** Assume the results of this study indicated that the practice session had a positive effect (led to higher test scores). Identify one characteristic of the experimentally accessible population about which additional information should be obtained before a generalization to all third-grade students could be justified. Explain.

................................................................................................................

................................................................................................................

................................................................................................................

**11.3.5** Is a sampling distribution a probability distribution? Explain.

................................................................................................................

................................................................................................................

................................................................................................................

................................................................................................................

**11.3.6** Let $T$ represent some statistic and let $\theta$ represent the corresponding parameter.

    **a** What does $\sigma_T$ represent?..............................................................

    ..............................................................................................................

    **b** What is $\sigma_T$ called? ....................................................................

    **c** What does $T - \theta$ represent? ........................................................

    ..............................................................................................................

    **d** What does $\sigma_{T-\theta}$ represent?..................................................

    ..............................................................................................................

    **e** Does $\sigma_{T-\theta}$ differ from $\sigma_T$? Explain. (*Hint:* Remember, $\theta$ is a constant; see Section 8.4.)...............................................................

    ..............................................................................................................

    ..............................................................................................................

    **f** What does $\mu_T$ represent?..............................................................

    ..............................................................................................................

    **g** Suppose $\mu_T = \theta$. What is said to be true of the statistic $T$ in this situation? ..............................................................................

    ..............................................................................................................

    **h** Suppose $\mu_T = \theta$. How does the sampling distribution of $T$ differ from that of $T - \theta$? Compare in terms of mean, standard deviation, and shape. ..................................................................

    ..............................................................................................................

    ..............................................................................................................

    ..............................................................................................................

    ..............................................................................................................

**11.3.7** B operates a weight-guessing concession. Over a period of time, he keeps a record of the absolute magnitude of the error involved in each guess.

**a** Without using any statistical concept more advanced than the mean or median, how could you use B's error data to secure a quantitative index of his reliability as a weight guesser? Explain how your suggested index should be interpreted.

..............................................................................................................

..............................................................................................................

..............................................................................................................

**b** How could you use B's error data to estimate an amount such that in the long run the magnitude of B's errors could be expected to exceed this amount about half the time?

.................................................................................................................

**c** Patrons of B's concession pay a certain price to have their weight guessed. If B's guess is in error by more than a specified amount, they receive a prize. B, of course, does not wish to give out too many prizes. But he knows that if he never gives out a prize, his concession will soon cease to attract customers. How could you use B's error data to determine approximately how far off B's guess should be for a customer to qualify for a prize, if B decides he wants to award prizes only about 20 percent of the time in the long run?

.................................................................................................................

.................................................................................................................

**d** C, who operates a similar concession, claims to be a more reliable guesser than B. As a test, both guess the weight of the same individual, and in this case B's error proves to be less than half as large as C's. Explain why this does not prove that B is the more reliable guesser.

.................................................................................................................

.................................................................................................................

.................................................................................................................

.................................................................................................................

**11.3.8** In a study of family expenditures for newspapers and periodicals in a given community, the investigator recognized the impracticability of securing the required data from each family in the community. She therefore decided to select a sample and to generalize the facts derived from it to all families in the community. She selected her sample at random from a complete list of home owners supplied her by a local tax official. She then visited each family thus identified to collect the necessary data for the sample.

**a** In view of the purpose of the investigation, is this sample random or biased? Why?

.................................................................................................................

.................................................................................................................

.................................................................................................................

.................................................................................................................

.................................................................................................................

.................................................................................................................

**b** If the investigator were to repeat this study with a second sample selected independently but by the same method as the first sample, would you expect the facts for this second sample to agree exactly with those for the first? Why?

..................................................................................................................................

..................................................................................................................................

..................................................................................................................................

..................................................................................................................................

**c** Why are the sampling errors in these samples due partly to chance and partly to bias?

..................................................................................................................................

..................................................................................................................................

..................................................................................................................................

..................................................................................................................................

..................................................................................................................................

**d** Would it be possible in this situation for a given sample to be free from sampling error? Why?

..................................................................................................................................

..................................................................................................................................

..................................................................................................................................

**e** Would it be possible in this situation for the sampling error arising in the case of a particular sample to be in a direction opposite that of the bias? Why?

..................................................................................................................................

..................................................................................................................................

..................................................................................................................................

..................................................................................................................................

**f** Describe the population to which this investigator's sample findings could be generalized without bias.

..................................................................................................................................

..................................................................................................................................

**11.3.9** In a study of guidance programs in Illinois high schools, an investigator mailed a questionnaire (for voluntary reply) to the principal of each high school in the state. He received replies from 40 percent of the principals. He decided to regard the replies as though randomly sampled and to generalize his findings to all Illinois high schools. How are the data thus secured likely to be biased?

..........................................................................................................................

..........................................................................................................................

..........................................................................................................................

**11.3.10** A local television station conducts a poll on its late-night news show. Each evening a question is given and the viewing audience is invited to indicate their response by telephoning one number if their answer is "Yes" and a different number if their answer is "No." At the end of the show, the results of the poll are given to the audience.

One evening the question was: "Should the state legislature pass the bill that would allow alcoholic beverages to be sold in grocery stores?" At the end of the show the following data were given:

$$\text{Yes} = 55\% \qquad \text{No} = 45\%$$

Explain why it is absolutely impossible to attach any meaning to these data.

..........................................................................................................................

..........................................................................................................................

..........................................................................................................................

**11.3.11a** If a sample value (statistic) differs from the corresponding population value (parameter) because the sampling procedure introduces bias, is the difference between the two values still known as a sampling error? Explain.

..........................................................................................................................

..........................................................................................................................

..........................................................................................................................

..........................................................................................................................

**b** What is meant by a *random error* in sampling or a *random sampling error*?

..........................................................................................................................

..........................................................................................................................

..........................................................................................................................

..........................................................................................................................

c Is a random sampling error an "error" in the usual sense of an avoidable mistake on the part of the investigator, or is it due to factors beyond the investigator's control?

......................................................................................................................

......................................................................................................................

d What is the difference between a *random error in sampling* and an *error due to failure to secure a random sample*?

......................................................................................................................

......................................................................................................................

......................................................................................................................

......................................................................................................................

......................................................................................................................

......................................................................................................................

......................................................................................................................

**11.4.12** Consider the 100 scores of Table 3.A (p. 13) as a population. Let it be required to select a simple random sample of 10 scores from this population.

a Suppose that each score is written on a slip of paper, that these slips are inserted into identical capsules, and that the 100 capsules are placed in a bowl and thoroughly mixed. If 10 capsules are then taken in succession from the bowl, would the resulting 10 numbers constitute a simple random sample from the population?

......................................................................................

b Now identify all the scores in Table 3.A with the numbers 00, 01, 02, . . . , 99. (Begin with the first score in the first column, number *down* the column, then move to the next column, and so on.) Now use Table III, Appendix C, of the text to select the required random sample of 10 scores. Assume that row 22, columns 67 and 68, is the arbitrarily selected starting point and that the identification numbers of the sample scores are read from these columns in *upward* succession. In the blanks that follow, write the values of the 10 scores selected in the order of their selection. If the same two-digit number occurs more than once in the table of random numbers, reject it and move up to the next one. (This does not mean that the same score value from Table 3.A can be selected only once, because there are *different* individuals making scores that have the same value.)

1 ...............    3 ...............    5 ...............    7 ...............    9 ...............

2 ...............    4 ...............    6 ...............    8 ...............    10 ...............

**c** Why was it necessary to identify the 100 scores in the population by the numbers 00, 01, 02, . . . , 99, rather than by the numbers 1, 2, 3, . . . , 100?

..................................................................................................................

..................................................................................................................

**d** How many random two-digit identification numbers was it necessary to read in order to obtain the 10 sample scores?

..................................................................................................................

**e** What is the advantage of the selection scheme of part **b** over the scheme described in part **a**?

..................................................................................................................

..................................................................................................................

..................................................................................................................

**f** What is the mean of the sample selected in part **b**?

$$\overline{X} = \text{.................................................}$$

**g** The mean of all 100 scores is 26.17. What is the sampling error in the mean of the sample selected in part **b**?

$$E = \text{.................................................}$$

**h** The data for parts **b**, **f**, and **g** are given in Table 11.A (sample 1). Assume the procedure of part **b** is repeated eight more times using the starting points listed for samples 2 through 9. The obtained mean values and the sampling errors for these repetitions are given in Table 11.A. Obtain $\overline{X}$ and $E$ for a tenth sample using the starting point given in the table. [Remember to read *upward* from the starting point. If there are not enough rows above the starting point, continue by going to the last row (row 99) of Table III.]

**11.5.13a** On the scale for the figure for 11.5.13a, construct the histogram for the relative frequency distribution of the ten $\overline{X}$-values of Table 11.A.

### Table 11.A

| | Starting Point in Table III: | | | |
|---|---|---|---|---|
| Sample | Row | Columns | $\overline{X}$ | $E$ |
| 1 | 22 | 67 and 68 | 25.4 | − .77 |
| 2 | 39 | 83 and 84 | 26.0 | − .17 |
| 3 | 04 | 76 and 77 | 27.4 | +1.23 |
| 4 | 78 | 37 and 38 | 25.2 | − .97 |
| 5 | 67 | 83 and 84 | 29.2 | +3.03 |
| 6 | 35 | 20 and 21 | 25.4 | − .77 |
| 7 | 89 | 74 and 75 | 25.1 | −1.07 |
| 8 | 01 | 64 and 65 | 26.3 | + .13 |
| 9 | 79 | 05 and 06 | 26.5 | + .33 |
| 10 | 81 | 26 and 27 | | |

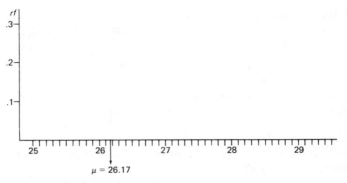

Figure 11.5.13a

**b** From what universe might these ten $\overline{X}$-values be regarded as having been sampled?

............................................................................................................................................

............................................................................................................................................

............................................................................................................................................

**c** Does Rule 11.1 of the text provide a description of the universe referred to in **b**? Why?

............................................................................................................................................

............................................................................................................................................

**d** Give two reasons why Rule 11.2 of the text does not apply to the universe referred to in **b**.

............................................................................................................................................

............................................................................................................................................

............................................................................................................................................

**11.5.14** The $X$-score distribution given in Table 11.B is an approximately normal distribution with $\mu = 7$ and $\sigma = 2$. Since the $rf$-values are expressed in thousandths, the distribution may be viewed as involving 1,000 $X$-scores. Each of these scores is identified by a number from 000 through 999 as shown in the third column of Table 11.B. Thus, the three of the 1,000 scores that have the value 13 are identified by the numbers 000, 001, and 002. There is no need to specify which of these three scores is identified by which of these three numbers, since they all have the same value, 13. If a list of three-digit numbers is selected from a table of random numbers and one or *more*[2] of the numbers thus selected are 000, 001, or

---

[2] Here the same random number may be included in the list more than once since it designates a score value rather than a particular score. This population actually consists of an infinity of scores.

**Table 11.B**

| X | rf | Identification Numbers | Number of Id. Numbers |
|---|---|---|---|
| 13 | .003 | 000–002 | 3 |
| 12 | .009 | 003–011 | 9 |
| 11 | .028 | 012–039 | 28 |
| 10 | .066 | 040–105 | 66 |
| 9 | .121 | 106–226 | 121 |
| 8 | .175 | 227–401 | 175 |
| 7 | .196 | 402 | 196 |
| 6 | .175 | | 175 |
| 5 | .121 | | 121 |
| 4 | .066 | 959 | 66 |
| 3 | .028 | 960–987 | 28 |
| 2 | .009 | 988–996 | 9 |
| 1 | .003 | 997–999 | 3 |
| | 1.000 | | 1,000 |

002, the score 13 is designated as picked for each such number in the list. Similarly, the score 10 is taken for each identification number in the list from 040 through 105.

Table 11.C gives three of five starting points in the table of random numbers (Table III of Appendix C of the text). These starting points were themselves picked at random from Table III by the following procedure.

1 Row 60 and columns 25 and 26 were arbitrarily selected as a starting point for picking rows.
2 Beginning with this starting point and reading *down*, successive two-digit numbers were selected (these are the row numbers given in Table 11.C).
3 Row 15 and columns 37 and 38 were arbitrarily selected as a starting point for picking columns.
4 Beginning with this starting point and reading *down*, successive two-digit numbers were again selected. These were used as the column for the hundreds digit, and the next two columns to the right were used for the tens and units digits, respectively.

**Table 11.C** Randomly Selected Starting Points in Table III of Appendix C of the Text

| Sample | Row | Columns |
|---|---|---|
| 1 | 39 | 44, 45, 46 |
| 2 | 89 | 05, 06, 07 |
| 3 | 98 | 34, 35, 36 |
| 4 | | |
| 5 | | |

**Table 11.D**  Three of Five Sets ($S$) of Ten Random Three-Digit Numbers and the Corresponding $X$-Values from Table 11.B

| $S_1$ | $X$ | $S_2$ | $X$ | $S_3$ | $X$ | $S_4$ | $X$ | $S_5$ | $X$ |
|---|---|---|---|---|---|---|---|---|---|
| 222 | 9 | 263 | 8 | 537 | 7 | | | | |
| 848 | 5 | 068 | 10 | 042 | 10 | | | | |
| 068 | 10 | 356 | 8 | 569 | 7 | | | | |
| 165 | 9 | 853 | 5 | 523 | 7 | | | | |
| 391 | 8 | 003 | 12 | 965 | 3 | | | | |
| 255 | 8 | 854 | 5 | 262 | 8 | | | | |
| 523 | 7 | 118 | 9 | 272 | 8 | | | | |
| 860 | 5 | 573 | 7 | 620 | 6 | | | | |
| 609 | 6 | 939 | 4 | 505 | 7 | | | | |
| 887 | 5 | 728 | 6 | 162 | 9 | | | | |
| | $\overline{X} = 7.2$ | | $\overline{X} = 7.4$ | | $\overline{X} = 7.2$ | | | | |

Using the starting points given in Table 11.C and reading *down*, the sets of ten three-digit random numbers shown in Table 11.D were selected from Table III. (When—see sample 3—there are fewer than ten rows below the starting point, the reading may be continued from row 00.) The $X$-scores corresponding to these random numbers were then read from Table 11.B. The resulting sets of ten $X$-values constitute independently selected random samples from the given population, that is, from a normally distributed population having mean and standard deviation of 7 and 2, respectively.

**a** Fill in the identification numbers omitted from Table 11.B.

**b** Complete Table 11.C.

**c** Complete Table 11.D.

**d** The means of the five samples of the complete Table 11.D are 7.2, 7.4, 7.2, 7.2, and 6.5, respectively. Describe completely the population to which these five means belong.

........................................................................................................................................

........................................................................................................................................

........................................................................................................................................

**e** What is the sampling error in the mean of sample 2? of sample 5?

........................................................................................................................................

**f** What is the population referred to in **d** called?

........................................................................................................................................

**g** Suppose this procedure for selecting samples of ten cases from the population of Table 11.B were repeated 10,000 times and that the resulting 10,000 means were organized into a relative frequency distribution. Approximately what would you expect the form, mean, and standard deviation of this distribution to be?

Form ................................................................................................................

Mean ................................................................................................................

Standard deviation ........................................................................................

**h** Under what condition would your answers to **g** hold even if the population from which the samples were selected were not normally distributed? Include as part of your answer any necessary restrictions on the character of the population.

................................................................................................................

................................................................................................................

................................................................................................................

**i** Do these restrictions on the character of the population seriously limit the practical applicability of the sampling theory involved? Why?

................................................................................................................

................................................................................................................

................................................................................................................

................................................................................................................

................................................................................................................

................................................................................................................

**11.5.15** Consider the two types of error referred to in part **d** of 11.3.11. To which—if either—of these types of error does the sampling theory of Rule 11.2 apply?

................................................................................................................

**11.5.16** Suppose that each of 100 investigators wishes to determine the mean weight of all ten-year-old boys in Iowa. Each investigator, working entirely independently of all the others, selects a random sample of 100 boys from the entire population in question and computes the mean weight of the boys in the sample.

**a** Explain why you would expect these means to differ from sample to sample.

................................................................................................................

................................................................................................................

**b** Since these means differ, they must, of course, involve differing amounts of sampling error. Explain why all of these means are, nevertheless, equally reliable.

..............................................................................................................................

..............................................................................................................................

..............................................................................................................................

**c** If you knew the values of these 100 means, how could you use this information to obtain a quantitative index of the reliability of any one of them?

..............................................................................................................................

..............................................................................................................................

..............................................................................................................................

**d** The standard error of the mean of a given sample does not indicate the actual magnitude of the sampling error in this particular mean. What does it indicate?

..............................................................................................................................

..............................................................................................................................

..............................................................................................................................

..............................................................................................................................

**11.5.17a** Explain in what sense a given mean can be unreliable and yet actually be free of any sampling error. (Develop the analogy suggested by the statement "Even the poorest marksman will hit the bull's-eye on an occasional given shot," indicating what corresponds to the marksman, the bull's-eye, and the given shot.)

..............................................................................................................................

..............................................................................................................................

..............................................................................................................................

..............................................................................................................................

..............................................................................................................................

..............................................................................................................................

..............................................................................................................................

**b** Explain in what sense the mean of a sample can be highly reliable and yet contain a large sampling error. (Again use the analogy of the marksman and the bull's-eye.)

........................................................................................................................

........................................................................................................................

........................................................................................................................

........................................................................................................................

........................................................................................................................

**c** Correct the following incorrect statement: "A reliable mean is one that contains a small sampling error."

........................................................................................................................

........................................................................................................................

**11.5.18** Two samples are drawn independently at random from the *same* population. Sample A contains 100 cases and Sample B contains 400 cases.

**a** What is the ratio of $\sigma_{\bar{x}}$ for Sample B to $\sigma_{\bar{x}}$ for Sample A?

........................................................................

**b** In the space below superimpose on the same scales rough freehand sketches of the sampling distributions of the means of these two samples. (Label the curves A and B.)

**c** Explain why you cannot be certain that the mean of Sample B (the larger and hence more reliable sample) is closer to the population mean than is the mean of Sample A (the smaller and hence less reliable sample).

........................................................................................................................

........................................................................................................................

........................................................................................................................

........................................................................................................................

**d** Use the curves called for in **b** to indicate specific values of a particular pair of Sample A and Sample B means in which the mean for Sample A involves the lesser sampling error.

**11.5.19** A physical education teacher is interested in the mean weight of the girls in her class. She computes the mean and its standard error and finds that the standard error is quite large.

**a** Does this large standard error indicate that the obtained mean is likely to be an inaccurate indication of the average weight of the girls in the class?

.................................................................

**b** Is there any point in calculating the standard error of the mean in this situation?

.................................................................

**11.5.20** The misconception is sometimes acquired by beginning students of statistics that the calculation of the standard error of the mean should accompany the calculation of the mean itself in all careful statistical work. Explain why this is a misconception.

.................................................................

.................................................................

.................................................................

.................................................................

.................................................................

.................................................................

.................................................................

**11.5.21** Another misconception sometimes acquired by beginning students is that the principal need for the formula for the standard error of a mean arises from the impracticability of obtaining samples that are truly random. Explain why this is a misconception.

.................................................................

.................................................................

.................................................................

.................................................................

.................................................................

.................................................................

**11.5.22** The *true* mean and *true* standard deviation of a given normally distributed population are known to be 110 and 15, respectively. (*Note:* This situation is purely hypothetical. If in any actual situation the true mean and true standard deviation were known, no sampling would be necessary, and, of course, no sampling-error theory would be required.)

**a** What would be the standard deviation of an infinity of means, each obtained from a random sample of nine cases drawn from this population?

........................................................................

**b** Is the answer to part **a** an estimate? Why or why not? ........................

........................................................................

........................................................................

........................................................................

........................................................................

**c** In this hypothetical infinite universe of means, the probability is .99 that the value of $\overline{X}$ is within what distance of 110? (The standard error of this universe is 5.)

........................................................................

**d** How large a sample must be used if it is to be said of the sampling distribution of means that the probability of $\overline{X}$ being within 3 units of 110 is .95?

........................................................................

**11.6.23** The student government organization at a large university is interested in assessing student attitudes toward current educational practices on campus. The organization decides to conduct a survey of a random sample of 400 students. One question asked in this survey was:

> Should students be involved in the curriculum planning for their courses?

The student organization is interested in estimating the proportion of students who favor this proposal (would respond "Yes" to the question).

**a** What is the parameter of interest in the above situation?

........................................................................

........................................................................

**b** Why can the population of interest be labeled a dichotomous population?

........................................................................

........................................................................

........................................................................

**c** Assume that, unknown to the investigator, the population proportion of "Yes" responses ($\phi$) is .60. Describe the approximate sampling distribution of the proportion ($p$) of "Yes" responses in random samples of 400 students taken from this population. (*Note:* Leave $\sigma_p$ in square root terms.)

Shape (form) ..............................................................................................................

Mean ..............................................................................................................................

Standard deviation ................................................................................................

**d** Assume $\phi = .60$. What is the probability that the $p$-value for a sample of 400 will be less than .58? [*Note:* $\sigma_p = \sqrt{(.6)(.4)/400} \approx .02.$]

..........................................................................................

What is the probability that the $p$-value will be between .58 and .62?

..........................................................................................

**11.6.24** Given a population of pairs of fraternal twins one-half of which are of *mixed sex* (are boy-girl pairs) and the other half of which are the *same sex* (boy-boy or girl-girl pairs).

**a** What is the population unit?

..........................................................................................

**b** Identify the types of population units involved.

..........................................................................................

**c** What is a population of this kind called? Why?

..........................................................................................

..........................................................................................

**d** Describe completely the approximate sampling distribution of the proportion ($p$) of mixed-sex pairs of twins in random samples of 100 pairs of twins taken from this population.

..........................................................................................

..........................................................................................

..........................................................................................

**11.7.25** In the hypothetical, continuous, infinite population probability distribution pictured in the figure for 11.7.25, the ordinate (height) at the median is .07. Suppose that a "large" number of random samples, each containing 100 scores, is selected from this population, that the median of each such sample is obtained, and that these medians are organized into a relative frequency distribution.

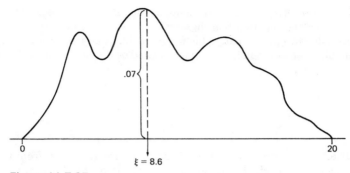

**Figure 11.7.25**

**a** What is the statistical name of this relative frequency distribution of sample medians?

...................................................................................................................

**b** What approximately is its mean?

...................................................................................

**c** What approximately is its standard deviation?

...................................................................................

**d** What approximately is its form?

...................................................................................

**e** What is the statistical name of the standard deviation called for in **c**?

...................................................................................................................

**f** Why was it necessary to use the word *approximately* in stating **b**, **c**, and **d**?

...................................................................................................................

...................................................................................................................

...................................................................................................................

**g** Suppose that the population probability distribution is itself a normal distribution with a standard deviation of 4.7. In this case what is the approximate standard deviation of the relative frequency distribution of sample medians ($N = 100$ as before)?

...................................................................................

**h** In the situation of **g**, would the median or the mean be the more reliable measure of central tendency? Why?

...................................................................................................................

...................................................................................................................

**i** Suppose the population probability distribution to be a symmetrical U-shaped distribution that dips very close to the score scale at its center. Explain why the median is highly unreliable (has a large standard error) in this situation. What, for example, would be the value of $\sigma_{Mdn}$ if $y_\xi = .001$ and $N = 100$?

.........................................................................................................................................

.........................................................................................................................................

.........................................................................................................................................

**11.8.26** Two random samples of the same size are drawn from the same population. By chance the standard deviation of the second sample turns out to be larger than that of the first.

**a** Would the estimated standard errors of the means ($\tilde{\sigma}_{\overline{X}}$) of both samples be the same? Explain.

.........................................................................................................................................

.........................................................................................................................................

.........................................................................................................................................

**b** Would the true standard errors of the means ($\sigma_{\overline{X}}$) be the same? Explain.

.........................................................................................................................................

.........................................................................................................................................

.........................................................................................................................................

**c** Would the two means be equally reliable? Explain.

.........................................................................................................................................

.........................................................................................................................................

.........................................................................................................................................

.........................................................................................................................................

**11.8.27** Consider the values of the ten means in Table 11.A (p. 111). The standard deviation of these ten mean values is 1.18. Since this is actually a standard deviation of a sample of means, we could represent this quantity symbolically as follows:

$$S_{\overline{X}} = 1.18$$

If we now multiply $S_{\overline{X}}$ by $\sqrt{N/(N-1)}$ we have $\sqrt{10/9}(1.18) \approx 1.25$. [*Note:* It is coincidental here that the number of means (ten) is the same as the size of the sample on which each mean value is based (also ten). The appropriate $N$ in this situation is the number of means rather than the number of scores in each sample.]

**a** Explain what this value of 1.25 represents.

.................................................................................

.................................................................................

.................................................................................

**b** What symbol have we used to represent the quantity described in **a**?

.................................................................................

**11.8.28a** The standard deviation of the five means given in 11.5.14**d** is approximately .31 (i.e., $S_{\bar{X}} = .31$). Use this information to find $\tilde{\sigma}_{\bar{X}}$.

.................................................................................

.................................................................................

**b** If you worked part **a** correctly and multiplied $\sqrt{5/4}$ by .31, your answer is approximately .35. Using just the ten scores of the first sample of Table 11.D (p. 114), estimate the standard error of the sampling distribution of $\bar{X}$. [*Note:* The value of the standard deviation, $S$, for these ten scores is 1.78.]

.................................................................................

**c** What is the true standard error of this sampling distribution? (Recall that for the population from which the samples are drawn, $\sigma = 2$.) [*Note:* $\sqrt{10} \approx 3.162$.]

.................................................................................

**d** Use the value of $S$ for the first sample ($S = 1.78$) to estimate the value of $\sigma$ for the population (i.e., to obtain $\tilde{\sigma}$). [*Note:* $\sqrt{10/9} \approx 1.054$.]

.................................................................................

**e** Use the value of $\tilde{\sigma}$ called for in **d** to estimate the standard error of the sampling distribution referred to in **a**, **b**, and **c**.

.................................................................................

**f** The results of **e** and **b** are the same. Will the standard error of a mean as estimated by these two procedures always be the same?

.................................................................................

**11.8.29** Consider the five samples of Table 11.D (exercise 11.5.14) as a single sample of 50 cases. The variance of this sample, $S^2$, is 4.01.

**a** What is the sampling error involved in this value of $S^2$? ($E = S^2 - \sigma^2$.)

.................................................................................

**b** Using $S^2 = 4.01$, estimate the variance of the population (i.e., find $\tilde{\sigma}^2$). [*Note:* $50/49 \approx 1.02$.]

.................................................................................

**c** What is the sampling error in the estimate called for in **b**?

............................................................................

**d** In this case $S^2$ involved less error than $\tilde{\sigma}^2$ as an estimate of $\sigma^2$. Why, then, as a matter of consistent practice, do we use $\tilde{\sigma}^2$ rather than $S^2$ as an estimator of the parameter $\sigma^2$?

............................................................................

............................................................................

............................................................................

............................................................................

............................................................................

............................................................................

**11.8.30** The superintendent of a large city school system wishes to determine the mean scholastic achievement, as measured by a certain test battery, of all sixth-grade pupils in the system. He cannot afford to test them all, so he resorts to sampling and uses as a sample three intact sixth-grade classes selected at random from all such classes in the system.

**a** Is the standard error of the mean of this sample, as computed by formula (11.19) of the text, a valid measure of the reliability of the mean? Why?

............................................................................

............................................................................

............................................................................

**b** How should the superintendent have selected his sample so as to justify the use of this formula?

............................................................................

............................................................................

............................................................................

**11.8.31** A pupil personnel worker wishes to determine the mean reading achievement score on a particular achievement test of all Mexican school children enrolled in the sixth grade of the public elementary schools of California. She induces several of her friends who are in school systems highly similar to her own to administer the test to all sixth-grade Mexican children in their particular systems. She computes the mean of this sample. She recognizes that the sample thus selected may not be considered a random sample from the population consisting of all Mexican sixth-grade pupils in the public schools of California. Nevertheless, she estimates the standard error of this mean by formula (11.19) of the text and uses the result to describe the reliability of the obtained mean. Is the obtained value of this standard error likely to be too big or too small for its intended purpose? (Consider "neither" as a possible response.) Explain. (*Hint:* How would the variability in the reading scores of these Mexican children from highly similar communities be likely to compare with that of California Mexican children in general?)

..................................................................................................................

..................................................................................................................

..................................................................................................................

..................................................................................................................

..................................................................................................................

**11.8.32a** Consider the investigation described in 11.6.23 but assume that the population parameter $\phi$ is not known. Also assume that of the 400 students in the sample, 236 ($p = .59$) responded "Yes" to the given question. Using this information, describe the approximate sampling distribution of $p$. [*Note:* $\tilde{\sigma}_p = \sqrt{(.59)(.41)/399} \approx .025$.]

Shape ...........................................................................................................

Mean ............................................................................................................

Standard deviation ..........................................................................................

**b** Why is this description of the sampling distribution of $p$ only approximate?

..................................................................................................................

..................................................................................................................

..................................................................................................................

**11.8.33a** Consider the situation described in 10.1.1. Assume the mean score ($\overline{X}$) for the random sample of 400 ninth-grade students was 58.3. Also assume that the standard deviation for these 400 scores was 12. Describe the approximate sampling distribution of $\overline{X}$. (*Note:* $\tilde{\sigma}_{\overline{X}} = 12/\sqrt{399} \approx .60$.)

Shape ...........................................................................................................

Mean ............................................................................................................

Standard deviation ..........................................................................................

**b** Why is this description of the sampling distribution of $\overline{X}$ only approximate?

..................................................................................................................

..................................................................................................................

..................................................................................................................

**11.8.34** There is probably no "real-life" collection of scores that follows a normal curve exactly. Why, then, is this mathematical model of interest in inferential statistics?

...........................................................................................................................................

...........................................................................................................................................

...........................................................................................................................................

...........................................................................................................................................

# 12

# Testing Statistical Hypotheses: The Classical Hypothesis Testing Procedure

**12.4.1** A certain elementary school supervisor administered a vocabulary test to all 145 fourth-grade pupils in a school system at the opening of the school term in the fall and found the mean score to be 40. This corresponded exactly not only with the national average on this test for beginning fourth-grade pupils, but also with the average for beginning fourth-grade pupils who had attended this particular school system over the past ten years. The supervisor knew that over a period of six months in the normal classroom environment, the mean score on this test should advance 6 points, a point for each month in the classroom. The supervisor believed that she had invented a program that would, without in any way sacrificing other classroom activities, and without any risk of actually retarding normal vocabulary growth, speed up this rate of vocabulary development. She introduced this program into all the fourth-grade classrooms of the system. After six months, during which this program was in operation, she again administered the vocabulary test and found the mean of the scores to be 49, and the standard deviation to be 15.

Being aware of the possibility that this gain of 3 points in excess of the normal 6 might be peculiar to this particular collection of pupils, the supervisor decided that, before recommending her program for use with future fourth-grade groups in the system, she would investigate the likelihood of a mean gain of this magnitude occurring in the case of a random sample of 145 taken from a population for which the mean gain was the normal 6 points. This, of course, amounted to testing a hypothesis about the mean of a certain population.

**a** What is the hypothetical value of the mean of the population in question?

...............................................................

**b** What is the alternative possibility (or alternative possibilities) to this hypothetical mean value?

..................................................................................................................................

**c** Identify the individuals who make up this population.

..................................................................................................................................

..................................................................................................................................

**d** Does the supervisor know that the group of fourth-grade pupils currently enrolled (the experimentally accessible population) is a random sample from this target population, or must the randomness of this group be assumed? If the latter, under what conditions is such an assumption justifiable?

..................................................................................................................................

..................................................................................................................................

..................................................................................................................................

..................................................................................................................................

..................................................................................................................................

..................................................................................................................................

..................................................................................................................................

**e** Assume the supervisor selected .01 as the level of significance. In terms of the $\overline{X}$-scale, what is the critical region? (*Note:* $\tilde{\sigma}_{\overline{X}} = S/\sqrt{N-1} = 15/\sqrt{144} = 1.25$.)

..................................................................................

**f** What is the outcome of the test of the hypothesis in question?

..................................................................................

**g** What course of action by the supervisor is indicated by this outcome?

..................................................................................................................................

..................................................................................................................................

..................................................................................................................................

**h** At what point in the process of testing this hypothesis did the supervisor assume that the sampling distribution of the test statistic ($\overline{X}$) was a normal distribution?

..................................................................................................................................

..................................................................................................................................

..................................................................................................................................

..................................................................................................................................

**i** Granting the randomness of the sample, is the assumption of a normal sampling distribution of $\overline{X}$ exactly or only approximately satisfied? Explain. If your answer is "approximately," indicate whether or not the degree of approximation is sufficiently close for practical purposes. Why?

..................................................................................................................

..................................................................................................................

..................................................................................................................

..................................................................................................................

..................................................................................................................

..................................................................................................................

..................................................................................................................

**j** Does the supervisor have evidence that would warrant recommending applying the course of action called for in part **g** to fourth-grade pupils in other school systems? Why? If your answer is "no," indicate what additional evidence would be needed to justify such a recommendation.

..................................................................................................................

..................................................................................................................

..................................................................................................................

..................................................................................................................

..................................................................................................................

..................................................................................................................

..................................................................................................................

..................................................................................................................

**12.5.2a** Suppose that the supervisor in 12.4.1 had elected to use $z$ ($ND$: $\mu_z = 0$, $\sigma_z = 1$) instead of $\overline{X}$ as the test statistic. In terms of the $z$-scale, what is the critical region?

..................................................................................................

**b** Determine the value of this test statistic $z$ for the given sample data.

..................................................................................................

**c** How does the outcome of the test based on the use of $z$ as the test statistic compare with that of the test based on $\overline{X}$?

..................................................................................................................

**12.6.3** In the situation of 12.4.1, suppose that under normal classroom conditions it is the *median* rather than the mean score that advances at a rate of one point per month. Suppose that it is also reasonable to assume that the vocabulary scores yielded by this test are normally distributed for the hypothetical population involved.

**a** If, like the mean, the median for beginning fourth-grade pupils in this system as well as across the country is 40, state the hypothetical value of the median of the population under investigation.

..............................................................................................................

**b** What is(are) the alternative possibility(ies) to this hypothetical median value?

..............................................................................................................

**c** Again using $\alpha = .01$, specify in terms of the scale of values of the sample median the critical region appropriate for testing the hypothesis in question. (Assume, as in 12.4.1, that for the sample at hand $S = 15$.) [*Note*: $\tilde{\sigma}_{Mdn} = 1.25\, S/\sqrt{N-1} = (1.25)(1.25) \approx 1.56$.]

..............................................................................................................

**d** Assume that for the sample at hand $Mdn = 49$. What is the outcome of this statistical test?

..............................................................................................................

**e** Specify the appropriate critical region for this test in terms of the scale of values of the test statistic $z$.

..............................................................................................................

**f** What is the value of the test statistic $z$ for the data at hand?

..............................................................................................................

**g** In 12.4.1 the sample mean indicated a gain of 3 points in excess of normal. In this exercise the sample median also indicated a gain of 3 points in excess of normal. Explain why the two tests (the one based on $\overline{X}$, the other on $Mdn$) differed in outcome.

..............................................................................................................

..............................................................................................................

..............................................................................................................

..............................................................................................................

..............................................................................................................

..............................................................................................................

**12.6.4a** It is hypothesized that the median of a certain population is 50. The alternative possibility is $\xi > 50$. A significance level of .001 is adopted, so that in terms of the scale of values of $z$ (a test statistic that you may presume to be fully appropriate in the given situation) the critical region is $z \geq +3.09$. The value of $z$ for the given sample data turned out to be $+.6$, so that retention of the hypothesis is clearly indicated. Why does this finding not constitute proof of the hypothesis (i.e., proof of the fact that $\xi = 50$)?

..................................................................................................

..................................................................................................

..................................................................................................

..................................................................................................

..................................................................................................

**b** What, then, does it indicate about the possibility that $\xi = 50$?

..................................................................................................

..................................................................................................

..................................................................................................

..................................................................................................

**12.7.5** Again consider the situation of 12.4.1. Assume that everything is as before (i.e., $\overline{X} = 49$ and $S = 15$) except for the fact that the investigation is carried out with 50 instead of 145 pupils.

**a** If, as before, $\alpha = .01$, specify the critical region in terms of $z$ as a test statistic.

..................................................................................................

**b** What is the value of $z$ for the given sample data? (*Note:* $\tilde{\sigma}_{\overline{X}} = S/\sqrt{N-1} = 15/\sqrt{49} \approx 2.14$.)

..................................................................................................

**c** What is the outcome of the test?

..................................................................................................

**d** Explain why this outcome differs from that of 12.4.1 (see **f**) in spite of the fact that the sample mean and standard deviation are precisely the same in both instances.

..................................................................................................

..................................................................................................

..................................................................................................

..................................................................................................

..................................................................................................

..................................................................................................

**12.8.6** In the situation of 12.6.3 (which in turn refers to that of 12.4.1), it was supposed that the median score would advance 6 points in a normal classroom environment. Now suppose that the supervisor views the population as a dichotomous one, consisting of some pupils who *do* and others who *do not* gain 6 or more points during the six months her experimental program is in operation. As an index of the success of her program, she now elects to use the proportion of children in the sample ($N = 145$) who, at the close of the six-month trial period, show gains of *at least* 6 points in performance on the vocabulary test.

**a** What should she use as the hypothetical value of the proportion of pupils in this dichotomous population who gain 6 or more points?

**b** Specify the alternative(s) to this hypothesis.

**c** If a significance level of .01 is used, indicate in terms of the scale of values of $p$ (the sample proportion) the critical region for testing the hypothesis called for above. [*Note:* $\sigma_p = \sqrt{(\phi)(1 - \phi)/145} = \sqrt{(.5)(.5)/145} \approx .04$.]

**d** Suppose that 87 of the 145 pupils were found to have made gains of 6 or more. What is the value of the test statistic?

**e** What is the outcome of the test?

**f** Suppose that $z$ is used as a test statistic. Specify the critical region.

**g** What is the value of $z$ for the given sample?

**12.10.7** A psychologist read a statement in a journal article to the effect that on a learning task involving a list of ten paired adjectives of a certain type (e.g., high-cold or dark-hard), the probability of a correct response for a given pair on the trial immediately following the first reinforcement (i.e., the first correct response) had been empirically established as .7 for a specified population of subjects. That is to say, seven-tenths of the population may be expected to respond correctly to the stimulus member of a given pair of adjectives on the trial immediately following that on which a correct response is first made for this pair. The psychologist had no preconceived notion regarding the direction of any possible error in this determination, but he felt strongly that it needed further investigation. He constructed a list of ten paired adjectives according to the specifications described in the article and selected at random one pair. This he designated as the experimental pair. He ran the list with 100 subjects randomly selected from the specified population and found that 60 of these subjects responded correctly to this particular experimental pair on the trial immediately following the one on which their first correct response to it occurred. He then tested the hypothesis represented by the article statement.

**a** State this hypothesis.

..............................................................

**b** Specify the alternative(s) to it.

..............................................................

**c** Specify the critical region in terms of $z$ as a test statistic if $\alpha = .05$.

..............................................................

**d** What is the value of $z$ for the sample data? [*Note:* $\sigma_p = \sqrt{(.7)(.3)/100} \approx .046$.]

..............................................................

**e** The outcome of this test indicates rejection of the hypothesis. What is the acceptable alternative?

..............................................................

**12.10.8** For each of the hypothesis tests in Table 12.A, record in the table:

   **1** The appropriate critical region, $R$, in terms of the scale of values of the test statistic $z$
   **2** The outcome of the test—whether the test indicates *retention* (Ret.) or *rejection* (Rej.) of $H_0$
   **3** If the outcome is rejection, the alternative indicated

**12.11.9a** Suppose the program of vocabulary development referred to in 12.4.1 is extremely simple and inexpensive to implement. Which of the two types of error involved in testing statistical hypotheses would be the more serious under these circumstances?

..............................................................

### Table 12.A

| $H_0$ | Alternatives to $H_0$ | $\alpha$ | $R$ | Sample $z$-Value | Outcome | Indicated Alternative |
|---|---|---|---|---|---|---|
| $\phi = .5$ | $\phi < .5, \phi > .5$ | .05 | | $+1.85$ | | |
| $\mu = 20$ | $\mu < 20$ | .01 | | $-2.75$ | | |
| $\xi = 50$ | $\xi < 50, \xi > 50$ | .001 | | $+3.60$ | | |
| $\mu = 25$ | $\mu < 25, \mu > 25$ | .10 | | $-2.00$ | | |
| $\phi = .6$ | $\phi > .6$ | .05 | | $-2.10$ | | |

**b** In this situation, should the supervisor use a small, medium, or relatively large probability value as a level of significance?

..................................................

**12.11.10a** Suppose the probability of .7 cited by the journal article referred to in 12.10.7 is based on very extensive research and is widely accepted by leading psychologists. In this case the publication of a different value, if later proved wrong, would be very costly to the psychologist's professional reputation. Which of the two types of error involved in testing statistical hypotheses would be the more serious under these circumstances?

..................................................

**b** In this situation should a small, medium, or relatively large probability value be used as a level of significance?

..................................................

**12.12.11** Suppose that a statistical test is to be made of a hypothesis about a population mean and suppose that, unknown to the investigator, this hypothesis is false. Assume .05 is to be used as the level of significance.

**a** What is the probability of a Type I error in this situation? Explain.

..................................................

..................................................

..................................................

**b** In this situation will the obtained value of the test statistic always fall into the critical region? That is, will the test always lead to rejection of the false hypothesis being tested? Explain.

..................................................

..................................................

..................................................

..................................................

**c** The following statement is fallacious: "If a sample mean does not fall into the critical region, the difference between it and the hypothesized value of the population mean *is entirely due to chance*." Revise the italicized part of this statement in such a way as to make the entire statement true.

..................................................

**12.12.12a** If .01 is used as the level of significance in the situation of 12.4.1, and if the actual value of the population parameter is 50, what is the probability of a Type II error?

..................................................

**b** What would this probability be if .05 had been used as the level of significance?

.................................................................

**c** What would be the answer to part **a** if a sample of 65 had been used instead of a sample of 145? (Assume $S = 15$ as before.)

.................................................................

**d** What would be the answer to part **a** if the actual value of the population parameter were 49 instead of 50?

.................................................................

**12.12.13** Indicate how the probability of a Type II error associated with the test of a statistical hypothesis is affected by:

    **a** The magnitude of the difference between the hypothesized and the actual value of the population parameter

.................................................................

.................................................................

    **b** The magnitude of the level of significance

.................................................................

.................................................................

    **c** The size of the sample

.................................................................

.................................................................

    **d** The magnitude of the standard error of the statistic used

.................................................................

.................................................................

**12.12.14** Suppose that a particular statistical hypothesis is true and that the sampling-error theory applied in testing it is appropriate. Indicate how the probability of a Type I error is affected by:

    **a** The magnitude of the standard error of the statistic used

.................................................................

    **b** The size of the sample beyond the minimum necessary to make the sampling theory appropriate or applicable

.................................................................

    **c** The magnitude of the level of significance

.................................................................

.................................................................

.................................................................

**Table 12.B**

| D | Ex. 12.4.1 P | Ex. 12.6.3 P | Ex. 12.7.5 P |
|---|---|---|---|
| 1 | .063 | .046 | .031 |
| 2 | .233 | .149 | .081 |
| 3 | . . . | .345 | .176 |
| 4 | .808 | . . . | .323 |
| 5 | .953 | .811 | . . . |
| 6 | .993 | .936 | .681 |
| 7 | | .985 | .826 |
| 8 | | .997 | .921 |
| 9 | | | .969 |
| 10 | | | .990 |
| 11 | | | .998 |

**12.13.15** In Table 12.B, the column headed $D$ gives selected values of differences between hypothesized and possible actual values of the population parameter involved in the statistical tests of exercises 12.4.1, 12.6.3, and 12.7.5. The next three columns give the approximate values of the power ($P$) of each of these tests for given values of $D$. (Approximate because the sample $S$ was used in each case to estimate the population $\sigma$ and also, of course, because the sampling distributions involved are only approximately normal.)

**a** Enter in Table 12.B the three omitted $P$-values.

**b** What is the limit of each of these $P$-values as $D$ approaches zero?

........................................................................................................................

**c** Using the grid of the figure for 12.13.15c, sketch the power curves for each of these tests. Label the curves for the tests of 12.4.1, 12.6.3, and 12.7.5 as 1, 3, and 5, respectively.

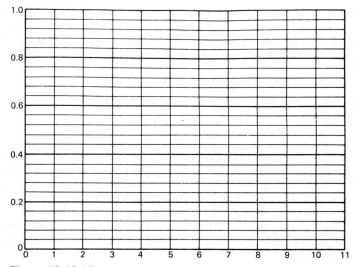

**Figure 12.13.15c**

**d** Suppose that the supervisor does not feel her program to be worth the trouble involved in setting it up unless the population parameter is at least 10 points greater than the value hypothesized for it. Which of the three tests should she use? Why?

........................................................................................................................................

........................................................................................................................................

........................................................................................................................................

........................................................................................................................................

........................................................................................................................................

........................................................................................................................................

**e** Suppose that the supervisor feels that it would be a serious mistake *not* to introduce her program should the parameter exceed the hypothesized value by 3 points. Which of the three tests should she use? (Consider "none" as a possible answer.) Explain.

........................................................................................................................................

........................................................................................................................................

........................................................................................................................................

........................................................................................................................................

........................................................................................................................................

f Suppose that the supervisor wants a test sufficiently powerful to detect a discrepancy of 5 points between the actual and hypothesized values of the parameter at least 95 times out of 100 in the long run. Which, if any, of the three tests should she use?

..........................................................................................................................

g Which of the three tests would best prevent rejection of a true hypothesis?

..........................................................................................................................

**12.15.16** Suppose it is required to test the hypothesis that the mean of a certain population is 50 against the alternatives that it is either greater or less than 50. Suppose further that it is desired to conduct this test with a level of significance of .05 and also with a $\beta$-value of .05 should the actual value of the parameter differ from 50 by as much as 5. Roughly, what size sample is necessary to meet these requirements if a small preliminary sample of 17 cases selected from the population is found to have a standard deviation of 12?

..........................................................................

**12.15.17** The problem is to determine roughly what size sample is needed in the situation of 12.8.6 with $\alpha = .01$. It is desired that the probability of a Type II error not be more than .01 should the actual population proportion of children gaining at least 6 points exceed the value hypothesized for it by as much as .10.

..........................................................................

# 13

# Sampling Theory as it Applies to Difference Between Means and Proportions: Large Samples

**13.2.1** An investigator wished to determine if there is any difference in average intelligence between the 13-year-old boys and the 13-year-old girls enrolled in a large city school system. He selected a random sample of 50 cases from each of the two populations. He obtained a mean IQ of 121 for the sample of boys and of 118 for the sample of girls.

**a** May the investigator safely conclude from this evidence that the mean IQ for the entire population of boys is higher than that for the entire population of girls? How might the difference of 3 between the obtained (sample) means be accounted for other than by a real difference between the means of the two populations?

..................................................................................................................

..................................................................................................................

..................................................................................................................

..................................................................................................................

..................................................................................................................

..................................................................................................................

..................................................................................................................

**b** Suppose that, unknown to the investigator, the means of the two populations are in fact equal: $\mu_B = \mu_G$. Suppose also that the standard deviations of both populations are 15: $\sigma_B = \sigma_G = 15$. Describe the sampling distribution of $\overline{X}_B - \overline{X}_G$.

Shape ......................................................................................................

Mean ......................................................................................................

Standard deviation or standard error ....................................................

..................................................................................................................

**c** In the sampling distribution described in part **b**, determine the probability of $|\overline{X}_B - \overline{X}_G| \geq 3$. (*Note:* $\sigma_{\overline{X}_B - \overline{X}_G} = 3$.)

.................................................................

**d** Assuming the populations to have equal means and considering the probability value called for in part **c**, would you say that the obtained difference of 3 was a likely or unlikely finding? Why?

........................................................................................................

........................................................................................................

........................................................................................................

........................................................................................................

**13.2.2** Fill in the blanks in the following statement.

The standard error of the difference between the proportions of A's arising from a pair of random samples, one drawn from each of two populations consisting of objects that are A's and not-A's, can be approximated directly (without using the formula) by selecting a "large"

number of such ......................... of ......................... from these

.................................. by computing the difference between the

.................................. for each ......................... of .........................,

organizing these ......................... into a frequency distribution,

and computing the ......................... of this distribution.

**13.2.3a** Is it assumed at the beginning of the statement of the foregoing exercise (13.2.2) that both samples of a pair are of the same size? That is, if the sample from one population contains 100 cases, must the sample from the other population contain 100 cases also?

.................................................................

**b** Is it assumed, later in this statement, that all samples selected from the same population are of the same size? Explain.

........................................................................................................

........................................................................................................

........................................................................................................

........................................................................................................

........................................................................................................

........................................................................................................

........................................................................................................

**13.2.4** The standard error of the difference between the means of two samples of 50 cases, each drawn at random from one of two populations, is 3.

**a** Assuming the actual difference between the population means to be 10, draw a freehand sketch of the sampling distribution of such differences. (Use the space allowed for the figure for 13.2.4.) Designate the values of the points on the scale that are one standard error apart.

**b** Two investigators, working independently, select random samples of 50 cases from each of these same two populations. Each investigator then determines the difference between the means of her pair of samples. Investigator A reported an obtained difference of 3. Investigator B reported an obtained difference of 18—six times as large. Is this possible? Explain. Show where these differences would lie on the scale of the figure called for in **a**.

.................................................................................................................

.................................................................................................................

.................................................................................................................

**13.2.5** A freshman class of high school pupils consists of 25 boys and 30 girls. The mean age of the boys is 170 months and the mean age of the girls is 167 months.

**a** May one safely conclude that *these* boys are on the average older than *these* girls without computing the standard error of this difference in means? Why?

.................................................................................................................

.................................................................................................................

.................................................................................................................

.................................................................................................................

**b** When should the standard error of a difference be computed?

.................................................................................................................................................

.................................................................................................................................................

**13.3.6a** Consider the situation described in 13.2.1. Assume the following data were found for the two samples.

| Boys | Girls |
|------|-------|
| $n_B = 50$ | $n_G = 50$ |
| $\overline{X}_B = 121$ | $\overline{X}_G = 118$ |
| $S_B = 16$ | $S_G = 14$ |

On the basis of this information describe the approximate sampling distribution of $\overline{X}_B - \overline{X}_G$. (Leave the answer related to standard deviation or standard error in terms of the square root sign.)

Shape .........................................................................................................................

Mean ..........................................................................................................................

Standard deviation or standard error .........................................................................

.................................................................................................................................................

**b** Why is this distribution approximate?

.................................................................................................................................................

.................................................................................................................................................

.................................................................................................................................................

**13.3.7** Using a random sample of 126 from the public high school seniors in City A, a school psychologist finds that one-fourth ($p_A = .25$) of them have experienced at least one academic failure at some time since beginning first grade. Using a similar random sample of 211 seniors from City B he finds that three-tenths ($p_B = .3$) have experienced at least one such failure. Using this information, sketch in the space allowed for the figure for 13.3.7 the *approximate* sampling distribution of the difference between these proportions, that is, of the difference $p_B - p_A$. (Designate the value of $\tilde{\sigma}_{p_B - p_A}$ and designate selected values on the $p_B - p_A$ scale after the manner of Figure 13.2 of the text.) *Note:*

$$\tilde{\sigma}_{p_B - p_A} = \sqrt{\frac{(p_B)(1 - p_B)}{n_B - 1} + \frac{(p_A)(1 - p_A)}{n_A - 1}}$$

$$= \sqrt{\frac{(.3)(.7)}{210} + \frac{(.25)(.75)}{125}} \approx .05$$

**13.4.8** A psychologist wished to compare two populations of individuals with respect to mean performance on the complex perceptual-motor task provided by the Iowa Pursuitmeter.[1] Briefly, the apparatus consisted of two elements: (1) a target moving in an irregular path, and (2) a spot of light that a subject could move by pushing, pulling, and twisting in a properly coordinated manner two control handles having pistol-type grips. The task consisted simply of manipulating the control handles so as to keep the spot of light continuously on the bull's-eye of the moving target. The criterion or performance score was the total time in seconds on bull's-eye in two successive 30-second trials after ten practice trials. All trials—practice and test—were separated by 30-second rest intervals.

Both populations consisted of male undergraduate students, but here the similarity ended. The members of one population had solved block-design problems of a certain type in an analytical way, and were referred to as *analyzers*. The other population consisted of individuals who did not attack these block-design problems in an analytical fashion and, hence, were described as *nonanalyzers*. The psychologist had no definite preconceived notion as to which, if either, of these populations would be superior to the other in the performance of the task. The means and standard deviations of the test scores for random samples from each of these populations are given in Table 13.A.

**Table 13.A**

|                          | Analyzers | Nonanalyzers |
|--------------------------|-----------|--------------|
| Sample size ($n$)        | 50        | 55           |
| Mean ($\bar{X}$)         | 15.1      | 10.8         |
| Standard deviation ($S$) | 5.57      | 5.23         |

[1] Although the situation described in this exercise is imaginary, it is based on an article by Guy H. Miles and Don Lewis ["Relation of Grade-Point Averages and Placement Test Scores to Analytic Tendency and to Performance on the Iowa Pursuitmeter," *Proceedings of the Iowa Academy of Science*, 65 (November 20, 1958), 370–376].

**a** If $\mu_A$ and $\mu_{NA}$ represent the mean scores on the criterion task for the two populations under investigation, state the statistical hypothesis involved.

................................................................................................................

**b** Cite the alternative(s) to this hypothesis.

................................................................................................................

................................................................................................................

**c** Assuming the hypothesis to be true, describe the following aspects of the sampling distribution of the statistic $\overline{X}_A - \overline{X}_{NA}$. (Leave your answer about the standard error in terms of the square root sign.)

Mean ..........................................................................................................

Standard error ............................................................................................

Form ..........................................................................................................

**d** Assuming the hypothesis to be false, indicate in what respects the sampling distribution of $\overline{X}_A - \overline{X}_{NA}$ would differ from that of **c**.

................................................................................................................

................................................................................................................

................................................................................................................

................................................................................................................

................................................................................................................

**e** If .01 is used as the level of significance, specify the critical region appropriate to a test of the hypothesis in question in terms of the scale of values of the test statistic $z$.

................................................................................................................

**f** What is the value of $z$ for the given sample data? (*Note:* $\tilde{\sigma}_{\overline{X}_A - \overline{X}_{NA}} \approx 1.07$.)

................................................................................

**g** What is the outcome of the test? If it is rejection, cite the alternative indicated by this outcome.

................................................................................................................

**h** Again using .01 as the level of significance, specify the critical region in terms of the scale of values of the test statistic $\overline{X}_A - \overline{X}_{NA}$.

................................................................................................................

**i** What is the value of $\overline{X}_A - \overline{X}_{NA}$ for the given sample data?

................................................................................

**13.4.9** Consider the speed reading experiment described in Section 9.1 of the text. Assume that 50 students were randomly assigned to the speed reading course (the experimental group) and 50 students served as control subjects. When a reading comprehension test was administered to both groups, the following results were found.

| Experimental Group | Control Group |
|---|---|
| $n_E = 50$ | $n_C = 50$ |
| $\overline{X}_E = 48$ | $\overline{X}_C = 46$ |
| $S_E = 5$ | $S_C = 7$ |

**a** Recall that the purpose of the experiment was to test the effectiveness of the speed reading course. If the course has no effect (either positive or negative), how do $\mu_E$ and $\mu_C$ compare?

...........................................................................................................................

...........................................................................................................................

**b** Assume the statistical hypothesis is $H_0: \mu_E - \mu_C = 0$. Why is it reasonable to have two alternatives in this situation (i.e., $H_1: \mu_E - \mu_C > 0$ and $H_2: \mu_E - \mu_C < 0$)?

...........................................................................................................................

...........................................................................................................................

...........................................................................................................................

**c** What is the estimated standard error of the sampling distribution of $\overline{X}_E - \overline{X}_C$? (*Note:* Leave your answer in terms of square root sign.)

...........................................................................................................................

**d** Assume $\alpha = .05$. Specify the $R$ appropriate to a test of $H_0$ (part **b**) in terms of the scale of values of the test statistic $z$.

...........................................................................................................................

**e** What is the value of $z$ for the given sample data? (*Note:* $\tilde{\sigma}_{\overline{X}_E - \overline{X}_C} \approx 1.2$.)

...........................................................................................................................

**f** Given your answers to parts **d** and **e**, what is the outcome of this test? If it is rejection, what alternative is indicated by this outcome?

...........................................................................................................................

...........................................................................................................................

**13.4.10** In the experiment described in the previous exercise, there are two *hypothetical* sets of scores on the reading comprehension test. Briefly describe the distributions of these two sets of scores.

..................................................................................................................................

..................................................................................................................................

..................................................................................................................................

..................................................................................................................................

**13.4.11** Assume the following results were obtained for the two samples of students described in 11.2.3:

| Group I (IQ Directions) | Group II (Routine Directions) |
|---|---|
| $n_I = 40$ | $n_{II} = 40$ |
| $\overline{X}_I = 119$ | $\overline{X}_{II} = 110$ |
| $S_I = 16$ | $S_{II} = 15$ |

**a** Why is $H_0: \mu_I - \mu_{II} = 0$ a reasonable hypothesis to test in this situation?

..................................................................................................................................

..................................................................................................................................

**b** Justify the possible use of only one alternative hypothesis in this situation.

..................................................................................................................................

..................................................................................................................................

**c** Justify the use of two alternatives in this situation.

..................................................................................................................................

..................................................................................................................................

..................................................................................................................................

**d** Assume $\alpha = .10$ and a one-tailed test is used (assume $H_1: \mu_I - \mu_{II} > 0$). What is the $R$ in terms of the scale of the test statistic $z$?

..................................................................................

**e** What is the particular value of $z$ for the given data? (*Note:* $\tilde{\sigma}_{\overline{X}_I - \overline{X}_{II}} \approx 3.5$.)

..................................................................................

**f** On the basis of the results in **d** and **e**, what is the outcome of the test?

..................................................................................................................................

..................................................................................................................................

**13.4.12** An elementary school supervisor wished to compare the average effectiveness of two methods (A and B) of teaching a certain unit of material in fifth-grade arithmetic. Method A, the conventionally used method, was tried out on a random sample of 122 fifth-grade pupils. Method B, a novel experimental method, was tried out on a similar sample of 50 pupils. After the instructional period was completed, the same criterion test was administered to the pupils of both samples. The mean and standard deviation of the scores made by the pupils who studied under Method A were 105 and 33, respectively. The corresponding values for the other group of pupils were 115 and 28.

**a** What is the standard error of the sampling distribution of $\overline{X}_B - \overline{X}_A$?

..........................................................................................

**b** The supervisor wishes to test the hypothesis that $\mu_B - \mu_A = 0$ against the alternatives that $\mu_B - \mu_A < 0$ or $\mu_B - \mu_A > 0$. If .05 is selected as the level of significance, specify the critical region in terms of the scale of values of:

$z$ ...............................................................

$\overline{X}_B - \overline{X}_A$ .............................................

**c** What is the particular value of $z$ for the data given? ..............................

**d** What is the outcome of the test? If it is rejection, cite the alternative indicated by this outcome.

..........................................................................................

**e** Suppose that it is desired to test the hypothesis that $\mu_B - \mu_A = 15$ against the alternatives that $\mu_B - \mu_A < 15$ or $\mu_B - \mu_A > 15$. If .05 is used as the level of significance, specify the critical region in terms of the scale of values of:

$z$ ...............................................................

$\overline{X}_B - \overline{X}_A$ .............................................

**f** In this case, what is the particular value of $z$ for the data given?

..........................................................................................

**g** What is the outcome of this test? If it is rejection, cite the alternative indicated by this outcome.

..........................................................................................

**13.4.13** Suppose the outcome of the test of the hypothesis stated in 13.4.12b indicated rejection and consequent adoption of the alternative that the mean of the hypothetical population taught by the experimental Method B is larger than that of the one taught by the conventional Method A. A number of possible explanations exist for the *observed* difference of 10 in favor of the Method B sample. Some of these are listed below.

    **1** The pupils in Sample B might have had a higher average intelligence than those in Sample A.

    **2** The pupils in Sample B might on the average have known more arithmetic before the experiment than those in Sample A.

    **3** The pupils in Sample B might have acquired better study habits before the experiment began than those in Sample A.

    **4** The pupils in Sample B might have had more expert teachers during the experiment.

    **5** During the experiment the pupils in Sample B might have been receiving incidental instruction in the arithmetic in question in another subject while those in Sample A did not.

    **6** The teachers using Method A might have been prejudiced against it.

    **7** Method B is actually more effective than Method A.

**a** Cite two other possible explanations for the observed difference in favor of Method B.

........................................................................................................................

........................................................................................................................

........................................................................................................................

........................................................................................................................

........................................................................................................................

........................................................................................................................

........................................................................................................................

........................................................................................................................

........................................................................................................................

**b** Does the fact that random samples were used eliminate any of the possible explanations suggested above?

........................................................................

**c** Which of the possible explanations in the list of seven that introduce this exercise might be described as due to chance fluctuations arising from the use of random samples?

........................................................................

**d** Which, if any, of the above explanations may be ruled out as a result of the rejection of the statistically tested hypothesis?

...................................................................

**e** Does rejection of this hypothesis imply that explanation 7 is the only reasonable explanation of the consequent alternative? Explain.

...................................................................................................
...................................................................................................
...................................................................................................
...................................................................................................
...................................................................................................
...................................................................................................

**13.5.14** Does college make students more liberal? To answer this question, an investigator selected a random sample of freshmen and a random sample of seniors. Each group was administered an instrument purported to measure "liberalism." The investigator found that the mean score was much higher for seniors than for freshmen; the seniors sampled were more liberal. By application of the techniques for testing statistical hypotheses, he determined that rejection of the hypothesis of equal mean scores for the two populations represented was clearly indicated. He thereby concluded that college increases the degree of liberalism in students. Give another possible explanation of the observed differences between the sample means.

...................................................................................................
...................................................................................................
...................................................................................................
...................................................................................................
...................................................................................................

**13.5.15** From the population of all pupils graduating from high school during a given year in a given state, a random sample was drawn from the subpopulation of those who had completed three years of a foreign language. Another random sample was drawn from the subpopulation of those who had not studied any foreign language. The pupils in both samples were given the same comprehensive test in English correctness. The mean score on this test was considerably higher for the sample of pupils who had had three years of a foreign language than for the sample of those who had not. Application of the appropriate sampling theory suggested that the observed difference between the sample means was statistically significant. It was concluded that instruction in a foreign language leads to improvement in English correctness.

**a** To state that an observed difference between sample means is *statistically significant* is equivalent to stating that a statistical test indicates rejection of what hypothesis?

.........................................................................................................................................

.........................................................................................................................................

**b** What might be another and perhaps better reason for the observed difference than the one expressed in the conclusion given?

.........................................................................................................................................

.........................................................................................................................................

.........................................................................................................................................

.........................................................................................................................................

.........................................................................................................................................

.........................................................................................................................................

**13.5.16** An investigator wished to determine in the case of a certain large city whether or not there is any relationship between the intelligence of children and the ages of their mothers at parturition. Using as a data source the school records of this city, he listed all 10-year-old pupils whose mothers were 35 or older when the child was born. Similarly, he listed the names of all 10-year-old pupils whose mothers were 20 or younger when the child was born. He then made a purely random selection of 50 names from each list and administered a reliable intelligence test to both sets of pupils. He found the mean intelligence to be considerably higher for the sample of children born to the older mothers, and by appropriate statistical techniques he found the difference between the means of the two samples to be highly statistically significant. His conclusion was that to ensure high intelligence in their offspring women should postpone childbearing until late in life.

**a** What does the fact that the observed difference was statistically significant mean in this case?

.........................................................................................................................................

.........................................................................................................................................

.........................................................................................................................................

**b** Point out the possible fallacy in the conclusion.

...........................................................................................................

...........................................................................................................

...........................................................................................................

...........................................................................................................

...........................................................................................................

...........................................................................................................

...........................................................................................................

**13.5.17** Discriminate between *significant* when used as a technical term in statistics and when used with its ordinary nontechnical meaning.

...........................................................................................................

...........................................................................................................

...........................................................................................................

...........................................................................................................

...........................................................................................................

...........................................................................................................

**13.5.18** Is the absolute magnitude of the test statistic $z$ necessarily indicative of, or proportional to, the importance or general (nontechnical) significance of the difference between two sample means? For example, if a $z$ of 6 arises from the observed difference between one pair of sample means and a $z$ of 3 from another pair, is the first difference necessarily of greater importance or even necessarily of greater magnitude than the second? Explain.

...........................................................................................................

...........................................................................................................

...........................................................................................................

...........................................................................................................

...........................................................................................................

...........................................................................................................

**13.5.19** Consider the problem of the principal and the superintendent described in Sections 12.1 and 12.4 of the text. Assume that instead of selecting a sample of 65 students to take an individually administered intelligence test (the WISC), the superintendent decides to administer a group intelligence test such as the Thorndike-Hagen Cognitive Abilities Test to all 1,601 students in the principal's school. These 1,601 students are assumed to be a random sample from the population of students who will be enrolled in this school over the next ten years. The mean on this group test for a national standardization sample is 100. Therefore, the superintendent decides to test $H_0: \mu = 100$. Assume the results for the 1,601 students are

$$\overline{X} = 94 \quad \text{and} \quad S = 20$$

(*Note:* These are the same values as used in Section 12.4.)

**a** What is the value of the test statistic in terms of $z$? (*Note:* $\tilde{\sigma}_{\overline{X}} \approx .5$.)

.................................................................

**b** The $z$-value found in **a** was $-12$. What information does this give the superintendent? Does it tell her anything about the importance of the difference between the observed mean and the hypothesized mean?

.................................................................

.................................................................

.................................................................

**c** Assume that instead of $\overline{X} = 94$, the mean for these 1,601 students was 99. If $S = 20$ (and hence $\tilde{\sigma}_{\overline{X}} \approx .5$), what is the test statistic in terms of $z$?

.................................................................

**d** If $\alpha = .05$ had been selected and a one-tailed test performed, the $z$-value in part **c** would have fallen in the $R$ on the $z$-scale. Therefore, $H_0: \mu = 100$ would have been rejected and $H_1: \mu < 100$ would have been accepted as the only remaining possibility. Explain how this example illustrates the proposition that although statistical significance is a necessary condition for practical significance, it is not a sufficient condition.

.................................................................

.................................................................

.................................................................

**13.7.20** Summaries of the reported results of several statistical investigations are given in Table 13.B. This table simply gives: (1) the statement of the statistical hypotheses tested, (2) the alternatives to these hypotheses, (3) the levels of significance used by the several investigators, (4) the

**Table 13.B**

| Hypothesis | Alternative | $\alpha$ | $z$ | Outcome |
|---|---|---|---|---|
| $\phi = .5$ | $\phi > .5$ | .01 | $+1.90$ | Retain |
| $\mu = 100$ | $\mu < 100, \mu > 100$ | .001 | $-2.70$ | Retain |
| $\xi = 50$ | $\xi < 50, \xi > 50$ | .01 | $+2.75$ | Reject |
| $\mu_1 - \mu_2 = 0$ | $\mu_1 - \mu_2 < 0$ | .05 | $-1.85$ | Reject |

**Table 13.C**

| Reader's $\alpha$ | EA | Outcome |
|---|---|---|
| .05 | | |
| .01 | | |
| .001 | | |
| .01 | | |

obtained sample values of $z$, the test statistic, and (5) the outcomes of the tests.

Table 13.C gives the values that a reader of the reports of these investigations feels should have been used as the levels of significance instead of those adopted by the original investigators. For each of these investigations this reader determined the extreme area (EA) and compared it with the level of significance he deemed appropriate. Determine these EA-values and indicate what the outcome of each investigation would be if this reader's standards regarding levels of significance were applied. Enter the results in Table 13.C.

**13.7.21** An investigation of the difference between the means of two populations gives rise to an EA of .021. Another investigation concerned with two different populations results in an EA of .00001. Does this necessarily mean that the second difference is of greater importance than the first? Explain.

..........................................................................................................

..........................................................................................................

..........................................................................................................

..........................................................................................................

..........................................................................................................

**13.7.22** When you read the literature in your area of interest, you may not find each step of the hypothesis testing procedure listed. Rather, you will very often find a summary table of the findings. It is common practice to include in these summary tables a value for the extreme area. Consider the situation of 13.4.11. As part of the research article reporting these results, you might find the following table.

| | Mean | S | z | |
|---|---|---|---|---|
| Group I ($N = 40$) | 119 | 16 | | |
| (IQ directions) | | | 2.57 | $p < .015$ |
| Group II ($N = 40$) | 110 | 15 | | |
| (Routine directions) | | | | |

**a** In the preceding table the value of $p$ (i.e., $EA$) is interpreted as follows:

$$p = P(|z| \geq 2.57 \mid ND: \mu = 0; \sigma = 1) < .015$$

*Remarks:*
(1) A two-tailed test is assumed.
(2) The value of $p$ will vary from one run of the experiment to another and, hence, $p$ may be thought of as a random variable.

If a reader of this study decided that an $\alpha$-level of .05 was appropriate, what would be the outcome (retain or reject) of the test?

............................................................

The summary table described above is not the only type that you may encounter as you read the research literature. Another very common type of summary table is shown below for the same data as given above.

|  | Mean | $S$ | $z$ |
|---|---|---|---|
| Group I ($N = 40$) | 119 | 16 | |
| (IQ directions) | | | $2.57^a$ |
| Group II ($N = 40$) | 110 | 15 | |
| (Routine directions) | | | |

*[a] Significant at .05 level*

In this table, the extreme area is not given. Instead the $\alpha$-level selected by the experimenter is indicated.

**b** Assume you encounter a research article reporting the following data:

|  | Mean | $S$ | $z$ | |
|---|---|---|---|---|
| Experimental group | 68.4 | 3 | 4.0 | $p < .0001$ |
| Control group | 65.0 | 4 | | |

What does the $p$-value ($p < .0001$) indicate about the practical significance of these results? (Consider your answer to 13.5.18.)

............................................................................................

............................................................................................

............................................................................................

............................................................................................

............................................................................................

............................................................................................

**13.8.23a** The psychologist referred to in 13.4.8 wished to determine whether the average gain in performance recorded for the "analyzers" from practice trials 7 and 8 to test trials 11 and 12 was statistically significant or simply a chance characteristic of his particular sample of 50 analyzers. In other words, he wished to determine whether the learning curve for analyzers on this task had leveled off—reached an asymptote—as early as the seventh and eighth practice trials. This implies testing the hypothesis that there is no difference between the means of two hypothetical populations of scores. Describe these populations.

..................................................................................................

..................................................................................................

..................................................................................................

..................................................................................................

**b** In this situation should one or two alternatives to the hypothesis be considered? Explain. If your answer is "one alternative" indicate which one should be considered.

..................................................................................................

..................................................................................................

..................................................................................................

..................................................................................................

..................................................................................................

..................................................................................................

..................................................................................................

..................................................................................................

**13.8.24** The data collected by the psychologist in order to answer the question raised in the foregoing exercise (13.8.23) are given in Table 13.D. For each subject a difference score was computed, and the following values were found.

$$\bar{D} = \bar{X}_{11-12} - \bar{X}_{7-8} = 2.54 \qquad S_D \approx 3.0$$

**a** What is the estimated standard error of the sampling distribution of $\bar{X}_{11-12} - \bar{X}_{7-8}$?

..................................................................

**b** What is the particular value of the test statistic $z$ for the given data that provides a test of the hypothesis of concern to the psychologist (see 13.8.23**a**).

..................................................................

**c** If .01 is used as the level of significance, what is the outcome of the test?

..................................................................

**Table 13.D**   Times on Bull's-Eye in Seconds for 50 Analyzers on Practice Trials 7 and 8 and Test Trials 11 and 12

| Subject | 7–8 | 11–12 | Subject | 7–8 | 11–12 | Subject | 7–8 | 11–12 |
|---------|-----|-------|---------|-----|-------|---------|-----|-------|
| 1 | 14 | 20 | 18 | 20 | 22 | 35 | 9 | 14 |
| 2 | 16 | 16 | 19 | 8 | 10 | 36 | 10 | 15 |
| 3 | 11 | 10 | 20 | 14 | 13 | 37 | 17 | 21 |
| 4 | 11 | 10 | 21 | 7 | 10 | 38 | 9 | 12 |
| 5 | 13 | 13 | 22 | 15 | 16 | 39 | 12 | 16 |
| 6 | 15 | 18 | 23 | 4 | 6 | 40 | 2 | 2 |
| 7 | 20 | 24 | 24 | 11 | 14 | 41 | 15 | 24 |
| 8 | 4 | 3 | 25 | 9 | 16 | 42 | 14 | 15 |
| 9 | 19 | 21 | 26 | 20 | 18 | 43 | 7 | 5 |
| 10 | 14 | 18 | 27 | 21 | 23 | 44 | 12 | 17 |
| 11 | 9 | 11 | 28 | 8 | 22 | 45 | 9 | 10 |
| 12 | 10 | 11 | 29 | 20 | 23 | 46 | 16 | 22 |
| 13 | 10 | 13 | 30 | 17 | 19 | 47 | 14 | 15 |
| 14 | 7 | 9 | 31 | 10 | 12 | 48 | 14 | 17 |
| 15 | 9 | 9 | 32 | 12 | 16 | 49 | 17 | 17 |
| 16 | 16 | 14 | 33 | 15 | 23 | 50 | 8 | 9 |
| 17 | 20 | 25 | 34 | 14 | 16 | | | |

**d** Explain the implications of this outcome with respect to the psychological problem involved.

...................................................................................................................................

...................................................................................................................................

...................................................................................................................................

...................................................................................................................................

...................................................................................................................................

**13.8.25** Consider the speed reading experiment described in Section 9.1 of the text. The results of one experimental procedure are given in 13.4.9. In that procedure, independent groups were used. Now suppose the experimental procedure outlined on p. 305 of the text is used with college entrance examination scores as the matching or control variable. Assume that 50 pairs of students, matched on entrance scores, are formed and that one member of each pair is assigned by some random process to the speed reading course. Assume the following results were obtained. (Note that the value for $\bar{D}$ is the same as the value found in 13.4.9.)

$$\bar{D} = \bar{X}_E - \bar{X}_C = 2 \qquad S_D = 5.6 \qquad \tilde{\sigma}_{\bar{D}} = .8$$

**a** What is the hypothesis of interest in this situation?

...................................................................................................................................

...................................................................................................................................

**b** If $\alpha = .05$ and a two-tailed test is used, what is $R$ in terms of the scale of values of the test statistic $z$?

..........................................................................................

**c** What is the value of $z$ for the given sample data?

..........................................................................................

**d** Parts **c** and **b** indicate rejection of $H_0$. What alternative is indicated?

..........................................................................................

..........................................................................................

**e** In the previous solution to this speed reading problem (exercise 13.4.9) using independent random samples, the same mean difference (2 units) was not statistically significant ($\alpha = .05$, two-ended). Explain why these two different outcomes are possible.

..........................................................................................

..........................................................................................

..........................................................................................

..........................................................................................

**13.9.26** An investigator wished to compare pupils from groups of low and high socioeconomic status with regard to their attitudes toward high school. She selected a random sample of 200 pupils from the low socio-economic population and a similar sample of 100 from the high socioeconomic population. She then administered to these 300 subjects an attitude inventory designed to assess various aspects of attitude toward high school. Among the items involved was the question, "Are you satisfied with your social life in high school?" This question was answered "yes" by 120 of the subjects in the low socioeconomic sample and by 72 of the subjects in the high socioeconomic sample. The problem is to determine whether the observed difference in the proportion of "yes" responses is actually characteristic of the two populations or is simply a random characteristic of the two particular samples investigated. This, of course, amounts to testing a statistical hypothesis regarding the relative magnitudes of the proportions of individuals in these two populations who would give a "yes" response to this question.

**a** State the statistical hypothesis involved. (Let $\phi_H$ and $\phi_L$ represent the proportions for the high and low populations, respectively.)

..........................................................................................

**b** State the alternative(s) to this hypothesis.

..........................................................................................

**c** What is the value of $p_H - p_L$ for the given data?

..........................................................................................

**d** What is the estimated standard error of the sampling distribution of $p_H - p_L$?

...............................................................

**e** What is the value of the test statistic $z$ for the given data? (*Note:* $\tilde{\sigma}_{p_H - p_L} \approx .059$.)

...............................................................

**f** If .05 is used as the level of significance, what is the outcome of the test? If this outcome is rejection, specify the alternative indicated.

...............................................................

**g** For the given data, what is the particular value of the extreme area associated with this statistical test?

...............................................................

**13.9.27** An instructor of a large introductory sociology class at a certain university was interested in assessing the effect of labeling a movie as X-rated on the decision of students to see it. As one part of a larger survey related to student attitudes toward types of books and movies, the instructor provided a brief description of the plot of and the actors in a movie as yet to be released. One-half of the instruments, designated as the experimental form, indicated that the movie was X-rated. The other half, designated the control form, had exactly the same description except no mention was made of the rating of the film. In each case the students were asked to indicate (check "Yes" or "No") whether they wanted to see this movie.

There were 202 students in the class. The survey instruments were distributed in such a manner that every other student in a row received the experimental form (the one with the X-rated designation). The following results were obtained:

| Experimental Group (X-rated) | Control Group |
|---|---|
| $n_E = 101$ | $n_C = 101$ |
| $p_E = .50$ | $p_C = .60$ |

where $p_E$ = proportion of experimental sample checking "Yes," and $p_C$ = proportion of control sample checking "Yes."

**a** State the statistical hypothesis of interest in this situation. Let $\phi_E$ and $\phi_C$ represent the population proportions.

...............................................................

**b** Assuming $\tilde{\sigma}_{p_E - p_C} = .07$, what is the value of the test statistic $z$ for these data?

...............................................................

**c** If $\alpha = .10$ and a two-tailed test is used, what is the outcome of this test?

...............................................................

**d** Assume the outcome is retain $H_0$. Does this prove that $\phi_E = \phi_C$? Explain.

.......................................................................................................................

.......................................................................................................................

.......................................................................................................................

**e** Assume that the outcome is reject $H_0$ and that as a consequence the sociologist reports that people in this age group tend to avoid X-rated movies. Granting that the students in this class are indeed a random sample of college students of this age group, explain why the above generalization may not be valid.

.......................................................................................................................

.......................................................................................................................

.......................................................................................................................

.......................................................................................................................

**13.10.28** In a study comparing team teaching with "traditional" teaching, the following statement was made.

> Parents of children attending the team school and parents of children attending the traditional school were found to be equally favorable in their opinions of school effectiveness.

Assume this statement was made because the hypothesis of equal population means was not rejected. Explain the fallacy of this statement.

.......................................................................................................................

.......................................................................................................................

.......................................................................................................................

.......................................................................................................................

.......................................................................................................................

# 14
# Interval Estimation

**14.1.1** A number of situations requiring some form of data analysis have been described in earlier exercises in this study manual. Several of these situations have been identified below by exercise number. For each situation, you are asked to go back to the exercise and decide whether the primary interest of the researcher would be in estimating parameters (E) or in testing hypotheses (H). Then, briefly explain your choice.

**a** Exercise 3.7.19 ............................................................

................................................................................

................................................................................

................................................................................

**b** Exercise 3.7.20 ............................................................

................................................................................

................................................................................

................................................................................

**c** Exercise 11.2.1 ............................................................

................................................................................

................................................................................

................................................................................

**d** Exercise 11.2.2 (*Note:* This exercise is concerned with the speed reading experiment described in Section 9.1 of the text.)

................................................................................

................................................................................

................................................................................

................................................................................

**e** Exercise 12.4.1 ............................................................

................................................................................

................................................................................

................................................................................

**f** Exercise 12.10.7 ...........................................................

.................................................................................................

.................................................................................................

.................................................................................................

**g** Exercise 13.4.8 ...........................................................

.................................................................................................

.................................................................................................

.................................................................................................

**14.3.2** Consider the vocabulary experiment discussed in 12.4.1. Assume that the researcher established a 90 percent confidence interval for $\mu$, the population mean. Further assume that this interval was 45.6–52.4.

**a** What is the value of $\gamma$? ...........................................................

**b** Is $\mu$ between 45.6 and 52.4? ...........................................................

**c** Briefly describe how this information should be interpreted from a relative frequency viewpoint.

.................................................................................................

.................................................................................................

.................................................................................................

.................................................................................................

**d** If a 95 percent confidence interval had been computed, would the width of the interval be greater or less than that of the 90 percent interval?

...........................................................

**14.4.3** Suppose that a certain statistic $T$ is known to be approximately normally distributed with a standard deviation of 2, but that the mean of its sampling distribution is unknown. Figure 14.4.3 pictures this distribution. In the figure, points $A$ and $B$ have been located 1.28 standard deviations below and above $\mu$, respectively.

**a** What is the value of $P(T > B)$? ...........................................................

**b** What is the value of $P(T < A)$? ...........................................................

**c** What is the value of $P(A \leq T \leq B)$? ...........................................................

**d** What is the value of $P(\mu - 2.6 \leq T \leq \mu + 2.6)$? ...........................................................

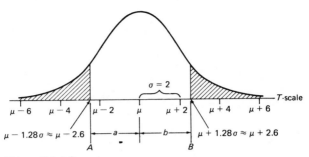

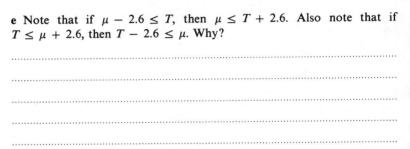

**Figure 14.4.3**

**e** Note that if $\mu - 2.6 \leq T$, then $\mu \leq T + 2.6$. Also note that if $T \leq \mu + 2.6$, then $T - 2.6 \leq \mu$. Why?

..............................................................................................................................

..............................................................................................................................

..............................................................................................................................

..............................................................................................................................

..............................................................................................................................

**f** The statements $\mu \leq T + 2.6$ and $T - 2.6 \leq \mu$ may be combined into a statement regarding the location of $\mu$:

*Statement I: $T - 2.6 \leq \mu \leq T + 2.6$*

This statement was derived algebraically from a similar statement regarding the location of $T$, namely,

*Statement II: $\mu - 2.6 \leq T \leq \mu + 2.6$*

It follows that for given values of $T$ the statement regarding the location of $\mu$ will be true whenever the statement regarding the location of $T$ is true. That is, if II is true, I is true, and if II is not true, I is not true. What is the probability of I being true? That is, what is the value of $P(T - 2.6 \leq \mu \leq T + 2.6)$? Why?

..............................................................................................................................

..............................................................................................................................

..............................................................................................................................

**g** An experimental check on the answer to **f** may be made with a distribution having a known value of $\mu$. Such a distribution is given in Table 11.B of exercise 11.5.14; here, $\mu = 7$. Of course, this distribution is only approximately a normal distribution, because a true normal distribution is continuous whereas the score values of the distribution in the table are all integers (whole numbers). Table 11.D gives three samples, each consisting of 10 score values selected at random from the distribution of Table 11.B. There should also appear in Table 11.D two additional similar samples that you yourself selected. Consider these 50 values as a single random sample from the approximately normal universe of Table 11.B. These 50 values are given in Table 14.A. For the first 25 values, 2.6 has been subtracted from and added to each value. Complete Table 14.A by computing the remaining 25 values ±2.6.

Consider these 50 pairs of values. How many contain between them the value 7 (i.e., $\mu$)?

...............................................................

**h** According to the theory developed in the foregoing parts of this exercise, how many of these pairs would be expected to contain the value 7?

...............................................................

**i** Apart from the fact that the distribution used in this experimental check was only approximately a normal distribution, explain why you would not expect the answers to **g** and **h** to agree exactly.

...............................................................

...............................................................

...............................................................

...............................................................

...............................................................

**j** The pairs of values obtained in answer to **g** are confidence interval estimates of the value of $\mu$ for the given distribution. (Note that to establish these intervals it was not necessary to know that the value of $\mu$ was 7. The only use we made of our knowledge of the fact that $\mu = 7$ was to check experimentally on the number of these intervals that did in fact contain 7.) What is the value of the confidence coefficient associated with these interval estimates?

...............................................................

**k** The value of the first score in the first set of Table 11.D is 9. Hence, the interval estimate for $\mu$ based on this particular score is 6.4–11.6. Does this mean that $P(6.4 \leq \mu \leq 11.6) \approx .8$? Explain.

...............................................................

...............................................................

...............................................................

...............................................................

...............................................................

...............................................................

...............................................................

**Table 14.A** A Set of 50 Random Values from a Normal Distribution with $\mu = 7$ and $\sigma = 2$

| Random Value | Value $\pm 2.6$ | Random Value | Value $\pm 2.6$ |
|:---:|:---:|:---:|:---:|
| 9 | 6.4, 11.6 | 8 | |
| 5 | 2.4, 7.6 | 8 | |
| 10 | 7.4, 12.6 | 6 | |
| 9 | 6.4, 11.6 | 7 | |
| 8 | 5.4, 10.6 | 9 | |
| 8 | 5.4, 10.6 | 3 | |
| 7 | 4.4, 9.6 | 8 | |
| 5 | 2.4, 7.6 | 7 | |
| 6 | 3.4, 8.6 | 8 | |
| 5 | 2.4, 7.6 | 5 | |
| 8 | 5.4, 10.6 | 11 | |
| 10 | 7.4, 12.6 | 9 | |
| 8 | 5.4, 10.6 | 5 | |
| 5 | 2.4, 7.6 | 8 | |
| 12 | 9.4, 14.6 | 8 | |
| 5 | 2.4, 7.6 | 9 | |
| 9 | 6.4, 11.6 | 7 | |
| 7 | 4.4, 9.6 | 5 | |
| 4 | 1.4, 6.6 | 8 | |
| 6 | 3.4, 8.6 | 6 | |
| 7 | 4.4, 9.6 | 9 | |
| 10 | 7.4, 12.6 | 5 | |
| 7 | 4.4, 9.6 | 5 | |
| 7 | 4.4, 9.6 | 4 | |
| 3 | 0.4, 5.6 | 7 | |

**l** Let $\underline{\mu}_1$ and $\bar{\mu}_1$ represent the lower and upper limits of an 80 percent confidence interval for the mean of the distribution of Figure 14.4.3. Let $T_1$ represent a particular value of $T$ randomly selected from this distribution. Write formulas for $\underline{\mu}_1$ and $\bar{\mu}_1$ in terms of $T_1$, $a$, and $b$ (see Figure 14.4.3).

$\underline{\mu}_1 =$ .................................................        $\bar{\mu}_1 =$ .................................................

**m** Write formulas for these values of $a$ and $b$ in terms of $\sigma$.

$a =$ .................................................        $b =$ .................................................

**n** Suppose it is desired to establish for the distribution of Figure 14.4.3 an interval estimate of the value of $\mu$ that is open at the top end. That is, it is desired to present a value of which it can be said with a certain degree of confidence that $\mu$ is not less than this value. If .8 is used as the confidence coefficient, write formulas for $a$ and $b$ in terms of $\sigma$.

$a =$ .................................................        $b =$ .................................................

**o** In the situation of **n**, what is the value of:

    **1** $P(T > B)$?      .................................................

    **2** $P(T < A)$?      .................................................

    **3** $P(A \leq T \leq B)$?      .................................................

**p** Explain why the system (universe) of confidence intervals that could be generated by repeated application of the formulas called for in **l** and **m** is not the only system for which the confidence coefficient is .8.

.................................................................................................................

.................................................................................................................

.................................................................................................................

.................................................................................................................

**q** What feature of the system of confidence intervals given by the formulas of **l** and **m** makes it in general preferable to other systems having the same confidence coefficient?

.................................................................................................................

.................................................................................................................

.................................................................................................................

.................................................................................................................

**14.5.4a** The elementary school supervisor referred to in 12.4.1 obtained a mean vocabulary test score of 49 for the 145 pupils who studied under her vocabulary development program for a period of six months. The standard deviation of these pupils' test scores was 15. For these data, what are the limits of the 99 percent confidence interval for the population mean? (*Note*: $\tilde{\sigma}_{\overline{X}} = S/\sqrt{N-1} = 15/\sqrt{144} = 1.25$.)

..............................................

**b** Suppose that the supervisor wished to establish *only* a lower limit for the population mean. What is the value of such a lower limit that results from the given data if a confidence coefficient of .99 is associated with it?

..............................................

**c** Suppose that test score data were available for only 50 instead of 145 pupils, but that the obtained mean and standard deviation are 49 and 15 as before. What are the limits of the 99 percent confidence interval for the population mean? (*Note*: $\tilde{\sigma}_{\overline{X}} = 15/\sqrt{49} \approx 2.14$.)

..............................................

**14.6.5a** Again consider the problem of the elementary school supervisor as reviewed in 14.5.4a. Suppose, however, that the value 49 is the median rather than the mean of the 145 scores. What are the limits of the 99 percent confidence interval for the population median? [*Note*: $\tilde{\sigma}_{Mdn} = 1.25\tilde{\sigma}_{\overline{X}} \approx (1.25)(1.25) \approx 1.56$.]

..............................................

**b** For a given confidence coefficient, what governs the accuracy of an interval estimate? That is, what determines the width of the interval?

..............................................

..............................................

**14.7.6a** Again consider the problem of the elementary school supervisor. In 12.8.6, the supervisor viewed the population involved as dichotomous. Specifically, she viewed it as consisting of pupils who do and do not gain 6 or more points in performance on a vocabulary test during the six-month period her program is in operation. If 87 out of a random sample of 145 pupils do make gains of 6 or more test score points, what are the limits of the confidence interval of the proportion of the population making such gains if the confidence coefficient is *approximately* .99? [*Note*: $\tilde{\sigma}_{p} = \sqrt{(.6)(.4)/144} \approx .0408$.]

..............................................

**b** Assuming the sampling theory to be completely appropriate, what further requirement regarding the determination of the distances added to and subtracted from the statistic in establishing a confidence interval must be met, if the specified confidence coefficient is to be correct?

................................................................................................

................................................................................................

**c** Is this requirement satisfied when the population characteristic to be estimated is a proportion? Why?

................................................................................................

................................................................................................

................................................................................................

................................................................................................

**14.7.7** Use the findings of the psychologist referred to in 12.10.7 to establish the limits of the confidence interval for the population proportion in question if the confidence coefficient is *approximately* .95. [*Note:* $\tilde{\sigma}_p = \sqrt{(.6)(.4)/99} \approx .049.$]

................................................................................................

**14.8.8** Use the data of 13.4.8 (see Table 13.A) to establish the limits of the 99 percent confidence interval for the difference between the means of the performance scores of populations of analyzers and nonanalyzers (i.e., for the true difference $\Delta = \mu_A - \mu_{NA}$). (*Note:* $\tilde{\sigma}_{\overline{X}_A - \overline{X}_{NA}} \approx 1.07.$)

................................................................................................

**14.8.9** Given the data of 13.4.12, determine the limits of the 95 percent confidence interval for the difference between the means of the two populations involved (i.e., for the true difference $\Delta = \mu_B - \mu_A$). (*Note:* $\tilde{\sigma}_{\overline{X}_B - \overline{X}_A} = 5.$)

................................................................................................

**14.8.10** A test of the hypothesis that the means of two populations, $\mu_1$ and $\mu_2$, are equal resulted in a value of $z$, the test statistic used, of $+8.0$. The observed difference between the two sample means was 24.

**a** Is the observed difference statistically significant?

................................................................................................

**b** What is the estimated standard error of $\overline{X}_1 - \overline{X}_2$?

................................................................................................

**c** What are the limits of the 99 percent confidence interval for the true difference $\Delta = \mu_1 - \mu_2$?

................................................................................................

**d** Does the unusual $z$-value of $+8.0$ mean that the observed difference, $\bar{D} = \bar{X}_1 - \bar{X}_2 = 24$, is a good estimate of the true difference, $\Delta = \mu_1 - \mu_2$? Explain.

..................................................................................................................

..................................................................................................................

..................................................................................................................

..................................................................................................................

..................................................................................................................

**14.8.11** Use the data of 13.8.24 (see Table 13.D) to establish the 99 percent confidence interval for the difference between the mean of the hypothetical population of performance scores made by analyzers on test trials 11 and 12 and the mean of the hypothetical population of performance scores made by this same population of analyzers on practice trials 7 and 8 (i.e., for the true difference $\mu_D = \mu_{11-12} - \mu_{7-8}$). [*Note:* $\tilde{\sigma}_{\bar{D}} \approx .43$.]

..................................................................................

**14.8.12** Given the data of Table 14.B for independent random samples from Populations 1 and 2.

**a** What is the estimated standard error of the sampling distribution of $\bar{X}_1 - \bar{X}_2$?

..................................................................................

**b** Suppose that it is desired to test the hypothesis that $\mu_1 - \mu_2 = 0$ against the alternative that $\mu_1 - \mu_2 < 0$. If .05 is used as the level of significance, what is the critical region in terms of the scale of values of $\bar{X}_1 - \bar{X}_2$?

..................................................................................

**c** What are the limits of the two-ended 95 percent confidence interval for $\mu_1 - \mu_2$?

..................................................................................

**d** Explain why a two-ended confidence interval might properly be desired in a situation that appropriately calls for a test of a hypothesis against a single alternative.

..................................................................................................................

..................................................................................................................

..................................................................................................................

..................................................................................................................

..................................................................................................................

..................................................................................................................

..................................................................................................................

## Table 14.B

|        | Sample from 1 | Sample from 2 |
|--------|---------------|---------------|
| $n$    | 75            | 100           |
| $\overline{X}$ | 150   | 160           |
| $S^2$  | 1,110         | 990           |

**e** If in the situation of this exercise a one-ended confidence interval were desired, which end do you think should be established? Why?

..............................................................................................................................

..............................................................................................................................

..............................................................................................................................

..............................................................................................................................

..............................................................................................................................

..............................................................................................................................

..............................................................................................................................

**f** Establish the appropriate end of this one-ended confidence interval using a confidence coefficient of .95.

.................................................................................

**g** What are the limits of the two-ended 99 percent confidence interval for $\mu_1 - \mu_2$?

.................................................................................

**h** Explain the meanings of the plus and minus signs associated with the values of the limits called for in part **g**.

..............................................................................................................................

..............................................................................................................................

..............................................................................................................................

..............................................................................................................................

..............................................................................................................................

..............................................................................................................................

# 15

# Some Small-Sample Theory and Its Application

**15.1.1** The following is an imaginary rule about an imaginary statistic, $W$.

> RULE For random samples of size $N$ from any population, the sampling distribution of the statistic $W$ is normal with mean equal to a population parameter $\theta$, and a standard error of $2\theta/\sqrt{10N}$.

**a** An investigator hypothesizes the value of $\theta$ for a particular population to be 25. If this hypothesis is true, describe the sampling distribution of $W$ for random samples of ten cases ($N = 10$) from this population by indicating its:

Form ...................................................................................................................

Mean ...................................................................................................................

Standard deviation ...........................................................................................

**b** Assuming this hypothesis ($\theta = 25$) is true, are the descriptive facts called for in **a** exactly or only approximately correct?

...................................................................................................................

**c** Suppose that the actual value of $\theta$ could be either more or less than the value of 25 hypothesized for it. If .05 is used as the level of significance, specify the appropriate critical region in terms of the scale of values of $W$ for a sample of size 10.

...................................................................................................................

**d** If the hypothesis $\theta = 25$ is in fact true, what is the probability of occurrence of a Type I error in the case of the test of part **c**?

...................................................................................................................

**e** Is the probability called for in part **d** exactly or only approximately correct?

...................................................................................................................

**f** Is the statistical test of part **c** an exact or an approximate test? Why?

...................................................................................................................

...................................................................................................................

...................................................................................................................

**15.1.2** Let it be required to use a small random sample ($N \leq 10$) to test a hypothesis about the mean of a population *known* to be normally distributed and having a *known* finite variance, $\sigma^2$. The test statistic to be used is

$$z = \frac{\overline{X} - \mu_H}{\sigma_{\overline{X}}}$$

where $\sigma_{\overline{X}} = \sigma/\sqrt{N}$.

**a** If the actual value of $\mu$ can be either greater or less than the value hypothesized for it, specify the critical region in terms of the scale of values of $z$ if .05 is used as the level of significance.

................................................................................................................................

**b** If the hypothesized value of $\mu$ is in fact true, is the probability of a $z$ in this critical region exactly or approximately .05? Explain.

................................................................................................................................

................................................................................................................................

................................................................................................................................

................................................................................................................................

................................................................................................................................

................................................................................................................................

................................................................................................................................

**c** Is this statistical test exact or approximate? Why?

................................................................................................................................

................................................................................................................................

................................................................................................................................

**15.1.3** Let it be required to use a random sample to test a hypothesis about the mean of a population that is *known* to be normally distributed but that has a finite variance of *unknown* magnitude. The test statistic to be used is

$$z = \frac{\overline{X} - \mu_H}{\tilde{\sigma}_{\overline{X}}}$$

where $\tilde{\sigma}_{\overline{X}} = S/\sqrt{N - 1}$. This $z$ is to be interpreted as a normally distributed random variable having a mean of 0 and a standard deviation of 1.

**a** Assuming the hypothesized value of $\mu$ to be true, is this interpretation of the test statistic $z$ exact or approximate? Explain.

.......................................................................................................................................

.......................................................................................................................................

**b** Under what condition(s) would this interpretation of this test statistic be sufficiently accurate for most practical purposes?

.......................................................................................................................................

.......................................................................................................................................

**15.1.4** Let it be required to use a random sample to test a hypothesis about the mean of a large *nonnormal* population that has a finite variance of *known* magnitude, $\sigma^2$. The test statistic to be used is

$$z = \frac{\overline{X} - \mu_H}{\sigma_{\overline{X}}}$$

where $\sigma_{\overline{X}} = \sigma/\sqrt{N}$. This $z$ is to be interpreted as a normally distributed random variable having a mean of 0 and a standard deviation of 1.

**a** Assuming the hypothesized value of $\mu$ to be true, is this interpretation of the test statistic $z$ exact or approximate? Explain.

.......................................................................................................................................

.......................................................................................................................................

.......................................................................................................................................

**b** Under what condition(s) would this interpretation of this test statistic be sufficiently accurate for most practical purposes?

.......................................................................................................................................

.......................................................................................................................................

.......................................................................................................................................

**15.1.5** Consider the typical practical situation that calls for a test of a hypothesis about the mean of some population. Assume $z$ is used as a test statistic.

**a** How is such a situation likely to differ from that of 15.1.3?

.......................................................................................................................................

.......................................................................................................................................

**b** How is such a situation likely to differ from that of 15.1.4?

.......................................................................................................................................

**c** In this typical practical situation, how does the accuracy of the interpretation of the test statistic $z$ as a normally distributed random variable having a mean of 0 and a standard deviation of 1 compare with that of this same interpretation as applied in the situations of 15.1.3 and 15.1.4? Is it more, less, or equally accurate for a sample of a given size? Explain.

.................................................................................................................

.................................................................................................................

.................................................................................................................

.................................................................................................................

.................................................................................................................

**15.3.6a** In general terms, how does the sampling distribution of the statistic $t$ for $df = 3$ differ from that of $z$—that is, from a normal distribution having a mean of 0 and a standard deviation of 1?

.................................................................................................................

.................................................................................................................

.................................................................................................................

**b** In what respects are these two sampling distributions alike?

.................................................................................................................

.................................................................................................................

.................................................................................................................

**15.3.7** Why do you think the $t$-curve for $df = 29$ was not included in Figure 15.1, page 338, of the text?

.................................................................................................................

.................................................................................................................

.................................................................................................................

.................................................................................................................

**15.3.8** In general terms, how does the $t$-curve for $df = 3$ differ from the $t$-curve for $df = 15$?

.................................................................................................................

.................................................................................................................

.................................................................................................................

.................................................................................................................

.................................................................................................................

**15.5.9** Use Table IV, Appendix C, of the text to determine the value of $t_1$ and $t_2$ in the following probability statements.

   **a** $P(t \geq t_1 \mid t\text{-distribution for } df = 7) = .01$

$$t_1 = \dots\dots\dots$$

   **b** $P(t \leq t_1 \mid t\text{-distribution for } df = 10) = .05$

$$t_1 = \dots\dots\dots$$

   **c** $P(t \leq t_1 \text{ or } t \geq t_2 \mid t\text{-distribution for } df = 5) = .01$

$$t_1 = \dots\dots\dots$$

$$t_2 = \dots\dots\dots$$

   **d** $P(t_1 \leq t \leq t_2 \mid t\text{-distribution for } df = 12) = .95$

$$t_1 = \dots\dots\dots$$

$$t_2 = \dots\dots\dots$$

**15.5.10** Use Table IV, Appendix C, of the text to determine each of the following probability values.

   **a** $P(t \leq -2.13 \mid t\text{-distribution for } df = 4)$

$$\dots\dots\dots$$

   **b** $P(t \geq -2.09 \mid t\text{-distribution for } df = 20)$

$$\dots\dots\dots$$

   **c** $P(t \geq +3.25 \mid t\text{-distribution for } df = 9)$

$$\dots\dots\dots$$

   **d** $P(-.92 \leq t \leq +.92 \mid t\text{-distribution for } df = 5)$

$$\dots\dots\dots$$

   **e** $P(t \leq -3.00 \text{ or } t \geq +3.00 \mid t\text{-distribution for } df = 7)$

$$\dots\dots\dots$$

**15.6.11** An investigator used a *random* sample of ten $X$-values from a population of such values to test the hypothesis that the mean of the population is 50. He used the $t$ given by formula (15.3) of the text as a test statistic, and, on the assumption that the hypothesis was true, he interpreted this $t$ as a random variable having a sampling distribution modeled by the $t$-curve for 9 degrees of freedom.

**a** Under what condition(s) is this interpretation exactly correct?

$$\dots\dots\dots$$

$$\dots\dots\dots$$

**b** If .05 was the level of significance used, specify the appropriate critical region in terms of the scale of values of $t$ if the alternative to $\mu = 50$ is:

**1** $\mu < 50$. ............................................................................................

**2** $\mu > 50$. ............................................................................................

**3** $\mu < 50$ or $\mu > 50$. ............................................................................

**c** Suppose that the standard deviation ($S$) of the sample selected is 12. What is the estimated value of the standard error of $\overline{X}$ that is appropriate for use with $t$-distribution sampling theory?

............................................................................

**d** If the value of $\overline{X}$ for this sample is 40, what is the particular value of $t$ for this sample?

............................................................................

**e** What is the outcome of this test when the alternative to $\mu = 50$ is:

**1** $\mu < 50$? ............................................................................................

**2** $\mu > 50$? ............................................................................................

**3** $\mu < 50$ or $\mu > 50$? ..............................................................................

**15.6.12** It is necessary to use a sample of only five scores to test the hypothesis that the mean of a certain population of $X$-values is 25. The alternatives to be considered are $\mu < 25$ or $\mu > 25$, and the level of significance desired is .05. The random sample selected yielded the score values 19, 15, 25, 17, and 19 with $\overline{X} = 19$ and $S = 3.347$.

**a** What is the estimated value of the standard error of $\overline{X}$ that is appropriate for use with $t$-distribution sampling theory?

............................................................................

**b** What is the number of degrees of freedom of this estimate?

............................................................................

**c** What is the appropriate critical region in terms of the scale of values of the test statistic $t$?

............................................................................

**d** What is the value of $t$ for this particular sample?

............................................................................

**e** What is the outcome of the test? If it is rejection, what alternative is indicated?

............................................................................

**f** Under what condition(s) is this statistical test exact?

.............................................................................................

**g** Specify the critical region in terms of the scale of values of $\overline{X}$.

.............................................................................

**15.6.13** Reconsider the situation of 12.4.1. Imagine, however, that the supervisor tries out her special vocabulary-development program on a single small group of 17 pupils. Suppose that after the six-month experimental period the mean and standard deviation of the vocabulary test scores of these 17 pupils are found to be 49 and 15, respectively. These are the same values as were used in 12.4.1. Again, the sample mean exceeds by three points the expected minimum value of 46.

**a** If .01 is again used as the level of significance, specify the appropriate critical region for a test of the hypothesis in question in terms of the scale of values of the test statistic $t$.

.............................................................................

**b** What is the estimated value of the standard error of $\overline{X}$ that is appropriate for use with $t$-distribution sampling theory?

.............................................................................

**c** What is the particular value of $t$ for the given sample data?

.............................................................................

**d** What is the outcome of the test?

.............................................................................

**e** Suppose that the mean of this sample of 17 subjects had been 55 (a mean gain of 15 points over the initial status or a mean gain of 9 points in excess of the expected 6 points). If $S = 15$ as before, what is the value of $t$ for the sample data?

.............................................................................

**f** Given the situation of part **e**, what is the outcome of the test?

.............................................................................

**g** Assuming $S$ remains 15, how large would $\overline{X}$ have to be in order to indicate rejection of the hypothesis? (*Note:* Answering this question simply amounts to establishing the critical region for $\alpha = .01$ in terms of the scale of values of $\overline{X}$ as the test statistic.)

.............................................................................

**h** In 12.4.1, $\overline{X} = 49$ was found to differ sufficiently from the hypothesized value of the population mean to warrant rejection. Explain why in the present exercise not even a difference three times greater is judged, in terms of the sampling theory used, as sufficient to warrant rejection. Why, in other words, is the test of this exercise so much less powerful than that of 12.4.1? Is its weakness in any way due to a weakness of the $t$-theory itself?

...........................................................................................................................

...........................................................................................................................

...........................................................................................................................

...........................................................................................................................

...........................................................................................................................

...........................................................................................................................

...........................................................................................................................

...........................................................................................................................

...........................................................................................................................

...........................................................................................................................

**i** How does the normal-curve sampling theory as applied in the case of 12.4.1 ($N = 145$) compare with the $t$-curve theory applied in this exercise ($N = 17$) insofar as control over a Type I error is concerned, if the population distribution is normal? If the population distribution is not normal?

...........................................................................................................................

...........................................................................................................................

...........................................................................................................................

...........................................................................................................................

...........................................................................................................................

...........................................................................................................................

...........................................................................................................................

...........................................................................................................................

...........................................................................................................................

...........................................................................................................................

...........................................................................................................................

**j** When a hypothesis about the mean of a population of unknown variance is being tested, the test statistics $z$ and $t$ are given by precisely the same formula; that is, for a given collection of sample data, both would have the same value. If, in this exercise ($N = 17$), the value of $t$ (or $z$) were evaluated in terms of normal-curve sampling-error theory, how would the probability of a Type I error compare in magnitude with that which would obtain under the $t$-curve sampling theory?

................................................................................................

**15.7.14** Consider the speed reading experiment described in Section 9.1 of the text. Assume that 15 students, the experimental subjects, were assigned to the speed reading course and 15 students served as control subjects. Assume further that a reading comprehension test was administered to both groups with the following results:

| Experimental | Control |
|---|---|
| $n_E = 15$ | $n_C = 15$ |
| $\overline{X}_E = 48$ | $\overline{X}_C = 46$ |
| $S_E = 5$ | $S_C = 7$ |

**a** If it is desirable to test the hypothesis that $\mu_E - \mu_C = 0$, what is the estimated standard error of the difference $\overline{X}_E - \overline{X}_C$ that is appropriate for use with $t$-distribution sampling theory? (*Note:* Express the answer in terms of the square root sign.)

................................................................................................

**b** What is the number of degrees of freedom of this estimate?

................................................................................................

**c** If the mean of the population represented by the experimental sample could be either greater or less than that of the population represented by the control sample, specify the appropriate critical region for a test of the hypothesis in question in terms of the scale of values of the test statistic $t$, given .05 as the level of significance.

................................................................................................

**d** What is the particular value of $t$ for the given data? (*Note:* $\tilde{\sigma}_{\overline{X}_E - \overline{X}_C} \approx 2.3$.)

................................................................................................

**e** What is the outcome of the test? If it is rejection, what alternative is indicated? (Express this outcome both symbolically and verbally.)

................................................................................................

................................................................................................

................................................................................................

................................................................................................

................................................................................................

**15.7.15** Suppose that in a situation similar to that of 13.4.8 the means and standard deviations reported in Table 13.A were based on samples of 8 analyzers and 12 nonanalyzers.

**a** What is the estimated value of the standard error of the difference $\bar{X}_A - \bar{X}_{NA}$ that is appropriate for use with $t$-distribution sampling theory? (*Note:* Leave answer in terms of square root sign.)

.................................................

**b** What is the number of degrees of freedom of this estimate?

.................................................

**c** If .01 is used as the level of significance, specify the critical region appropriate to a test of the hypothesis of 13.4.8 in terms of the scale of values of the test statistic $t$.

.................................................

**d** What is the value of $t$ for the given sample data? (*Note:* $\tilde{\sigma}_{\bar{X}_A - \bar{X}_{NA}} \approx$ 2.58.)

.................................................

**e** What is the outcome of the test? If it is rejection, what alternative is indicated?

.................................................

**f** Under what condition(s) is this test exact?

.................................................

.................................................

**15.7.16** The developers of a new ninth-grade algebra course wished to compare its effectiveness with that of the traditional course in general use.[1] Forty-three teachers from schools throughout the United States agreed to participate in the experiment. Twenty-one of these were randomly selected to teach the new course while the other 22 continued teaching the traditional course. At the end of the experimental year, students in all 43 classrooms were given a test published by Educational Testing Service and a new test based on the principles incorporated into the new course.

In this experiment the classroom is the sampling unit (see Section 11.3), and the mean score for each classroom is used as the classroom score. The means, variances, and standard deviations of these classroom scores are shown in Table 15.A.

---

[1] The situation described in this exercise is based on information given in chapter 28 of the *Handbook of Multivariate Experimental Psychology*, edited by R. B. Cattell (Rand McNally, Chicago, 1966). The particular set of data reported in Table 15.A was fabricated for purposes of illustration. However, these data do conform to the data given in Cattell.

**Table 15.A**

|  | New Course $(n_N = 21)$ | Traditional Course $(n_T = 22)$ |
|---|---|---|
| Traditional Test | Mean $= 12$<br>$S^2 = 36$<br>$S = 6$ | Mean $= 18$<br>$S^2 = 25$<br>$S = 5$ |
| New Test | Mean $= 18$<br>$S^2 = 16$<br>$S = 4$ | Mean $= 12$<br>$S^2 = 4$<br>$S = 2$ |

*Note:* Parts **a** through **e** refer to the data of the traditional test.

**a** Let $\mu_N$ represent the mean on the traditional test of a population of classes taking the new course and $\mu_T$ represent the mean on the traditional test of a population of classes taking the traditional course. What is the estimated standard error of the difference $\overline{X}_T - \overline{X}_N$ that is appropriate for use with $t$-distribution sampling theory? (*Note:* Leave answer in terms of square root sign.)

..................................................................................

**b** What is the number of degrees of freedom of this estimate?

..................................................................................

**c** If $\alpha = .05$ is used as the level of significance specify the critical region appropriate to a test of the hypothesis $\mu_T - \mu_N = 0$ in terms of the scale of values of the $t$-statistic. (Use a two-tailed critical region.)

..................................................................................

**d** What is the value of $t$ for the given data for the traditional test? (*Note:* $\tilde{\sigma}_{\overline{X}_T - \overline{X}_N} \approx 1.72$.)

..................................................................................

**e** What is the outcome of the statistical test? If it is rejection, what alternative is indicated?

..................................................................................

..................................................................................

*Note:* Parts **f** through **h** refer to the data of the new test.

**f** The standard error of the difference $\overline{X}_T - \overline{X}_N$ that is appropriate for use with $t$-distribution theory is approximately .98. Assume the experimenters wish to test the hypothesis $\mu_T - \mu_N = 0$. What is the value of the $t$-statistic for the observed data?

..................................................................................

**g** If $\alpha = .05$ (two-tailed), what is the outcome of the test? If it is rejection, what alternative is indicated?

........................................................................................................................

........................................................................................................................

**h** On the basis of the data for the new test in Table 15.A, what condition necessary for an exact test of $H_0: \mu_T - \mu_N = 0$ is probably not met?

........................................................................................................................

**i** Given the results in Table 15.A and the outcomes of parts **e** and **g**, what conclusion seems reasonable?

........................................................................................................................

........................................................................................................................

........................................................................................................................

**15.7.17** Consider the situation of 13.8.23. Suppose it is necessary to test the hypothesis in question using only the data given for the first ten subjects in Table 13.D (exercise 13.8.24).

**a** What is the estimated value of the standard error of the difference $\overline{X}_{11-12} - \overline{X}_{7-8}$ that is appropriate for use with $t$-distribution sampling theory? (*Note:* $\overline{X}_{11-12} - \overline{X}_{7-8} = \overline{D} = 1.6$, $S_D = 2.42$.)

........................................................................................................................

**b** What is the number of degrees of freedom of this estimate?

........................................................................................................................

**c** If .01 is used as the level of significance, specify the appropriate critical region in terms of the scale of values of $t$ as a test statistic.

........................................................................................................................

**d** What is the particular value of $t$ for the given data?

........................................................................................................................

**e** What is the outcome of the test? If it is rejection, what alternative is indicated?

........................................................................................................................

**f** Under what condition(s) is this test exact?

........................................................................................................................

........................................................................................................................

**15.9.18** The data from three experiments are shown below. For each situation decide whether $t$-distribution theory, large-sample normal theory, or some other procedure should be used to test $H_0: \mu_E = \mu_C$.

### Experiment 1

| E | C |
|---|---|
| $\overline{X}_E = 17.1$ | $\overline{X}_C = 19.6$ |
| $S_E^2 = 5.3$ | $S_C^2 = 24.9$ |
| $n_E = 28$ | $n_C = 25$ |

### Experiment 2

| E | C |
|---|---|
| $\overline{X}_E = 33.6$ | $\overline{X}_C = 25.8$ |
| $S_E^2 = 6.3$ | $S_C^2 = 8.9$ |
| $n_E = 14$ | $n_C = 14$ |

### Experiment 3

| E | C |
|---|---|
| $\overline{X}_E = 100.3$ | $\overline{X}_C = 90.5$ |
| $S_E^2 = 50.0$ | $S_C^2 = 10.0$ |
| $n_E = 5$ | $n_C = 20$ |

**15.9.19** Consider the situation described in 15.7.16. From Table 15.A, as it applies to the new test, it may be seen that the variance of the classes taking the new course is approximately four times that of the classes taking the traditional course. Assume these sample facts do, in fact, indicate that the populations are not equally variable with respect to the new test scores. In part **g** of 15.7.16, an $\alpha$-level of .05 was selected to test $H_0: \mu_T - \mu_N = 0$.

**a** Is the true $\alpha$-level exactly .05?

**b** Consider the conclusions listed on page 359 of the text. Which of these best supports the use of the $t$-test of $H_0: \mu_T - \mu_N = 0$?

**c** Why is it difficult to apply the conclusion selected in **b** to the present situation?

**15.9.20** A guidance counselor was interested in ascertaining "whether a group of students (E's) could be effectively motivated, through individual and group guidance activities, to achieve significantly higher results on a standardized achievement test than another group of students (C's) who were not offered the same guidance services."[2] Regarding the hypothesis $\mu_E = \mu_C$, the investigator wrote: "The statistical technique used for comparing the two groups was the $t$-test of differences between two means with separate group variance."

**a** There were 135 students in each group. According to the text, what procedure should have been used to test $H_0 : \mu_E = \mu_C$?

..............................................................................................................................

**b** Did the experimenter use the procedure you identified in **a**? Explain.

..............................................................................................................................

..............................................................................................................................

..............................................................................................................................

..............................................................................................................................

..............................................................................................................................

**15.10.21** The mean of a random sample of ten scores is 40 and the standard deviation is 12.

**a** Use $t$-distribution theory to establish the limits of the 95 percent confidence interval for the mean of the population represented by this sample.

..............................................................................................................

**b** Under what condition(s) is the confidence coefficient associated with the universe of intervals to which this interval belongs exactly .95?

..............................................................................................................................

**15.10.22** Consider the problem of the elementary school supervisor as modified in 15.6.13 (i.e. $\overline{X} = 49$ and $S = 15$ for a random sample of 17).

**a** What are the limits of the 99 percent confidence interval for the mean of the population involved?

..............................................................................................................

**b** What would these limits be had the value of $\overline{X}$ been 55?

..............................................................................................................

**c** Suppose that the supervisor wished to establish *only* a lower limit for the population mean. If $\overline{X} = 49$ and if $\gamma = .99$, what is the lower limit of such a confidence interval?

..............................................................................................................

[2] C. P. Omvig, "Effects of Guidance on the Results of Standardized Achievement Testing," *Measurement and Evaluation in Guidance*, 4 (1971): 47–52.

**d** Suppose that $z$-distribution rather than $t$-distribution theory were erroneously used to establish the limits of the interval called for in part **a**. What would be the values of the resulting limits?

..................................................

**e** Consider the universe of intervals established in the manner of the one called for in part **d**. Would the probability that such intervals contain $\mu$ be less than, equal to, or greater than .99? Explain.

..................................................

..................................................

..................................................

..................................................

..................................................

**f** Compare the limits called for in 14.5.4a with those called for in part **a** above. Primarily, what accounts for the greater separation of the latter?

..................................................

**15.10.23** Consider the situation of 15.7.14. Let $\mu_E$ equal the mean of the population represented by the experi.nental sample and $\mu_C$ equal the mean of the population represented by the control sample.

What are the limits of the 95 percent confidence interval for the difference $\Delta = \mu_E - \mu_C$? (*Note:* $\tilde{\sigma}_{\bar{X}_E - \bar{X}_C} \approx 2.3$.)

..................................................

**15.10.24** Assume the means and standard deviations of Table 13.A (exercise 13.4.8) to have been based on samples of 8 analyzers and 12 nonanalyzers (see exercise 15.7.15). If the mean of the population of analyzers is represented by $\mu_A$ and that of the population of nonanalyzers by $\mu_{NA}$, what are the limits of the 99 percent confidence interval for the difference $\Delta = \mu_A - \mu_{NA}$? (*Note:* $\tilde{\sigma}_{\bar{X}_A - \bar{X}_{NA}} \approx 2.58$.)

..................................................

**15.10.25** Consider the situation of exercise 13.8.23 as modified in exercise 15.7.17. Let $\mu_{11-12}$ represent the mean of the population on test trials 11 and 12, and $\mu_{7-8}$ the mean of the population on practice trials 7 and 8. What are the limits of the 99 percent confidence interval for the difference $\mu_D = \mu_{11-12} - \mu_{7-8}$? (*Note:* $\tilde{\sigma}_{\bar{D}} \approx .81$.)

..................................................

**15.11.26** In the accompanying table specify the appropriate critical region using the criteria described on p. 367 of the text. For some problems, you will need to refer to Table 9.5 on text page 169.

| Hypothesis | Alternatives | $n$ | $\alpha$ | $R$ ($p$-scale) |
|---|---|---|---|---|
| $\phi = .40$ | $\phi > .40$ | 10 | .05 | |
| $\phi = .50$ | $\phi < .50; \phi > .50$ | 8 | .10 | |
| $\phi = .25$ | $\phi > .25; \phi < .25$ | 20[a] | .10 | |
| $\phi = .25$ | $\phi < .25$ | 10 | .05 | |
| $\phi = .25$ | $\phi > .25$ | 10 | .10 | |

[a] *See Table 15.6.*

**15.11.27** Assume that the speed reading experiment described in Section 15.11 is modified as follows (a similar procedure for the speed reading experiment was described in 13.8.25).

**1** Select one student at random from all freshmen.
**2** Assume that scores on a particular college entrance examination are available for all freshmen. From those students with the same examination score as the student selected in step 1, select, at random, a second student.
**3** Repeat steps 1 and 2 until ten pairs of students are formed.
**4** By a random process (e.g., tossing a coin) assign one member of each pair to take the speed reading course.
**5** After the course is completed, give the reading comprehension test to all 20 students.
**6** Count the number of times the comprehension score was greater for the member of the pair who took the course than for the member of the pair who did not take the course.

**a** The six-step procedure given above describes a binomial experiment. Therefore, the binomial probability distribution can be used to assign probability values to outcomes of this experiment. What is $n$?

..................................................................

**b** Why is $H_0: \phi = .50$ the most reasonable hypothesis to test? ($\phi$ = the proportion of pairs in the population for which the scores on the criterion test are greater for the member who took the course.)

..........................................................................................................

..........................................................................................................

..........................................................................................................

..........................................................................................................

**c** If $\alpha = .05$ and a two-tailed test is run, what is the critical region on the $p$-scale? (*Note:* The binomial distribution for $n = 10$ and $\phi = .50$ is given in Table 9.5, page 169 of the text.)

..................................................................

**Table 15.B**    Results for Exercise 15.11.27

| Pair | Course | No course | Difference (Sign Only) |
|------|--------|-----------|------------------------|
| 1 | 50 | 48 | + |
| 2 | 37 | 34 | + |
| 3 | 42 | 47 | − |
| 4 | 33 | 32 | + |
| 5 | 47 | 40 | + |
| 6 | 55 | 50 | + |
| 7 | 36 | 38 | − |
| 8 | 52 | 48 | + |
| 9 | 51 | 45 | + |
| 10 | 29 | 26 | + |

**d** One possible set of results for this experiment is shown in Table 15.B. What is the value of the test statistic $p$?

.................................................................

**e** What is the outcome of the test of $H_0$?

.................................................................

**f** What is the extreme area ($EA$) for this experiment? (*Note: EA* is defined in Section 13.7.)

.................................................................

**15.11.28** Consider the experiment described on text pages 304 and 308. The results for one run of this experiment are shown in Table 15.3 (p. 351). For this exercise assume that the experimenter is interested only in the sign of the difference scores and not in the magnitude of this difference.

**a** Let $\phi$ = proportion of pairs in the population for which the scores on the criterion measure are greater for the member who received the PB condition. Why is $\phi = .50$ a reasonable hypothesis to test?

.................................................................................................

.................................................................................................

.................................................................................................

.................................................................................................

**b** The modification of this experiment can be viewed as a binomial experiment. For the data shown in Table 15.3, what is the value of $n$?

.................................................................

**c** In Table 15.3, it can be seen that the difference between scores for pair 8 is zero. If the suggestion given in Remark 2 on p. 368 is followed, what is the new sample size?

.................................................................

**d** If $H_0: \phi = .50$ and if $n = 10$, what is the critical region on the $p$-scale if $\alpha = .10$ and a two-tailed test is conducted?

...............................................................

**e** What is the value of the test statistic, $p$?

...............................................................

**f** What is the outcome of the test of $H_0: \phi = .50$?

...............................................................

**15.11.29** Consider the problem of the principal and the superintendent as described in Section 12.9. In this instance, $A$-type objects are students with IQ scores below 100 and $\bar{A}$-type are students with IQ scores equal to or greater than 100. The hypothesis of interest is $H_0: \phi = .50$ and the alternative is $H_1: \phi > .50$ where $\phi$ = proportion of $A$-type objects in the population.

Assume the school psychologist is instructed to give the WISC to 20 students. If the hypothesis is true, the appropriate binomial distribution for assigning probability values to outcomes of this experiment (i.e., proportion of students with IQ < 100) has $\phi = .50$ and $n = 20$. This distribution is shown as Table 15.C.

**a** If $\alpha = .10$, what is the critical region on the $p$-scale?

...............................................................

**b** Assume 15 of the 20 students obtained scores below 100 on the WISC. What is the value of the test statistic, $p$?

...............................................................

**c** What is the outcome of the test of $H_0$?

...............................................................

**Table 15.C**    Binomial Distribution for $\phi = .50$ and $n = 20$

| Test Statistic ($p$) | Probability | Test Statistic ($p$) | Probability |
|---|---|---|---|
| .00 | .0000 | .55 | .1602 |
| .05 | .0000 | .60 | .1201 |
| .10 | .0002 | .65 | .0739 |
| .15 | .0011 | .70 | .0370 |
| .20 | .0046 | .75 | .0148 |
| .25 | .0148 | .80 | .0046 |
| .30 | .0370 | .85 | .0011 |
| .35 | .0739 | .90 | .0002 |
| .40 | .1201 | .95 | .0000 |
| .45 | .1602 | 1.00 | .0000 |
| .50 | .1762 | | |

**15.11.30** In the situation described in 12.8.6, a group of 145 fourth-grade students was given a vocabulary test at the beginning of the year and then six months later. The proportion of students who gained 6 or more points (6 points was the expected growth) was determined, and the hypothesis $\phi = .50$ (where $\phi$ represents the proportion of students in the population who gain 6 or more points) was tested using normal-curve theory. The use of normal-curve theory was appropriate even though the experiment could be viewed as a binomial experiment since the sample size was large. In this exercise we modify the experiment by assuming that only 20 students participate. This reduction in sample size makes feasible the use of the binomial model.

Assume the results shown as Table 15.D were found for this experiment.

**a** Considering the situation as described in 12.8.6, why is $H_0: \phi = .50$ a reasonable hypothesis?

................................................................................................................................

................................................................................................................................

................................................................................................................................

................................................................................................................................

**Table 15.D**    Results for Exercise 15.11.30

| Student | Beginning of Year | Six Months Later | Type[a] |
|---------|-------------------|------------------|---------|
| 1 | 38 | 45 | + |
| 2 | 39 | 46 | + |
| 3 | 40 | 45 | − |
| 4 | 41 | 47 | + |
| 5 | 42 | 47 | − |
| 6 | 43 | 50 | + |
| 7 | 43 | 49 | + |
| 8 | 44 | 51 | + |
| 9 | 37 | 41 | − |
| 10 | 36 | 44 | + |
| 11 | 35 | 38 | − |
| 12 | 42 | 49 | + |
| 13 | 43 | 50 | + |
| 14 | 41 | 47 | + |
| 15 | 40 | 44 | − |
| 16 | 40 | 47 | + |
| 17 | 38 | 43 | − |
| 18 | 39 | 46 | + |
| 19 | 37 | 45 | + |
| 20 | 39 | 47 | + |

[a] *Students who gained 6 or more points are classified as A-types and are noted with a +. Students gaining fewer than 6 points are $\bar{A}$-types and are noted with a −.*

**b** The binomial probability distribution for $n = 20$ and $\phi = .50$ is given in Table 15.C. If $\alpha = .10$ and a one-tailed test is conducted, what is the critical region on the $p$-scale?

......................................................................

**c** What is the value of the test statistic, $p$?

......................................................................

**d** What is the outcome of the test of $H_0$?

......................................................................

# 16

# Introduction to Bayesian Inference

**16.2.1** In exercise 13.7.22, two methods of summarizing the results of a particular experiment were given. In the first method, the test statistic and $EA$-value were given as shown below ($p$ was the extreme area).

*Method 1:* $z = 2.57, p < .015$

In the second method, the test statistic was given and the result of the hypothesis test was indicated:

*Method 2:* $z = 2.57^a$

[a] Significant at the .05 level.

Which of these methods would be labeled a Fisherian procedure and which a Neyman-Pearson procedure?

...................................................................................................................................

...................................................................................................................................

**16.2.2** In Section 14.5 of the text, a 99 percent confidence interval for the mean IQ of the population of school children in the principal and superintendent problem was found to be the interval 87.55–100.45. [i.e., $C(87.55 \leq \mu \leq 100.45) = 99\%$]. Assume the superintendent wishes to make a two-tailed test ($\alpha = .01$) of the hypothesis that $\mu$ is equal to some constant.

**a** Assume $H_0: \mu = 100$. Given the above information, is $H_0$ retained or rejected?

...................................................................

**b** Let $c$ equal the value being tested, so that the hypothesis is $H_0: \mu = c$. What values of $c$ would lead to the retention of $H_0$?

...................................................................

What values of $c$ would lead to the rejection of $H_0$?

...................................................................

**16.3.3** Which of the following statements would be permissible in a Bayesian data analysis but not in a Neyman-Pearson data analysis?

1 The probability that the true difference between $\mu_1$ and $\mu_2$ is greater than 0 is .80.

2 The probability that $\xi$ is between 95 and 100 is .75.

3 The probability that $\phi_1 - \phi_2$ is greater than .2 is .15.

4 The probability of rejecting the $H_0: \mu_1 - \mu_2 = 0$ when $\mu_1 - \mu_2 = 5$ is .90.

**16.3.4** Consider the probability distribution shown below:

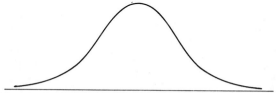

Now consider the following set of statistics and parameters:

$$\{\overline{X}, p, Mdn, \overline{X}_1 - \overline{X}_2, \overline{D}, \mu, \phi, \xi, \mu_1 - \mu_2, \mu_D\}$$

**a** In Neyman-Pearson and Fisherian procedures which of these quantities would be permissible labels for the horizontal axis of the above probability distribution?

**b** In Bayesian inference, which of these quantities would be permissible labels for the horizontal axis?

**c** Fill in the blanks in the following.

In Neyman-Pearson and Fisherian procedures, parameters are considered as fixed constants and statistics are considered as random variables.

However, in Bayesian procedures both ..................................... and

..................................... are considered as .....................................

**16.4.5** Consider Table 9.A on page 79. Situation 1 in Table 9.A involved the spinning of a pointer located at the center of a circle divided into four equal sectors of different colors (red, blue, green, and yellow).

**a** If the spinner is not biased, what are the propensities for the following outcomes?

    **1** Pointer stops in green sector.................................................................

    **2** Pointer stops in red sector....................................................................

    **3** Pointer stops in red or green sector.................................................

    **4** Pointer does not stop in green sector...............................................

    **5** Pointer stops in yellow, blue, or green sector.................................

**b** What odds should you receive if you want to bet on each of the outcomes listed in **a**?

    **1** .........................................................................................................

    **2** .........................................................................................................

    **3** .........................................................................................................

    **4** .........................................................................................................

    **5** .........................................................................................................

**c** Why are the values you gave in part **a** considered propensities?

........................................................................................................................

........................................................................................................................

........................................................................................................................

**16.4.6** Consider exercise 9.5.13.

**a** Why should the values you supplied in Table 9.B be considered propensities?

........................................................................................................................

........................................................................................................................

........................................................................................................................

**b** Using the values given in Table 9.B, what odds should you receive for betting on each of the following outcomes?

    **1** A 12                            ...................................................

    **2** A 7                              ...................................................

    **3** An 11                             ...................................................

    **4** A 2, 3, or 4                  ...................................................

    **5** A 7, 8, or 9                 ...................................................

**16.4.7** Consider the following statements.

  1 The probability of rain tomorrow is .80.
  2 The probability that our team will win the football game on Saturday is .80.

**a** Can the probability values be considered propensities? Briefly explain your answer.

.......................................................................................................................

.......................................................................................................................

.......................................................................................................................

**b** If the student making statement 2 were to bet on this game, what odds should he or she be willing to accept?

.......................................................................................................................

**16.5.8** Consider the experiment described in 9.5.13. Assume $A$ is the event "5 (i.e., 5 dots) on the first cast of the die" and $B$ is the event "5 on the second cast of the die." Answer parts **a**, **b**, and **c** without using any formulas. Use the equally likely model and find the indicated probabilities by counting.

**a** What is $P(A)$? (What is the probability that a 5 will occur on the first cast?)

.................................................................

**b** What is $P(A \text{ and } B)$? (What is the probability that both $A$ and $B$ will occur?)

.................................................................

**c** Assume $A$ has occurred. What is the probability that $B$ will occur?

.................................................................

**d** Using equation (16.1), find $P(B \mid A)$.

.................................................................

**16.5.9** At a particular university, the following facts are true for the current freshman class.

  1 60% are from urban areas.
  2 40% are from rural areas.
  3 20% have a grade-point average (gpa) of a B or better.
  4 10% have a gpa of a B or better and are from rural areas.

Let

$$B = \text{the event "gpa of B or better"}$$
$$R = \text{the event "from rural areas"}$$
$$R \text{ and } B = \text{the event "from rural areas and gpa of B or better"}$$

**a** For a student selected at random from this freshman class,

What is $P(B)$? .................................................................................

What is $P(R)$? .................................................................................

What is $P(R \text{ and } B)$? .................................................................

**b** In talking to a freshman you find out that she is from a rural area. What is the probability that she has a gpa of B or better?

.................................................................

**c** If $R$ and $B$ were independent events, how would $P(B \mid R)$ compare with $P(B)$?

.................................................................

**d** In parts **a** and **b** you found the probabilities $P(B) = .20$ and $P(B \mid R) = .25$. Briefly describe the meaning of the difference in probability values.

.................................................................................................

.................................................................................................

.................................................................................................

**16.5.10** In a certain statistics course two types of examinations are used: minimum competence examinations, and general achievement examinations. The minimum competence exams attempt to measure knowledge of basic skills and concepts; the general achievement exams attempt to measure the application of these skills and concepts to novel situations. If a student makes a score of 80 percent or higher on a minimum competence exam, he or she receives a grade of "pass"; otherwise, a grade of "fail" is assigned. The scores on the general achievement exam are used to assign letter grades (A, B, and so on) to students. On the basis of data gathered from previous classes, the following information is available.

1 $P(C) = .85$, where $C$ is the event "pass minimum competence exam"
2 $P(E) = .30$, where $E$ is the event "receive A or B on general achievement exam"
3 $P(C \text{ and } E) = .29$, where $C$ and $E$ is the event "pass minimum competence exam and receive A or B on the general achievement test"

**a** Verbally describe the event $E \mid C$.

.................................................................................................

**b** Assume the instructor wishes to provide students with information related to their chances of receiving a grade of A or B on the general achievement exam. If the data supplied above are used, what is $P(E)$?

.................................................................

What is $P(E \mid C)$? .................................................................

**c** Briefly describe the implications of the difference between the two probability values you listed in **b**.

...................................................................................................

...................................................................................................

...................................................................................................

**16.6.11** Consider the situation presented in 16.5.9. For events $B$ and $R$ as defined in that exercise, the following probabilities were given: $P(B) = .20$, and $P(R) = .40$.

**a** Verbally describe the event $R \mid B$.

...................................................................................................

...................................................................................................

**b** In talking to a person you find out that he is from a rural area. If $P(R \mid B) = .50$, what is the probability that this person has a gpa of B or better? [That is, $P(B \mid R) = ?$] Use equation (16.4).

...................................................................................................

**16.6.12** Consider the situation described in 16.5.10. Let

$C$ = event "pass minimum competence exam"
$E_1$ = event "receive a grade of A on general achievement exam"
$E_2$ = event "receive a grade of B on general achievement exam"
$E_3$ = event "receive a grade of C or lower on general achievement exam"

Assume that student performance over the last several years suggests that the following probability values hold.

$$P(E_1) = .10 \qquad P(C \mid E_1) = .99$$
$$P(E_2) = .20 \qquad P(C \mid E_2) = .90$$
$$P(E_3) = .70 \qquad P(C \mid E_3) = .70$$

**a** Are the events $E_1$, $E_2$, and $E_3$ mutually exclusive and exhaustive?

...................................................................

**b** Verbally describe the event $E_3 \mid C$.

...................................................................................................

...................................................................................................

**c** Using equation (16.5) and the notation above, write the formula for $P(E_3 \mid C)$. Keep $P(C)$ in the equation.

...................................................................................................

...................................................................................................

**d** Using the notation above, write the equation for finding $P(C)$.

................................................................................................................................

................................................................................................................................

What is the value of $P(C)$?................

**e** Using equation (16.5), compute $P(E_3 \mid C)$.

................................................................................................................................

**f** Using equation (16.5), compute $P(E_2 \mid C)$.

................................................................................................................................

**16.8.13** Why is the beta family of probability distributions a good choice for the representation of beliefs about $\phi$?

................................................................................................................................

................................................................................................................................

................................................................................................................................

**16.9.14** Consider the problem of the principal and the superintendent, described in some detail in Section 12.1 of the text; also, consider Solution V to this problem as discussed in Section 12.9. Here we shall use this solution, except that we shall have the superintendent instruct the school psychologist to select a sample of 50 children for testing rather than 100. In this solution of the problem, $\phi$ was defined as the proportion of the population of school children with IQs below 100.

**a** Since $\phi$ in this example can be any value from .0 to 1.0, the family of beta distributions in Figure 16.1 of the text (p. 392) may be used in a general way to characterize the superintendent's beliefs about $\phi$. If she says that graph G is a good representation of her beliefs, what is implied about her beliefs about $\phi$?

................................................................................................................................

................................................................................................................................

................................................................................................................................

**b** If she says that graph A characterizes her beliefs about $\phi$, what is implied about her beliefs?

................................................................................................................................

................................................................................................................................

................................................................................................................................

**c** Assume the superintendent feels very strongly that $\phi$ is near .5 and that if it differs from .5 it is more likely to be less than .5 than to be greater than .5. Which of the graphs in Figure 16.1 could be used to represent this set of beliefs?

..........................................................................................................................

**d** Assume that the superintendent's beliefs about $\phi$ can be represented by $\beta(31, 21)$. What is the approximate shape of this beta distribution (see Figure 16.1)?

..........................................................................................................................

**e** What are the summary statistics for this beta distribution?

Mean ....................................................................................................................

Mode ....................................................................................................................

Median .................................................................................................................

Variance ..............................................................................................................

Standard deviation ................................................................................................

**f** What is $P(\phi > .50)$ in this distribution? (*Note:* Use nearest tabled value. In this problem the tabled value nearest .50 is .5084.)

..............................................................................

**g** What is the 50% central credibility interval for $\beta(31, 21)$?

..............................................................................

What is the 50% *HDR* for $\beta(31, 21)$? ..............................................................

**h** If $\beta(31, 21)$ represents the superintendent's beliefs about $\phi$, what odds should she receive if she wants to bet that $\phi$ is between .55 and .60? (Use nearest tabled values.)

..............................................................................

What odds should she receive if she wants to bet that $\phi$ is between .578 and .622? (See Table 16.3.)

..............................................................................

**16.10.15** Again consider the problem of the principal and the superintendent. Assume the superintendent feels that the mean of her prior distribution of $\phi$ is .50 (i.e., $\mu = .50$). Furthermore, assume that she feels her prior information is worth just as much as the new information the school psychologist will gather. (As noted in 16.9.14, the school psychologist was directed to give the WISC to 50 students.)

**a** What beta distribution would describe the superintendent's prior beliefs?

$a =$ ................                $b =$ ..............

**b** In part **a** you should have found that $\beta(25, 25)$ would be an adequate representation of the superintendent's prior beliefs about $\phi$ given a mean value $\mu = .50$ and a sample size equivalence of 50. What are the following values for $\beta(25, 25)$?

    **1** $P(\phi > .50)$ ........................................................................

    **2** $P(.4522 \leq \phi \leq .5478)$ ........................................................

    **3** $P(\phi \leq .44)$ ........................................................................

    **4** The 75% $HDR$ ........................................................................

**c** Consider the following pairs of credibility intervals.

    **1** 50% $HDR$ and 50% central credibility interval
    **2** 75% $HDR$ and 75% central credibility interval
    **3** 90% $HDR$ and 90% central credibility interval

How do these values compare for $\beta(25, 25)$?

........................................................................

What is the shape of $\beta(25, 25)$?

........................................................................

**d** Assume that after examining the $\beta(25, 25)$ distribution the superintendent feels that it is not an adequate representation of her prior beliefs about $\phi$. What must she do?

........................................................................

........................................................................

........................................................................

........................................................................

**16.10.16** You may recall that the superintendent is not the only person interested in making probability statements about $\phi$. The principal is also concerned; in fact, he instigated the investigation. Given the nature of this situation we might suspect that the principal's initial beliefs about $\phi$ will differ somewhat from the superintendent's beliefs. Assume the principal believes that the mean ($\mu$) of his prior distribution of $\phi$ is .55 and that the sample size equivalence of his prior information is equal to the number of observations the school psychologist will gather (i.e., 50).

**a** What beta distribution should be an adequate representation of the principal's prior beliefs about $\phi$?

                    $a = $ ...............                $b = $ ...............

**b** In part **a** you should have found that $\beta(27.5, 22.5)$ would adequately represent the principal's prior beliefs about $\phi$ given a mean value of .55 and a sample size equivalence of 50. Find the following values for $\beta(27.5, 22.5)$. Use Tables 16.2 and 16.3. (*Note:* Use nearest values.)

    **1** $P(\phi > .50)$ ........................................................

    **2** $P(\phi \geq .55)$ ........................................................

    **3** $P(\phi \geq .60)$ ........................................................

    **4** $P(.5028 \leq \phi \leq .5979)$ ........................................

    **5** $P(.504 \leq \phi \leq .599)$ (see Table 16.3) ..................

    **6** $P(\phi \leq .41)$ ........................................................

**c** What is the 75% *HDR* for the principal's prior distribution?

..............................................................................

**d** If the principal and the superintendent have different prior beliefs about $\phi$, and if both incorporate the same observed data into their prior data, will their posterior beliefs about $\phi$ differ?

..............................................................................

**16.11.17** Again we consider the problem of the principal and the superintendent. In 16.10.15, we indicated that a beta distribution with $a = 25$ and $b = 25$ [i.e., $\beta(25, 25)$] was an adequate representation of the superintendent's prior beliefs about $\phi$ given a mean value of .50 and a sample size equivalence of 50. Now, assume that the school psychologist has administered the WISC to 50 students and finds that 30 of these have IQs below 100.

**a** Using the notation of Section 16.11, what is the particular observed value of $r$?

..............................................................................

What is the value of $n$? ..............................................

**b** What probability distribution can be used to assign probability values to the various possible values of $r$?

..............................................................................

**c** Before probability values can be assigned to possible $r$-values, what parameter must be known?

..............................................................................

**d** If $n = 50$ and $r = 30$, write the function for $P(r \mid \phi)$.

..............................................................................

**e** If a $\beta(25, 25)$ is our prior distribution for $\phi$, write the function for $P(\phi)$.

..............................................................................

**f** Given your answer to parts **d** and **e**, write the function for $P(\phi \mid r)$ using the form given by equation (d) on p. 403 of the text. [Keep $P(r)$ in the equation.]

..................................................................................................................

**g** In this example,

$$\binom{n}{r} = \binom{50}{30} \quad \text{and} \quad \beta(a, b) = \beta(25, 25)$$

According to the text, these two constants combine with the constant $P(r)$ to form a new constant. What is the new constant?

..................................................................

**h** Write the equation for $P(\phi \mid r)$ using the form of equation (16.8).

..................................................................................................................

**i** Given the result in part **h**, the superintendent's posterior beliefs about $\phi$ are characterized by what beta distribution?

..................................................................

**j** In part **i** you should have found that the superintendent's posterior beliefs about $\phi$ are represented by $\beta(55, 45)$. In this distribution, what is $P(\phi > .50)$? Use nearest tabled value.

..................................................................

**k** Given the result in part **j** and not considering any other factors (such as the losses associated with incorrect decisions), would the superintendent probably grant the funding for the special equipment and teachers that the principal requested? Why?

..................................................................................................................

..................................................................................................................

..................................................................................................................

..................................................................................................................

**l** In the prior distribution [$\beta(25, 25)$], $P(\phi > .50) = .50$. In the posterior distribution [$\beta(55, 45)$], $P(\phi > .50) \approx .85$. [*Note:* Using the nearest tabled value in $\beta(55, 45)$ you should have found $P(\phi > .50) \approx .833\frac{1}{3}$ for part **j** of this exercise. For the remaining exercises we shall use for this probability a value of .85, since it is more accurate and easier to manipulate.] This increase in probability seems logical, since .60 of the students in the sample (i.e., 30 out of 50) had IQs of less than 100. If the sample data had yielded an $r \leq 25$, would the $P(\phi > .50)$ be greater than or less than .85 in the superintendent's posterior distribution?

..................................................................

**16.11.18** In 16.10.16, we noted that if, instead of the superintendent, the principal were doing the analysis, the prior distribution for $\phi$ would be $\beta(27.5, 22.5)$ rather than $\beta(25, 25)$.

**a** Assume the principal uses the data gathered by the school psychologist ($n = 50$, $r = 30$) along with his prior beliefs to describe his posterior beliefs. What beta distribution will describe his posterior beliefs?

$$a = \quad\text{...............}\qquad\qquad b = \quad\text{...............}$$

**b** In part **a** you should have found that $\beta(57.5, 42.5)$ represents the principal's posterior beliefs about $\phi$. In this distribution, what is $P(\phi > .50)$? Use nearest tabled value.

....................................................................

**c** Given the result in part **b** and not considering any other factors (such as the losses associated with incorrect decisions), would the principal expect to receive the funding for the special equipment and teachers that he requested? Why?

....................................................................
....................................................................
....................................................................

**d** As noted in part 1 of 16.11.17, for the superintendent the posterior probability that $\phi > .50$ was approximately .85. From part **b** of the present exercise you know that for the principal the posterior probability that $\phi > .50$ was approximately .95. Why do these two probability values differ?

....................................................................
....................................................................
....................................................................

**e** The principal's prior beliefs about $\phi$ were represented by $\beta(27.5, 22.5)$. In this distribution $P(\phi > .50) \approx .75$. In the posterior distribution (see part **b**), $P(\phi > .50) \approx .95$. Based on the same data but different prior beliefs, the superintendent's probabilities that $\phi > .50$ change from .50 to about .85. Note that the probability values from the posterior distributions (.85 and .95) are closer than the probability values from the prior distributions (.50 and .75). Briefly explain why this result is reasonable.

....................................................................
....................................................................
....................................................................
....................................................................

**16.12.19** Assume that in the principal and superintendent problem, the superintendent has decided that if $\phi > .50$, she will grant the extra money to the principal. Of course, the superintendent does not know the value of $\phi$, and the best she can do in her Bayesian analysis is to make probability statements about $\phi$. She also realizes that any decision she makes must take into account both the probability that $\phi > .50$ and the losses associated with incorrect decisions. Her two possible decisions are:

1 Grant funds
2 Refuse funds

Assume that there is loss $K > 0$ associated with granting the money when it should not be granted (i.e., when the population of children is "normal" but funds are granted) and there is loss $L > 0$ associated with refusing the money when it should be granted. Also, assume there is no loss if the correct decision is made.

**a** Basing your entries on the conditions described above, complete the loss table below.

|  |  | Act as if Population Is | |
|---|---|---|---|
|  |  | Normal | Below Normal |
| Population of Children Is | Below Normal ($\phi > .50$) |  |  |
|  | Normal ($\phi \le .50$) |  |  |

**b** Since the superintendent's posterior distribution is $\beta(55, 45)$ we know that $P(\phi > .50) \approx .85$ and $P(\phi \le .50) \approx .15$. Find the expected loss, if she acts as if the population were normal.

$EL_N = $ ................................................................................................

**c** Find the expected loss if she acts as if the population is below normal.

$EL_{BN} = $ ................................................................................................

**d** In part **b**, $EL_N$ was defined as $L \cdot P(\phi > .50)$, or $.85L$. In part **c**, $EL_{BN}$ was defined as $K \cdot P(\phi \le .50)$, or $.15K$. Now, $EL_{BN} > EL_N$ if and only if

$$K \cdot P(\phi \le .50) > L \cdot P(\phi > .50)$$

or

$$.15K > .85L$$

Thus, if $.15K$ is greater than $.85L$, the superintendent should act as if the population is normal. Similarly, if $.15K$ is less than $.85L$, she should act as if the population were below normal. Now, $.15K$ will be greater than $.85L$ if and only if

$$\frac{.15}{.85} > \frac{L}{K} \quad \text{or} \quad \frac{1}{5.67} > \frac{L}{K}$$

Likewise, .15$K$ will be less than .85$L$ if and only if

$$\frac{1}{5.67} < \frac{L}{K}$$

Given these facts, complete the following statement:

The superintendent should act as if the population is "normal" if the loss involved in incorrectly identifying the population as "below normal" ($K$)

is ........................ times the loss involved in incorrectly identifying the population as "normal" ($L$).

# 17
# Correlation

**17.2.1** Simply on the basis of what you have casually observed about the following pairs of variables, try to visualize how the dots would be distributed on a scatter diagram for a random sample drawn from the specified population. In each instance, indicate, by placing a plus or a minus sign in the first blank, whether you believe the relationship to be positive or negative, and by writing H, M, or L in the second blank, whether you believe it to be high, medium, or low. Enter a zero in the first blank to indicate a complete absence of relationship.

   **a** Present age of husband and present age of wife, for all married couples now living in the United States

           .............................       .............................

   **b** Total population and total public school enrollment for all cities in the United States between 5,000 and 100,000 in population

           .............................       .............................

   **c** Height of father and height of eldest *adult* son, for all such living pairs of fathers and sons in a given state

           .............................       .............................

   **d** Age and time required to run the 100-yard dash, for all males in a given city who are between the ages of 7 and 20

           .............................       .............................

   **e** Shoe size and spelling ability, for all male college freshmen in a given state

           .............................       .............................

   **f** Ability in industrial arts and ability in first-year French, for ninth-grade pupils in the high schools of a given state

           .............................       .............................

   **g** Intelligence (IQ) and number of trials required to learn a list of paired adjectives, for college sophomores enrolled in an introductory course in psychology

           .............................       .............................

   **h** Sense of pitch (of musical tone) and intelligence (IQ) for high school pupils in a certain state

           .............................       .............................

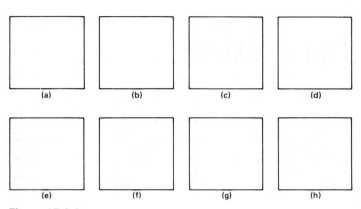

**Figure 17.2.2**

**17.2.2** In the boxes provided for the Figure for 17.2.2, sketch roughly the boundaries of the types of scatter diagrams you think would result from plotting the points for each of the eight situations of 17.2.1.

**17.2.3** Table 17.A contains the 30 pairs of scores made by a sample of 30 individuals on two hypothetical psychological variates $X$ and $Y$.

**a** On the grid prepared for Figure 17.2.3, plot the scatter diagram for the 30 pairs of scores given in Table 17.A.

**b** Would you describe the relationship between $X$ and $Y$ as high, medium, or low?

..............................................................................

**c** Is the relationship positive (direct) or negative (inverse)?

..............................................................................

**Table 17.A**

| Individual | X-Score | Y-Score | Individual | X-Score | Y-Score |
|---|---|---|---|---|---|
| 1 | 7 | 7 | 16 | 4 | 11 |
| 2 | 12 | 4 | 17 | 9 | 7 |
| 3 | 15 | 3 | 18 | 13 | 6 |
| 4 | 4 | 12 | 19 | 8 | 9 |
| 5 | 9 | 5 | 20 | 6 | 9 |
| 6 | 11 | 8 | 21 | 12 | 7 |
| 7 | 12 | 6 | 22 | 10 | 6 |
| 8 | 7 | 8 | 23 | 11 | 7 |
| 9 | 2 | 12 | 24 | 4 | 9 |
| 10 | 14 | 5 | 25 | 11 | 4 |
| 11 | 10 | 8 | 26 | 7 | 10 |
| 12 | 8 | 7 | 27 | 6 | 8 |
| 13 | 13 | 5 | 28 | 5 | 11 |
| 14 | 14 | 3 | 29 | 8 | 6 |
| 15 | 9 | 9 | 30 | 3 | 10 |

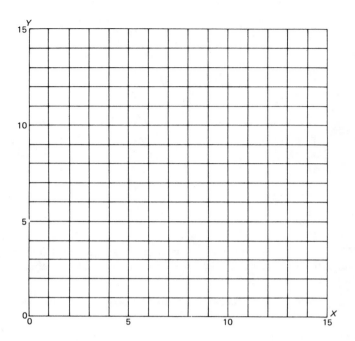

**17.3.4** What difficulty is one likely to encounter in plotting a scatter diagram for data of the type given in Table 17.A when a large number of individuals is involved?

.................................................................................................................................

.................................................................................................................................

.................................................................................................................................

.................................................................................................................................

**17.3.5** Organize the 30 pairs of scores given in Table 17.A into a grouped bivariate frequency table (use the framework provided for the figure for this exercise). Include the marginal distributions.

**17.4.6** Suppose that ten subjects make scores on Tests A, B, and C as shown in Table 17.B. For each subject compute the product of the scores on A and B and find the mean value of these products. Do the same for the scores on A and C. Note that the A and B scores of each pair are identical and that the column of C scores is identical with the column of A scores except for the transposition of two scores. The relationship between the A and B scores is perfect; that between the A and C scores is not.

**a** How does the mean of the products for A and C compare with that for A and B?

.................................................................................................................................

| X<br>Y | 0-2 | 3-5 | 6-8 | 9-11 | 12-14 | 15-17 | $f_y$ |
|---|---|---|---|---|---|---|---|
| 12-13 | | | | | | | |
| 10-11 | | | | | | | |
| 8-9 | | | | | | | |
| 6-7 | | | | | | | |
| 4-5 | | | | | | | |
| 2-3 | | | | | | | |
| $f_x$ | | | | | | | |

Figure 17.3.5

**b** Could you transpose any two scores in the B column without lowering the value of the mean of the products for A and B?

..................................................................

**c** When will such transposition have the least effect on the mean of the products?

.........................................................................................................................

.........................................................................................................................

**Table 17.B**

| Subject | A | B | C |
|---|---|---|---|
| 1 | 10 | 10 | 10 |
| 2 | 9 | 9 | 9 |
| 3 | 8 | 8 | 3 |
| 4 | 7 | 7 | 7 |
| 5 | 6 | 6 | 6 |
| 6 | 5 | 5 | 5 |
| 7 | 4 | 4 | 4 |
| 8 | 3 | 3 | 8 |
| 9 | 2 | 2 | 2 |
| 10 | 1 | 1 | 1 |

**d** Why may the mean of the products of pairs of scores of this kind be considered as an *index* of the degree of relationship between two such sets of scores?

..................................................................................................................

..................................................................................................................

..................................................................................................................

**17.4.7** It is desired to compare the degree of relationship between the heights (in inches) and IQs of a large group of high school senior boys with the relationship between their weights (in pounds) and IQs.

**a** Explain why the mean-product index suggested in 17.4.6d is unsatisfactory for this purpose.

..................................................................................................................

..................................................................................................................

..................................................................................................................

..................................................................................................................

..................................................................................................................

..................................................................................................................

..................................................................................................................

**b** How might the data be modified so as to make this mean-product index more suitable for such a comparison?

..................................................................................................................

..................................................................................................................

..................................................................................................................

..................................................................................................................

..................................................................................................................

..................................................................................................................

**17.4.8** Table 17.C contains fictitious measures of two traits ($X$ and $Y$) for each of a set of 30 subjects. The values of the $X$- and $Y$-columns are the original or raw scores. The $z_X$- and $z_Y$-columns contain most of the $z$-score equivalents of these raw scores. The $z_X z_Y$-column contains products of pairs of $z$-scores. Sums and sums of squares of the raw scores are given below $X$- and $Y$-columns.

**a** What is the value of $\sum x^2$? [See formula (7.6), p. 113 of the text.]

..................................................................................................

## Table 17.C

| Subject | X | Y | $z_X$ | $z_Y$ | $z_X z_Y$ |
|---------|-----|-----|-------|-------|-----------|
| 1 | 57 | 28 | .85 | .3 | .255 |
| 2 | 7 | 22 | | − .3 | |
| 3 | 31 | 23 | − .45 | − .2 | .090 |
| 4 | 19 | 13 | −1.05 | −1.2 | 1.260 |
| 5 | 52 | 31 | .60 | .6 | .360 |
| 6 | 60 | 37 | | | |
| 7 | 55 | 21 | .75 | | |
| 8 | 49 | 26 | .45 | .1 | .045 |
| 9 | 73 | 48 | 1.65 | 2.3 | 3.795 |
| 10 | 40 | 42 | | 1.7 | |
| 11 | 22 | 17 | − .90 | | |
| 12 | 29 | 24 | − .55 | − .1 | .055 |
| 13 | 49 | 32 | .45 | .7 | .315 |
| 14 | 46 | 24 | | | |
| 15 | 72 | 31 | 1.60 | .6 | .960 |
| 16 | 37 | 19 | − .15 | − .6 | .090 |
| 17 | 41 | 27 | .05 | .2 | .010 |
| 18 | 77 | 39 | 1.85 | 1.4 | 2.590 |
| 19 | 5 | 1 | −1.75 | −2.4 | 4.200 |
| 20 | 14 | 19 | −1.30 | − .6 | .780 |
| 21 | 24 | 37 | − .80 | 1.2 | − .960 |
| 22 | 62 | 24 | 1.10 | − .1 | − .110 |
| 23 | 26 | 30 | − .70 | .5 | − .350 |
| 24 | 32 | 19 | − .40 | − .6 | .240 |
| 25 | 64 | 29 | 1.20 | .4 | .480 |
| 26 | 33 | 24 | − .35 | − .1 | .035 |
| 27 | 10 | 10 | −1.50 | −1.5 | 2.250 |
| 28 | 53 | 29 | .65 | .4 | .260 |
| 29 | 16 | 9 | −1.20 | −1.6 | 1.920 |
| 30 | 45 | 15 | .25 | −1.0 | − .250 |
| Sums | 1,200 | 750 | | | |
| Sums of Squares | 60,000 | 21,750 | | | |

209

**b** What is the value of $\sum y^2$?

..................................................................

**c** What is the standard deviation of the $X$-scores?

..................................................................

**d** What is the standard deviation of $Y$-scores?

..................................................................

**e** Enter in Table 17.C the missing values of $z_X$, $z_Y$, and $z_X z_Y$.

**f** What is the sum of the 30 $z_X z_Y$-products of Table 17.C?

..................................................................

**g** What is the value of $r$ for the 30 pairs of $X$- and $Y$-scores of Table 17.C?

..................................................................

**17.5.9** Approximately what do you think the value of $r$ would be for the pairs of scores represented in the scatter diagram called for in 17.2.3a? (Do not compute this $r$; only your best judgment of its approximate magnitude is required here. See Figure 17.8, p. 427, in the text.)

..................................................................

**17.6.10a** For the bivariate frequency distribution of exercise 17.3.5, find (to the nearest tenth) the means of the $Y$-scores for each class of $X$-scores, and also the means of the $X$-scores for each class of $Y$-scores. Enter the results in Table 17.D.

**b** In Figure 17.3.5, plot points showing the approximate position of the $Y$-means of Table 17.D. Connect these points by solid straight lines. Do these points appear to fall roughly on the *same* straight line?

..................................................................

**c** In Figure 17.3.5, plot points showing the approximate position of the $X$-means of Table 17.D. Connect these points by dashed straight lines. Do these points appear to fall roughly on the *same* straight line as the $Y$-means?

..................................................................

**d** What do the findings of **b** and **c** indicate about the nature of the relationship between the pairs of $X$- and $Y$-values involved?

..................................................................

..................................................................

**Table 17.D**

| X-Classes | Y-Means | Y-Classes | X-Means |
|-----------|---------|-----------|---------|
| 15–17 | | 12–13 | |
| 12–14 | | 10–11 | |
| 9–11 | | 8–9 | |
| 6–8 | | 6–7 | |
| 3–5 | | 4–5 | |
| 0–2 | | 2–3 | |

**17.6.11** Given a random sample of 1,000 pairs of X- and Y-values from a population of such pairs. The relationship between X and Y for the population is positive and *perfectly* rectilinear.

**a** Does this mean that the value of r for the population is +1? Explain.

....................................................................................................................

....................................................................................................................

....................................................................................................................

....................................................................................................................

....................................................................................................................

....................................................................................................................

**b** Explain why in a sample this large some of the means of the Y-scores corresponding to a given X-score might deviate considerably from a straight-line pattern.

....................................................................................................................

....................................................................................................................

....................................................................................................................

....................................................................................................................

....................................................................................................................

....................................................................................................................

....................................................................................................................

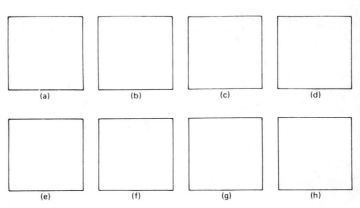

Figure 17.6.12

**17.6.12** In the boxes provided for Figure 17.6.12, sketch roughly the boundaries of the types of scatter diagrams you think would result from plotting points representing pairs of $X$- and $Y$-values related in the following ways.

    **a** Slightly curvilinear and high (i.e., a close relationship)
    **b** Markedly curvilinear and high
    **c** Slightly curvilinear and medium
    **d** Markedly curvilinear and medium
    **e** Linear, positive, and high
    **f** Linear, positive, and low
    **g** Linear, negative, and medium
    **h** A zero relationship

**17.7.13a** Classify (simply by showing the tally marks) the pairs of $X$- and $Y$-values given in Table 17.E in the appropriate cells of the grid provided for the figure for this exercise.

Table 17.E

| Pair | X | Y | Pair | X | Y | Pair | X | Y |
|------|---|---|------|---|---|------|---|---|
| 1 | 1 | 7 | 13 | 6 | 3 | 25 | 1 | 7 |
| 2 | 5 | 3 | 14 | 8 | 5 | 26 | 5 | 2 |
| 3 | 2 | 5 | 15 | 1 | 7 | 27 | 6 | 3 |
| 4 | 9 | 7 | 16 | 7 | 3 | 28 | 3 | 3 |
| 5 | 4 | 3 | 17 | 1 | 8 | 29 | 9 | 8 |
| 6 | 2 | 5 | 18 | 4 | 2 | 30 | 4 | 3 |
| 7 | 6 | 2 | 19 | 2 | 4 | 31 | 7 | 4 |
| 8 | 2 | 4 | 20 | 9 | 7 | 32 | 5 | 2 |
| 9 | 5 | 3 | 21 | 8 | 4 | 33 | 8 | 5 |
| 10 | 2 | 5 | 22 | 7 | 3 | 34 | 6 | 3 |
| 11 | 1 | 8 | 23 | 3 | 4 | 35 | 4 | 3 |
| 12 | 8 | 4 | 24 | 9 | 8 | 36 | 8 | 5 |

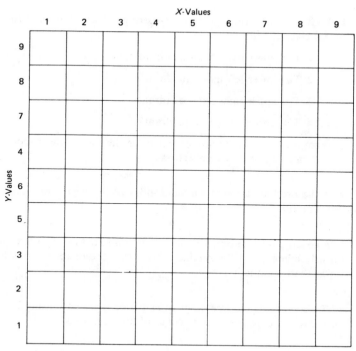

**Figure 17.7.13**

**b** What word indicates the *type* of relationship between these pairs of X- and Y-values?

...............................................................

**c** What word indicates the *degree* of relationship?

...............................................................

**d** The mean value of all the X-scores is 4.9 and that of all the Y-scores is 4.5. Draw vertical and horizontal lines across the grid at positions on the two scales corresponding to these mean values, thus dividing the table into four quadrants. How, *roughly*, does the number of tally marks in the lower right-hand quadrant compare with the number in the lower left-hand quadrant?

...............................................................

**e** How does the number in the upper right-hand quadrant compare, *roughly*, with the number in the upper left-hand quadrant?

...............................................................

**f** What would be the sign of all $z$-score products computed for pairs of scores classified in:

    **1** The lower right-hand quadrant? ....................................................

    **2** The lower left-hand quadrant? ....................................................

    **3** The upper right-hand quadrant? ....................................................

    **4** The upper left-hand quadrant? ....................................................

**g** What, *roughly*, would you expect to be the *sum* of the $z$-score *products* for *all* pairs in the entire collection?

....................................................

**h** Is the product-moment $r$ a valid index of the degree of relationship in this situation?

....................................................

**i** In general, if the product-moment $r$ is computed for data that are curvilinearly related, will the $r$-value suggest that the relationship is higher or lower than it actually is?

....................................................

**17.7.14a** Why would one describe as perfect the relationship between the volumes and edges of a set of cubes of different sizes?

....................................................

....................................................

**b** Why would the product-moment $r$ not be $+1$ for a set of such pairs of volumes and edges?

....................................................

**17.7.15a** Why does a product-moment $r$ of less than $+1$ not necessarily mean that the relationship is not perfect?

....................................................

**b** Explain why a product-moment $r$ of 1 always means a perfect relationship.

....................................................

....................................................

....................................................

....................................................

....................................................

**17.8.16** Consider the 30 pairs of scores given in Table 17.C. From parts **a** and **d** of 17.4.8 we have

$$\sum x^2 = 12,000; \ S_X = 20$$
$$\sum y^2 = 3,000; \ S_Y = 10$$

Also, from Table 17.C,

$$\sum X = 1,200; \ \sum X^2 = 60,000$$
$$\sum Y = 750; \ \sum Y^2 = 21,750$$

It is also true that $\sum XY = 34,081$. Therefore, $\sum xy = 4,081$ [see (17.7), p. 442 of the text.]

Given the above data, compute the product-moment correlation using the following formulas.

**a** $r = \dfrac{\sum xy}{NS_X S_Y} =$ ................................................

**b** $r = \dfrac{\sum xy}{\sqrt{(\sum x^2)(\sum y^2)}} =$ ................................................

**c** $r = \dfrac{Cov(XY)}{S_X S_Y} =$ ................................................

**d** $r = \dfrac{\sum XY - \dfrac{(\sum X)(\sum Y)}{N}}{\sqrt{\left(\sum X^2 - \dfrac{(\sum X)^2}{N}\right)\left(\sum Y^2 - \dfrac{(\sum Y)^2}{N}\right)}} =$ ................................

**17.8.17** Consider the situation of 13.8.23. In 15.7.17 you tested the hypothesis $\mu_D = 0$ using only the first ten subjects in Table 13.D. For these ten subjects $\overline{D} = \overline{X}_{11-12} - \overline{X}_{7-8} = 1.6$, and $S_D^2 \approx 5.84$ or $S_D \approx 2.42$.

**a** The variance of the first ten scores on trials 7 and 8 $(S_{7-8}^2)$ is 18.41. The variance for the first ten scores on trials 11 and 12 $(S_{11-12}^2)$ is 35.81. The covariance $(Cov)$ between the two sets of scores is 24.19. Find the value of the following quantity:

$$S_{7-8}^2 + S_{11-12}^2 - 2\ Cov$$
................................................

How does this value compare with $S_D^2$?

................................................

**b** Given the result in **a**, if an experimenter wished to test $H_0: \mu_{11-12} - \mu_{7-8} = 0$ using $t$-distribution theory, is it necessary for the experimenter to compute a set of difference scores to find $\tilde{\sigma}_{\overline{D}}$? Explain.

................................................
................................................
................................................

**17.8.18** The correlation between 100 pairs of $X$- and $Y$-values is .75.

**a** If $-10$ is added to each of the 100 $X$-values and $-5$ to each of the 100 $Y$-values, what is the correlation between the 100 new pairs of values thus derived?

......................................................................

**b** If each $X$-value is multiplied by 1/3 and each $Y$-value by 1/2, what is the correlation between the 100 new pairs of values?

......................................................................

**c** Explain the implication of your answers to parts **a** and **b** with regard to the computation of a correlation coefficient when computing machinery is not available.

......................................................................................................................

......................................................................................................................

......................................................................................................................

......................................................................................................................

**17.9.19** An investigator reported a correlation of .35 between IQ and height for a large group of 12-year-old girls. Would you describe this value as indicative of a high, medium, or low degree of relationship between these variables? Explain.

......................................................................................................................

......................................................................................................................

......................................................................................................................

**17.9.20** Two investigators measured the heights of the same large group of 10-year-old boys. In checking their results they discovered that their measurements were not always in agreement. They computed the correlation between the two height measures for these boys and obtained an $r$ of .92. Would you describe this value as indicative of a high, medium, or low degree of relationship in this situation? Why?

......................................................................................................................

......................................................................................................................

......................................................................................................................

......................................................................................................................

......................................................................................................................

**17.9.21** A science teacher constructed a set of 25 learning modules for one section of his course. Students were permitted to work through the modules at their own speed. After completing the 25 modules, they took a test covering the material in all the modules. In addition to the test score the instructor recorded the number of class periods each student took to complete the set of modules. The correlation between the test score and the time measure was −.70. Approximately what percentage of the variance of the test scores is accounted for by the variation in the time scores?

....................................................

**17.9.22** Consider Table 17.14 of the text (p. 448). Assume the correlation between college GPA (the criterion) and the Scholastic Aptitude Test (SAT) is .70 for a group of 4,000 freshmen at a large university. Approximately how many of the top 1,000 students on the SAT (predictor) had GPA's in the lowest quarter?

....................................................

Approximately how many of the lowest 1,000 students on the SAT had GPA's in the top quarter?

....................................................

**17.10.23** Two investigators, working independently, computed the coefficient of correlation between scores on a particular intelligence test and on a given test of reading comprehension. The first worked with a large group of 18-year-old college students and the second with an equally large sample of 18-year-olds selected at random from the whole population. Which investigator probably found the higher correlation? Why?

....................................................

....................................................

....................................................

**17.10.24** As part of a large-scale international study of the correlates of reading achievement, a reading comprehension test was given to a carefully selected sample of 14-year-olds in 15 countries.[1] For each country the mean reading comprehension score was obtained. This score was correlated with a number of other factors characteristic of the country. Two of these correlations were

| | |
|---|---|
| Reading vs. Number of books in the home | .85 |
| Reading vs. Hours watching TV or listening to radio | .92 |

**a** What is the sampling unit in this study (see Section 11.3)?

....................................................

[1] The information for this exercise was taken from R. L. Thorndike, "The Problems and Profits of Comparative Empirical Education," reported in *Frontiers of Educational Measurement and Information Systems—1973*, ed. William E. Coffman (Houghton Mifflin, Boston, 1973).

**b** For the variable "Number of books in the home," how were the values used to compute the correlation probably obtained?

.................................................................................................................

.................................................................................................................

.................................................................................................................

**c** Of the 15 countries used in this study, 12 were classified as developed countries and the other 3 as developing countries. When the correlations between the variables given in the introduction to this problem were computed for the 12 developed countries as a whole, the correlations were

<blockquote>
Reading vs. Number of books in the home      .17<br>
Reading vs. Hours watching TV or listening to radio   .28
</blockquote>

Explain why these correlations are markedly lower than those reported above.

.................................................................................................................

.................................................................................................................

.................................................................................................................

.................................................................................................................

.................................................................................................................

**d** In addition to illustrating the effect of the "range of talent" on the magnitude of the correlation coefficient, the results reported in the introduction and in part **c** illustrate the effect of one or two extreme scores on the magnitude of $r$ when the total sample size is small. Consider the scatter plot shown in the figure for 17.10.24d ($N = 15$). [Ignore, for the moment, the one dot with the circle around it.] Approximately what is the correlation between $X$ and $Y$ for the 14 scores? (You may want to refer to the graphs on pp. 427 and 428 of the text.)

.................................................................

**Figure 17.10.24d**

*Remark:* If the *X*- and *Y*-scores represented by the encircled dot are included in the calculation, the correlation between *X* and *Y* becomes approximately .65.

**17.11.25** An investigator found a substantial correlation between the IQ scores of a large group of children and the degree of open-mindedness of their parents' attitudes toward controversial issues. He concluded that bright children influence (cause) their parents to adopt such attitudes. Criticize this conclusion and suggest a more plausible explanation of the observed relationship.

.........................................................................................................................

.........................................................................................................................

.........................................................................................................................

.........................................................................................................................

.........................................................................................................................

.........................................................................................................................

.........................................................................................................................

.........................................................................................................................

**17.11.26** For a group of 9-year-old boys, it is found that there is no significant correlation between height and mental age. (*Note:* A 9-year-old boy whose mental age is measured as 10 years has made a test score that is average for 10-year-old boys.) For another group including boys of all chronological ages from 5 through 15, a substantial correlation is found between the same variables. What accounts for the correlation in the second group? (Do not explain in terms of increased "range of talent.")

.........................................................................................................................

.........................................................................................................................

.........................................................................................................................

.........................................................................................................................

.........................................................................................................................

**17.11.27** Explain why the correlation between height and weight for a group of 12-year-old children will be lower than that for a group including all ages from 5 to 21.

.........................................................................................................................

.........................................................................................................................

.........................................................................................................................

.........................................................................................................................

**17.11.28** For families in general in the United States there is a positive correlation between the amount of money spent annually for food and that spent for clothing. Is one of these the cause and the other the effect in a direct causal connection? How can you account for this correlation?

..................................................................................................................

..................................................................................................................

..................................................................................................................

**17.11.29** For a given group of high school students, it is found that there is a substantial correlation between ability in basketball and swimming ability. Does this fact mean that experience in swimming contributed to ability in basketball or that lots of basketball playing meant direct improvement in swimming ability? What would you consider to be a reasonable explanation of this relationship?

..................................................................................................................

..................................................................................................................

..................................................................................................................

..................................................................................................................

..................................................................................................................

**17.11.30** Researchers for some time have noted that a good predictor of initial success in reading is children's knowledge of the alphabet at the time they start school. The correlation between alphabet knowledge and reading success is usually around .60.

The following statement recently appeared in a magazine article. "To ensure that your children learn to read, all you need to do is teach them the alphabet before they start school." Discuss the appropriateness of this comment.

..................................................................................................................

..................................................................................................................

..................................................................................................................

**17.14.31** A random sample of 28 cases is selected from a normal bivariate population for which the correlation between the variates involved is $+.80$, and the value of $r$ is obtained for this sample. The process is repeated indefinitely.

**a** Describe the form of the sampling distribution of these $r$-values in general terms.

..................................................................................................................

..................................................................................................................

**b** Suppose that each sample $r$ were transformed to a Fisher $z$ (i.e., to $z_r$) and that these transformed values of $r$ were organized into a relative frequency distribution. Sketch this distribution in the space provided for Figure 17.14.31. On the scale of values of $z_r$, indicate (to the nearest tenth) the approximate value of the mean of this distribution, and also the approximate values of the points that are 1, 2, and 3 standard deviations above and below this mean.

**17.14.32** What value of $z_r$ corresponds to each of the following $r$-values?

    **a** $r = 0$ ..................................................................

    **b** $r = +.50$ ..............................................................

    **c** $r = -.50$ ..............................................................

**17.14.33a** What, to the nearest hundredth, is the value of $r$ that corresponds to each of the following $z_r$-values?

    **1** $z_r = +2$ ..............................................................

    **2** $z_r = -2$ ..............................................................

    **3** $z_r = 1.696$ ..........................................................

    **4** $z_r = 1.697$ ..........................................................

**b** Values of $r$ corresponding to given values of $z_r$ are usually recorded to the nearest hundredth. If this is so, what is the point of reporting $z_r$-values in Table V (Appendix C) that correspond to $r$-values such as .205, .215, .225?

..................................................................................................

..................................................................................................

..................................................................................................

..................................................................................................

..................................................................................................

**17.15.34** A random sample of 50 boys was selected from a particular high school. The correlation between the GPA for these students and the scores on an instrument that purportedly measured attitude toward school was .66.

It is desired to test the hypothesis that the population value of the correlation between the variates involved is .80. The actual population value may be either larger or smaller than the hypothesized value, and .05 is considered an appropriate value for the level of significance.

**a** Specify the critical region in terms of the scale of values of:

  **1** $z$ as a test statistic .................................................................

  **2** $z_r$ as a test statistic .................................................................

  **3** $r$ as a test statistic .................................................................

  **4** $EA$ as a test statistic
  (see Section 13.7) .................................................................

**b** For the given sample, what is the particular value of each of the following test statistics?

$z$ .................................................................

$z_r$ .................................................................

$r$ .................................................................

$EA$ .................................................................

**c** What is the outcome of this statistical test? If it is rejection, what is the alternative indicated?

.................................................................

**d** Does the choice of test statistic (see **a** and **b**) have any bearing on the outcome of the test?

.................................................................

**17.16.35** Given the sample of 17.15.34, establish the limits of the 95 percent confidence interval for the population value of the correlation coefficient.

.................................................................

**17.16.36a** With .99 as a confidence coefficient, an investigator wishes to be able to report that the population value of a correlation coefficient is not less than some specified value. In other words, he wishes to establish the value $\rho_1$ for a one-ended (or open-ended) 99 percent confidence interval for $\rho$. If for a sample of 40 cases randomly selected from the bivariate population in question the value of $r$ is .6, what is the value of this lower limit, $\underline{\rho}_1$?

.................................................................

**b** What is the value of $\overline{\rho}_1$?

.................................................................

**c** What might be true of this particular bivariate population that would result in the value of the confidence coefficient being highly inexact?

..................................................................................................................

**17.17.37** A random sample of 100 twelfth-grade public school pupils is selected from the population of such pupils in a certain state. For each of these 100 pupils the following scores or measures are available.

1 High school grade-point average
2 Elementary school grade-point average
3 IQ

The values of $r_{12}$ and $r_{13}$ are determined for the given sample. Assuming that both pairings of variates satisfy the conditions of the normal bivariate model for the population in question, is it appropriate to use these values of $r_{12}$ and $r_{13}$ in testing the hypothesis that $\rho_{12} = \rho_{13}$ by means of the technique described in Section 17.17 of the text? Explain.

..................................................................................................................

..................................................................................................................

..................................................................................................................

..................................................................................................................

..................................................................................................................

**17.17.38** A psychologist was interested in studying the relationship between "motivation" as measured by some valid instrument and reading achievement for inner-city elementary students. Specifically, she was interested in comparing the relationship between these two variables for boys and girls. As part of this study, she selected a sample of 23 boys and 28 girls from the fifth grade of an inner-city school. The correlations were .30 for boys and .60 for girls. She desires to test the hypothesis that $\rho_B - \rho_G = 0$ against the alternatives that $\rho_B - \rho_G < 0$ or $\rho_B - \rho_G > 0$.

**a** Using .01 as the level of significance, specify the critical region in terms of the scale of values of the test statistic $z$.

..................................................................................................................

**b** What is the particular value of $z$ for the given data?

..................................................................................................................

**c** What is the outcome of this statistical test? If it is rejection, what is the alternative indicated?

..................................................................................................................

# 18
# The Prediction Problem

**18.2.1** Table 18.A contains 20 pairs of measurements (scores) of two hypothetical traits ($X$ and $Y$) for each of 20 individuals selected at random from a population of such individuals. The individuals selected have been listed from high to low with respect to $X$.

**a** Suppose that a twenty-first randomly selected individual makes a score of 4 on trait $X$. Using the method suggested in Section 18.2 (pp. 464 and 465) of the text, estimate his $Y$-score.

..................................................................

**b** The estimate called for in part **a** is actually an estimate of a parameter of a certain subpopulation. Identify this subpopulation and parameter.

..................................................................

..................................................................

..................................................................

..................................................................

..................................................................

**c** Again using this method, estimate the value of $Y$ for a twenty-second randomly selected individual whose $X$-score is 5.

..................................................................

## Table 18.A

| Individual | $X$ | $Y$ | Individual | $X$ | $Y$ |
|------------|-----|-----|------------|-----|-----|
| 1 | 9 | 10 | 11 | 5 | 6 |
| 2 | 8 | 11 | 12 | 4 | 8 |
| 3 | 8 | 10 | 13 | 4 | 8 |
| 4 | 8 | 9 | 14 | 4 | 7 |
| 5 | 6 | 9 | 15 | 4 | 6 |
| 6 | 6 | 8 | 16 | 4 | 6 |
| 7 | 6 | 8 | 17 | 2 | 4 |
| 8 | 6 | 8 | 18 | 2 | 3 |
| 9 | 6 | 7 | 19 | 2 | 2 |
| 10 | 5 | 8 | 20 | 1 | 2 |

**d** Considered as estimates of subpopulation parameters, how do the estimates called for in parts **a** and **c** compare in reliability? Is the estimate of **a** more, less, or equally reliable? Explain.

.................................................................................................................................

.................................................................................................................................

.................................................................................................................................

**e** Explain why the method of estimation suggested in Section 18.2 of the text cannot be used with these data to estimate the $Y$-score of an individual whose $X$-score is 3.

.................................................................................................................................

.................................................................................................................................

.................................................................................................................................

.................................................................................................................................

**18.3.2a** Classify the 20 pairs of scores given in Table 18.A according to the cells of the figure for 18.3.2.

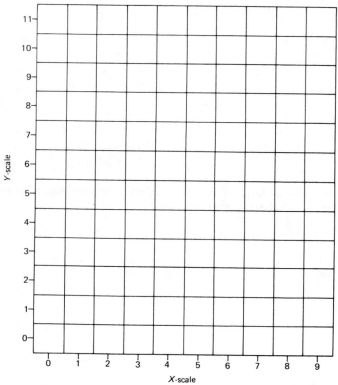

**Figure 18.3.2**

**b** In the figure, locate with a dot the mean of the $Y$-scores that are paired with an $X$-score of 2, and also the mean of the $Y$-scores paired with an $X$-score of 4. (Note that in the figure the unit points are at the centers of the cells.) Connect these dots by a straight line.

**c** Assuming that $X$ and $Y$ are linearly related for the population involved, use the two means called for in **b** to estimate the mean of the subpopulation of individuals who make $X$-scores of 3.

..................................................................................

**d** How might the means of the other subsamples of $Y$-scores (the means of $Y$-scores paired with $X = 1$, with $X = 5$, with $X = 6$, and so on) be used together with those for the subsamples of $Y$-scores paired with $X = 2$ and with $X = 4$ in order to improve the estimate called for in **c**? Explain why this use of these additional means ought to result in an improvement in the required estimate.

..................................................................................

..................................................................................

..................................................................................

..................................................................................

..................................................................................

..................................................................................

..................................................................................

..................................................................................

..................................................................................

..................................................................................

..................................................................................

**e** What would be a still better way of estimating the placement of the line along which these subpopulation $Y$-means fall? Why?

..................................................................................

..................................................................................

..................................................................................

..................................................................................

..................................................................................

..................................................................................

..................................................................................

..................................................................................

**18.4.3a** In the figure for 18.3.2, draw the line $Y = .4X + 5$. This may be done as follows. (1) Locate the $Y$-intercept, i.e., the point $X = 0$, $Y = 5$. (2) The slope of the line is .4, which is the same as 2/5, or a rise of 2 for a run of 5. Hence, locate a second point 5 units to the right of and 2 units above the $Y$-intercept. These two points determine the required line. (*Caution:* The unit points in the figure are at the centers of the cells.)

**b** Assume that the relationship between $X$ and $Y$ is linear for the population represented by the sample of Table 18.A, and that $Y = .4X + 5$ represents an estimate of the position of the line along which the subpopulation $Y$-means lie. What, then, is the estimated value of the mean of the subpopulation of $Y$-scores that are paired with an $X$-score of 8?

..............................................................

**c** If the estimate called for in **b** were used as an estimate of the $Y$-score for Individual 3 of Table 18.A, what would be the magnitude of the error involved in it?

..............................................................

**d** Table 18.B contains the $X$- and $Y$-values for the 20 individuals of Table 18.A. In addition, columns 4 and 5 of this table contain the predicted $Y$-scores ($\hat{Y}_i = .4X_i + 5$) and the error in prediction for the first ten individuals. Complete columns 4 and 5 for the last ten individuals, and find $G = \sum (Y_i - \hat{Y})^2$.

**e** Draw the line $Y = X + 2$ in the figure for 18.3.2.

**f** Columns 6 and 7 of Table 18.B contain the predicted $Y$-scores ($\hat{Y}_i = X_i + 2$) and the error in prediction for the first ten individuals of the experience pool. Complete columns 6 and 7 for the last ten individuals.

**g** What is the equation of the line that, according to the "least squares" criterion, provides the most accurate estimates of the $Y$-scores of the 20 individuals in Table 18.A? (*Note:* $\overline{X} = 5$, $\overline{Y} = 7$, $\sum x^2 = 96$, $\sum xy = 100$.)

..............................................................

**h** Columns 8 and 9 of Table 18.B contain the predicted $Y$-scores (using the least-squares equation, $\hat{Y}_i = 1.04X_i + 1.8$) and the error in prediction for the first ten individuals of the experience pool. Complete columns 8 and 9 for the last ten individuals.

**i** Consider columns 5, 7, and 9 in Table 18.B. Which of the three lines considered in this problem provides the *least* accurate estimates of the $Y$-scores for the 20 individuals in Table 18.A?

..............................................................

**j** What is the value of $G$ (i.e., the index of "goodness of fit") for the line $\hat{Y} = X + 2$?

..............................................................

**Table 18.B**

| Col. 1 | Col. 2 | Col. 3 | Col. 4 | Col. 5 Error |
|:---:|:---:|:---:|:---:|:---:|
| Individual | $X$ | $Y$ | $\hat{Y}_i = .4X_i + 5$ | $(Y_i - \hat{Y}_i)$ |
| 1 | 9 | 10 | 8.6 | 1.4 |
| 2 | 8 | 11 | 8.2 | 2.8 |
| 3 | 8 | 10 | 8.2 | 1.8 |
| 4 | 8 | 9 | 8.2 | .8 |
| 5 | 6 | 9 | 7.4 | 1.6 |
| 6 | 6 | 8 | 7.4 | .6 |
| 7 | 6 | 8 | 7.4 | .6 |
| 8 | 6 | 8 | 7.4 | .6 |
| 9 | 6 | 7 | 7.4 | − .4 |
| 10 | 5 | 8 | 7.0 | 1.0 |
| 11 | 5 | 6 | | |
| 12 | 4 | 8 | | |
| 13 | 4 | 8 | | |
| 14 | 4 | 7 | | |
| 15 | 4 | 6 | | |
| 16 | 4 | 6 | | |
| 17 | 2 | 4 | | |
| 18 | 2 | 3 | | |
| 19 | 2 | 2 | | |
| 20 | 1 | 2 | | |

| Col. 6 $\hat{Y}_i = X_i + 2$ | Col. 7 Error $(Y_i - \hat{Y}_i)$ | Col. 8 $\hat{Y}_i = 1.04X_i + 1.8$ | Col. 9 Error $(Y_i - \hat{Y}_i)$ |
|---|---|---|---|
| 11 | −1.0 | 11.16 | −1.16 |
| 10 | 1.0 | 10.12 | .88 |
| 10 | .0 | 10.12 | − .12 |
| 10 | −1.0 | 10.12 | −1.12 |
| 8 | 1.0 | 8.04 | .96 |
| 8 | .0 | 8.04 | − .04 |
| 8 | .0 | 8.04 | − .04 |
| 8 | .0 | 8.04 | − .04 |
| 8 | −1.0 | 8.04 | −1.04 |
| 7 | 1.0 | 7.00 | 1.00 |

**k** Since $\hat{Y} = 1.04X + 1.8$ is the best-fitting straight line by the least-squares criterion, how does the value of $G$ for this line compare to the value of $G$ for the line $\hat{Y} = X + 2$?

..................

**l** What is the value of $G$ for the line $\hat{Y} = 1.04X + 1.8$?

..................

**18.5.4** At the end of the school year, a reading readiness test was administered to a sample of 750 kindergarten children randomly selected from among all kindergartners in a certain state. At the end of first grade, these same children took a reading achievement test. The results of certain calculations carried out with the 750 readiness scores ($X$) and the 750 achievement scores ($Y$) are summarized in Table 18.C.

**a** Obtain the values of the following. [For the first three values, see formulas (7.6) and (17.7).]

**1** $\sum x^2$ ..................     **2** $\sum y^2$ ..................

**3** $\sum xy$ ..................     **4** $\overline{X}$ ..................

**5** $\overline{Y}$ ..................     **6** $S_X$ ..................

**7** $S_Y$ ..................     **8** $r_{XY}$ ..................

**b** Obtain an equation of the form of (18.2) for predicting $Y$ given $X$.

..................

**c** A particular kindergartener made a score of 40 on the readiness test. What is the predicted value of her reading achievement score?

..................

**d** Does this predicted score suggest that this particular pupil will be good, average, or poor in first-grade reading achievement? Explain.

..................

..................

..................

..................

..................

**e** What must be assumed about the *nature* of the relationship between the readiness and achievement scores if a prediction equation of the form of (18.2) is to be used in making predictions of the type called for in part **c**?

..................

**Table 18.C**

| Reading Readiness Scores (X) | Reading Achievement Scores (Y) |
|---|---|
| $\Sigma X = 45{,}000$ | $\Sigma Y = 15{,}000$ |
| $\Sigma X^2 = 2{,}775{,}000$ | $\Sigma Y^2 = 318{,}750$ |
| $\Sigma XY = 930{,}000$ | |

**f** Suggest a method of checking on the validity of this assumption.

..................................................................................................................................

..................................................................................................................................

..................................................................................................................................

..................................................................................................................................

..................................................................................................................................

**g** The prediction called for in part **c** is actually an estimate of a parameter of a particular population. Define this population and identify this parameter.

..................................................................................................................................

..................................................................................................................................

..................................................................................................................................

..................................................................................................................................

..................................................................................................................................

..................................................................................................................................

**h** Assume that the prediction called for in part **c** represents a good estimate of the parameter referred to in part **g**. Explain why this prediction may, nevertheless, be a poor prediction of the ultimate first-grade reading achievement of this particular pupil.

..................................................................................................................................

..................................................................................................................................

..................................................................................................................................

..................................................................................................................................

..................................................................................................................................

**18.5.5** In the previous exercises (and in the text), we have represented the so-called *independent* or *predictor* variable by $X$ and the *dependent* or predicted variable by $Y$. The situation is usually such that only one of the variates can properly be regarded as the variable to be predicted.

If for some reason it is desired to predict the value of a first variable from information about a second as well as that of the second from information about the first, the theory of Sections 18.1–18.5 still applies. Now, however, it is necessary to solve the problem twice, once with the first variate as the $Y$-variate and once with the second variate as the $Y$-variate. Suppose the variables involved are intelligence and reading ability. Ordinarily, we would be concerned with prediction of reading ability given information about intelligence and we would solve the problem designating reading ability as $Y$ and intelligence as $X$. Occasionally, however, we might encounter some individual for whom no intelligence score was available and for whom some estimate of such a score was badly needed—perhaps for quite some other purpose. If knowledge of this individual's reading score is available, we may use our experience pool for reading ability and intelligence to obtain an estimate of his intelligence. Such use, however, requires that we solve the problem a second time, designating intelligence as the $Y$-variate.

Actually it is a simple matter to restate the theory of Sections 18.1–18.5 with the dependent variable designated by $X$ instead of $Y$. After all, the choice of designation is purely arbitrary. To translate all our previous results into terms of a solution in which the dependent (predicted) variable is assigned the label $X$ and the independent (predictor) variable the label $Y$, it is necessary only to change all the $Y$'s of our previous results to $X$'s and all the $X$'s to $Y$'s. For example, we have seen (in Section 18.4) that the value of $b$ in (18.2) is given by

$$b_Y = \frac{\sum x_i y_i}{\sum x_i^2}$$

If we wish to translate this formula into a form that is appropriate for use with $X$ instead of $Y$ as the dependent variable, we simply write

$$b_X = \frac{\sum y_i x_i}{\sum y_i^2} \tag{a}$$

Similarly, the $c$ of (18.2) for predicting $Y$ is given by (18.5) as

$$c_Y = \overline{Y} - b_Y \overline{X}$$

To translate this formula into a form appropriate for use with $X$ as the dependent variable, we write

$$c_X = \overline{X} - b_X \overline{Y} \tag{b}$$

Note that the $b$-value in (b) is that given by (a) and not that given by (18.4). Now using (a) and (b) we obtain the following equation for predicting $X$, given $Y$.

$$\hat{X}_i = b_X Y_i + c_X \tag{c}$$

It is important that the student appreciate the fact that the best-fitting line for predicting $X$ is an entirely different line from the one for predicting $Y$. That is, the $X$-predictor equation cannot be derived from the $Y$-predictor equation simply by solving the latter for $X$ in terms of $Y$. The equation resulting from such a solution is still the equation—though in a different form—for the $Y$-predictor line. That is, it is still the locus of $Y$-means made by subgroups of individuals making the same $X$-score. To predict $X$, we need the locus of the $X$-means made by subgroups of individuals making the same $Y$-score. These subgroup $X$-means are not located along the same line as the subgroup $Y$-means.[1] In other words, a different prediction line is used to predict $X$, given $Y$, than is used to predict $Y$, given $X$. This different line is the one given by formulas (a), (b), and (c).

**a** Assume the following data are available for 200 fourth-grade students:

| Intelligence<br>Scores ($X$) | Reading Achievement<br>Scores ($Y$) |
|:---:|:---:|
| $\sum x^2 = 45{,}000$ | $\sum y^2 = 20{,}000$ |
| $\overline{X} = 105$ | $\overline{Y} = 60$ |

$$\sum xy = 15{,}000$$

Obtain an equation of the form of (18.2a) for predicting $Y$, given $X$ (i.e., $\hat{Y}_i = bX_i + c$).

.................................................................................................................

**b** Solve the equation obtained in answer to part **a** for $X$ in terms of $\hat{Y}$.

.................................................................................................................

**c** Obtain an equation of the form of equation (c) above for predicting $X$, given $Y$.

.................................................................................................................

**d** Are the equations called for in parts **b** and **c** the same?

.................................................................................................................

**e** Would the line representing the equation called for in part **a** (i.e., the equation for predicting $Y$, given $X$) be the same as the line representing the equation called for in part **c**?

.................................................................................................................

[1] Unless, of course, all pairs of $X$- and $Y$-values are on a straight line.

**f** The sample prediction line for predicting $Y$, given $X$, is the estimated locus of means of subpopulations of individuals making the same $X$-score. Of what is the sample prediction line for predicting $X$, given $Y$, the estimated locus?

..................................................................................................................

..................................................................................................................

**18.6.6** You know the $z$-score of an individual for one of two related variables and the coefficient of correlation between these variables for a sample from the population to which the individual belongs. How can you most simply estimate his $z$-score for the other variable?

..................................................................................................................

..................................................................................................................

**18.6.7** The following exercises refer to the data given in 17.4.8.

**a** A number of subjects, all of whom made a score of 60 on the $X$-test, were selected from the population from which the 30 subjects of Table 17.C may be presumed to have been randomly chosen. On the basis of the information available for the 30 subjects of Table 17.C (that is, using the value of $r$ called for in 17.4.8g), what do you estimate to be the value of the mean $z$-score on the $Y$-test for the selected group of subjects whose $X$-scores were 60?

..................................................................................

**b** Subject 6 (see Table 17.C) made a score of 60 on the $X$-test. If you did not know her score on the $Y$-test, what would you estimate its $z$-value to be?

..................................................................................

**c** What is the error in your estimate for **b**? That is, what is the difference between the *estimated* value of the $z$-score on the $Y$-test for Subject 6 and the *actual* value of this subject's $z$-score on this test?

..................................................................................

**d** Subject 27 made a raw score of 10 on the $X$-test. Use formula (18.9) to estimate his raw score on the $Y$-test.

..................................................................................

**e** What is the error in your estimate for **d**? That is, what is the difference between the estimated and actual $Y$-scores for Subject 27?

..................................................................................

**18.6.8** Two forms, A and B, of a test are given to a sample of students. The mean scores for Forms A and B are 98 and 112, respectively. The respective standard deviations are 10 and 12. The $r$ between the scores on the two forms is .80.

**a** A certain student is known to have made a score of 98 on Form A. Estimate her score, $B$, on Form B.

**b** Another student is known to have made a score of 75 on Form A. Estimate his score, $B$, on Form B.

**c** Write equations for estimating the $B$-scores from the $A$-scores. Your equations should be of the form of the following equations in the text.

**1** (18.2)

**2** (18.9)

**3** (18.10)

**4** (18.11)

**18.6.9** Consider again the situation of 18.6.8. Suppose that an equation of the form of (18.2) or (18.9) were used to obtain an estimate of the $B$-score of each of the students in the given sample. (*Note:* This situation is hypothetical. Since the actual $B$-score of each student in the sample is known, there is no practical reason for obtaining such estimates.)

**a** What is the mean of these estimated $B$-values?

**b** What is the standard deviation of these estimated $B$-values?

**18.6.10** An algebra test and a French test are administered to the same very large group of ninth-grade pupils. One hundred pupils of this large group made $z$-scores of $+.80$ on the algebra test. The mean of the $z$-scores of these 100 pupils on the French test was $+.60$. On the basis of this information, estimate the value of the coefficient of correlation between the algebra and French test scores for the entire group.

**18.7.11** The facts shown in Table 18.D have been determined for a sample of 100 subjects for each of whom an $X$- and a $Y$-score and also a predicted $Y$-score ($\hat{Y}$) are available.

**a** What is the correlation between $X$ and $Y$?

**Table 18.D**

|                    | X  | Y  | $\hat{Y}$ |
|--------------------|----|----|-----------|
| Mean               | 60 | 40 | 40        |
| Standard deviation | 10 | 5  | 3         |

**b** What is the correlation between $Y$ and $\hat{Y}$ ?

..........................................................

**c** In consideration of your answer to part **b**, justify the use of the coefficient of correlation between $X$ and $Y$ as an index of the accuracy with which $Y$-scores may be predicted from $X$-scores.

..........................................................

..........................................................

..........................................................

..........................................................

**18.7.12a** In a certain college the mean grade-point average of students upon completion of the first year is known to be 2.0. The standard deviation of the grade-point averages of all students who complete the first year is known to be .6. Suppose a counselor at this college knows these facts but knows nothing about a given individual except that he has completed his first year. What is the best guess (estimate) that the counselor can make about this student's first-year grade-point average?

..........................................................

**b** Suppose that this counselor is called upon to make many such estimates. What would be the standard deviation of these estimates?

..........................................................

**c** Now, suppose that the counselor knows further the value of the mean score on a certain entrance test for students who complete a year at this college, and also the standard deviation of these entrance scores. Suppose, also, that he knows the correlation between the entrance scores of such students and their first-year grade-point averages so that it is possible for him to set up an equation of the type of (18.9). Now if he is told the entrance scores of any students who complete a year at the college, his estimates of their first-year grade-point averages can be improved by taking these scores into account. What would be the standard deviation of his estimates if they were perfect (i.e., if the estimated and actual grade-point averages were the same for each individual)?

..........................................................

**d** How does the standard deviation of estimated grade-point averages change in value as the estimating procedure is improved in accuracy?

........................................................................................................................

........................................................................................................................

**e** Explain the basis for using the ratio of the standard deviation of estimated values to the standard deviation of actual values as an index of the accuracy of estimation.

........................................................................................................................

........................................................................................................................

........................................................................................................................

........................................................................................................................

**f** What would be the value of the ratio referred to in part **e** if the correlation between entrance scores and grade-point average was

.4? ...................................................

.6? ...................................................

**18.8.13a** Suppose that in a given situation the obtained prediction equation provides very good estimates of the $Y$-means of subpopulations of individuals making the same $X$-score. That is, suppose that the prediction line is so placed that the subpopulation $Y$-means come very close to falling on it. Explain why, even in this situation, an estimate of a particular individual's $Y$-score, as obtained by application of this equation, may involve a rather gross error and differ quite markedly from his actual $Y$-score.

........................................................................................................................

........................................................................................................................

........................................................................................................................

........................................................................................................................

........................................................................................................................

........................................................................................................................

........................................................................................................................

**b** How does the variability of the $Y$-scores of the subpopulation to which an individual belongs affect the likelihood that an estimate of that individual's $Y$-score will be accurate? Explain.

........................................................................................................................

........................................................................................................................

........................................................................................................................

........................................................................................................................

........................................................................................................................

**c** What name is given to the standard deviation of the $Y$-scores of a subpopulation consisting of individuals who make the same $X$-scores?

..............................................................................................................................

**d** Explain why it is generally not feasible to estimate the value of the standard deviation referred to in part **c** by using the known $Y$-scores of those members of such a subpopulation that are in the sample at hand.

..............................................................................................................................

..............................................................................................................................

..............................................................................................................................

..............................................................................................................................

..............................................................................................................................

..............................................................................................................................

**e** If a certain condition is satisfied, it is possible to use all the $Y$-scores in the entire sample to estimate the variance of the $Y$-scores of a particular subpopulation of individuals who make the same $X$-score, by finding a sort of an average of the estimates of the variances of all such subpopulations as are represented in the entire sample. Describe this condition.

..............................................................................................................................

..............................................................................................................................

**f** What is the statistical name of this condition?

..............................................................................................................................

**g** Assuming this condition to be satisfied, use the data of Table 18.A and formula (18.17) to estimate the standard deviation of the $Y$-scores of the subpopulations of individuals who make the following $X$-scores. [*Note:* You computed the numerator of (18.17) in part **l** of 18.4.3. Leave your answer in terms of the square root sign.]

$$X = 6 \quad ..............................................$$

$$X = 3 \quad ..............................................$$

**18.8.14** The equation for predicting $Y$ from $X$ in a given situation is determined to be $\hat{Y} = .9X + 16$.

**a** From this equation alone, can one say anything about the degree of relationship between $X$ and $Y$? Why or why not?

..............................................................................................................................

..............................................................................................................................

..............................................................................................................................

..............................................................................................................................

**b** Can one say anything about the magnitude of the standard error of estimate? Why or why not?

...................................................................................................................

...................................................................................................................

...................................................................................................................

**c** From this equation alone, what can be said about the accuracy of predictions based upon it? Explain.

...................................................................................................................

...................................................................................................................

...................................................................................................................

**18.9.15** For the data of Table 18.A, the following facts are true.

$$r_{XY}^2 \approx .826 \qquad S_Y^2 \approx 6.3$$

**a** Estimate $\tilde{\sigma}_{y \cdot x}^2$ using (18.20).

...................................................................

**b** What is the value of $\tilde{\sigma}_{y \cdot x}$? (Leave answer in terms of square root sign.)

...................................................................

**c** How should your answer to part **b** compare to the answer of part **g** of 18.8.13?

...................................................................

**18.9.16** Why, ordinarily, is the population estimate of a standard error of estimate to be preferred over the sample value as an index of accuracy of prediction?

...................................................................................................................

...................................................................................................................

...................................................................................................................

...................................................................................................................

...................................................................................................................

...................................................................................................................

...................................................................................................................

...................................................................................................................

**18.9.17** Consider the situation of 18.6.8. Suppose that the sample involved consisted of 50 students.

**a** What is the standard error of estimating $B$ from $A$ *for this sample*?

...................................................................

**b** Estimate (to the nearest tenth) the *population value* of this standard error.

.................................................................

**c** Assume the $B$-scores for the subpopulation of students whose $A$-scores are 110 to be normal in form. In the space provided for the figure for exercise 18.9.17, sketch the frequency curve for the $B$-score distribution for this subpopulation. On the score scale indicate the estimated value of the mean and the *estimated* values of the points 1, 2, and 3 standard deviations above and below the mean.

**d** A randomly selected student has an $A$-score of 110. What is the approximate probability that his $B$-score is above 133? In the curve sketched in answer to part **c**, shade the area representing the approximate proportion of this subpopulation of students whose $B$-scores are above 133.

.................................................................

**18.10.18** Suppose that the variables $X$ and $Y$ are linearly related for a certain population of subjects and that the condition of homoscedasticity is satisfied. The standard deviation of the $Y$-values for the entire population is 12. The standard deviation of $Y$-values for a subpopulation of individuals all of whom have the same $X$-value is 10. What is the coefficient of correlation between $X$ and $Y$ for the entire population?

.................................................................

**18.10.19** In a bivariate table involving the variables $X$ and $Y$, it is found that the standard deviation of all the $Y$-values is approximately twice as large as the standard deviation of the $Y$-values in any $X$-column. What, approximately, is the value of $r$ for the tabulated data?

.................................................................

**18.10.20** Suppose that for a given population the relationship between variables $X$ and $Y$ is linear and homoscedastic. Let the standard deviations of the $X$- and $Y$-distributions for a random sample from this population be represented by $S_X$ and $S_Y$.

**a** What is the sample standard error of estimating $Y$ from $X$ if the sample value of $r$ is zero?

.................................................................

**b** By what percentage is the standard error of estimate called for in part **a** reduced if the sample value of $r$ is increased to:

.30? ..........................................................

.50? ..........................................................

.90? ..........................................................

.95? ..........................................................

**c** Does an increase in the sample value of $r$ from .30 to .50 reduce the sample standard error of estimate as much as an increase in the sample value of $r$ from .90 to .95?

..............................................................

**d** How large must the sample value of $r$ be if the sample standard error of estimating $Y$ from $X$ is to be reduced to:

**1** One-half its value in **a**? ..............................................................

**2** One-third its value in **a**? ..............................................................

**3** Zero? ..............................................................

**e** In terms of the sample value of $r$, what is the value of the ratio of the sample standard error of estimating $Y$ from $X$ to the sample standard deviation of $Y$? (What is the value of the ratio $S_{y \cdot x}/S_Y$?)

..............................................................

**f** Does the ratio $S_{y \cdot x}/S_Y$ increase or decrease as the degree of relationship between $X$ and $Y$ increases?

..............................................................

**g** What is the maximum value of the ratio $S_{y \cdot x}/S_Y$, and what degree of relationship between $X$ and $Y$ gives rise to this maximum?

..............................................................

**h** What is the minimum value of the ratio $S_{y \cdot x}/S_Y$, and what degree of relationship between $X$ and $Y$ gives rise to this minimum?

..............................................................

**i** The ratio $S_{y \cdot x}/S_Y$ is sometimes referred to as the "coefficient of alienation" between $X$ and $Y$. Explain why.

..............................................................

..............................................................

..............................................................

..............................................................

..............................................................

**18.10.21** Again consider a sample collection of pairs of $X$- and $Y$-values. Assume the relationship between $X$ and $Y$ to be fairly high, positive, linear, and homoscedastic, and let the standard deviations of $X$ and $Y$ for the sample be represented by $S_X$ and $S_Y$.

**a** Suppose that those individuals whose $X$-scores are either very large or very small are withdrawn from the sample collection. What will be the effect on the values of the following variables?

$S_Y$ ................................................    $r$ ......................................................

$S_{y \cdot x}/S_Y$ ...............................    $S_{y \cdot x}$ ...............................................

**b** What is meant by the statement that the value of $r$ depends on the "range of talent"?

................................................................................................................................

................................................................................................................................

................................................................................................................................

**c** What is meant by the statement that the standard error of estimate is independent of the range of talent?

................................................................................................................................

................................................................................................................................

**d** What advantage does $S_{y \cdot x}$ have over $r$ as an index of accuracy of prediction?

................................................................................................................................

................................................................................................................................

**e** Suppose that is is desired to compare the accuracy of predicting college grade-point average from high school grade-point average with the accuracy of predicting occupational success as measured by monthly income in dollars from college grade-point average. Which index of accuracy, the correlation coefficient or the standard error of estimate, should be used? Why?

................................................................................................................................

................................................................................................................................

................................................................................................................................

................................................................................................................................

................................................................................................................................

**18.10.22** For a given population of 12-year-old girls, the mean weight ($\mu_W$) is 90 pounds, and the standard deviation of weights ($\sigma_W$) is 18 pounds. One individual is selected at random from this population.

**a** On the basis of just this information, what is the best estimate one can make of the weight of this individual?

..................................................................

**b** What is the standard error of this estimate?

..................................................................

**c** Now suppose it is known that the correlation between weight and height for this population ($\rho_{WH}$) is .75, and that the mean ($\mu_H$) and standard deviation ($\sigma_H$) of heights for this population are 60 and 3 inches, respectively. Suppose further that it is now known that the selected individual is 64 inches tall. With this additional information what is the best estimate one can make of the weight of this individual? [*Note:* Since population data are given, equation (18.9) can be written as

$$\hat{W} = (\rho_{WH})(\sigma_W/\sigma_H)(H - \mu_H) + \mu_W.]$$

..................................................................

**d** What is the standard error of this estimate? (*Note:* Since population data are given, we have $\sigma_{W \cdot H} = \sigma_W \sqrt{1 - \rho_{WH}^2}$.)

..................................................................

**e** Express the difference between the answers to **b** and **d** as a percentage of the answer to **b**.

..................................................................

**f** How does the result of **e** agree with the percentage of reduction in the standard error of estimate shown in Figure 18.9 (p. 492 of the text) for $r = .75$?

..................................................................

**g** The previous parts of this exercise were concerned with predicting weight from height. Assume it is desired to predict height from weight. (*Note:* Exercise 18.5.5 discussed, at some length, the idea of predicting $X$, given $Y$. In this part of the present exercise we extend this idea to the concept of standard error.) If $\sigma_{W \cdot H} = \sigma_W \sqrt{1 - \rho_{WH}^2}$, then $\sigma_{H \cdot W} = \sigma_H \sqrt{1 - \rho_{WH}^2}$. What is the standard error of estimating height given weight?

..................................................................

**h** The standard error of estimate in part **g** is smaller than the standard error for estimating weight given height (part **d**). Does this mean that it is possible to predict height from weight much more accurately than it is possible to predict weight from height? Why or why not?

.........................................................................................................................

.........................................................................................................................

.........................................................................................................................

.........................................................................................................................

.........................................................................................................................

**18.11.23** Assuming that the distribution of intelligence test scores for husbands has the same mean, standard deviation, and form as the distribution of intelligence test scores for wives, and assuming a linear relationship between the intelligence of husbands and wives, each of the following statements is true.

    **1** Women of superior intelligence tend to be married to men who are above average in intelligence but who, nevertheless, tend to be inferior in intelligence to their wives.

    **2** Men who are above average in intelligence tend to be more intelligent than their wives.

**a** Explain how, in spite of the apparent contradiction of these statements, it is nevertheless possible for both of them to be true.

.........................................................................................................................

.........................................................................................................................

.........................................................................................................................

.........................................................................................................................

.........................................................................................................................

.........................................................................................................................

.........................................................................................................................

.........................................................................................................................

.........................................................................................................................

.........................................................................................................................

.........................................................................................................................

.........................................................................................................................

**b** What statistical term is used to refer to this phenomenon?

.........................................................................................................................

**18.11.24** Scores on two achievement tests, X and Y, are linearly and positively related for a given population of pupils. Pupil A made a score on Test X that was two standard deviations above the population mean. Why would it not be a good guess that her score on Test Y would also be two standard deviations above the population mean?

...................................................................................................................................

...................................................................................................................................

...................................................................................................................................

...................................................................................................................................

**18.11.25a** Is there any positive relationship between achievement in algebra and achievement in French for ninth-grade pupils?

...................................................................................

**b** Are pupils who are very superior in algebra ordinarily equally superior in French?

...................................................................................

**c** Are pupils who are very superior in French ordinarily equally superior in algebra?

...................................................................................

**d** What phenomenon is involved in this and the two preceding exercises?

...................................................................................................................................

...................................................................................................................................

...................................................................................................................................

...................................................................................................................................

...................................................................................................................................

**18.11.26** An individual who has a mental age (MA) of 13 years as measured by a given intelligence test is one whose performance on the given test is the same as the average performance of 13-year-old children in general. Similarly, an individual who has an age equivalent (AE) of 13 years as measured by a given educational achievement test battery is one whose performance on the given test battery is the same as the average performance of 13-year-olds in general. A junior high school counselor wishes to identify, for special help, seventh-grade pupils who are "underachievers." He defines as underachievers children whose AE's are lower than their MA scores. In compiling his data he notices that many of the "dull" pupils (pupils whose MA scores are low in comparison to their chronological ages) tend to have AE scores that are higher than their MA scores. Conversely, he observes that many of the "bright" pupils (pupils whose MA scores are high in comparison to their chronological ages) tend to have AE scores that are lower than their MA scores. He concludes that the incidence of underachievement is much greater among bright than among dull pupils. Explain the fallacy in his definition of underachievement.

..........................................................................................................................

..........................................................................................................................

..........................................................................................................................

..........................................................................................................................

..........................................................................................................................

..........................................................................................................................

..........................................................................................................................

..........................................................................................................................

**18.11.27** Scores on two forms, A and B, of a third-grade reading comprehension test have means of 50 and standard deviations of 10. The correlation $r_{AB}$ is known to be .80.

The principal of a particular elementary school decides to use these tests as part of the evaluation of a remedial reading program. Form A is given to all 100 third-grade students in his school. On the basis of these test results students who have scores below 35 are assigned to the remedial program. The mean score on Form A for this remedial group was 30. After two months in the program the group is retested with Form B. The mean score for the remedial group on this form turned out to be 34. Assume the *difference* between 34 and 30 is statistically significant at the .05 level. Explain why it is unreasonable in this situation to interpret the significant difference between means as an indication that the remedial program was effective. (*Hint:* Consider what score you would predict on Test B for students with a score of 30 on Test A. This predicted score is expected even when no remedial program is employed.)

..........................................................................................................................

..........................................................................................................................

..........................................................................................................................

..........................................................................................................................

..........................................................................................................................

..........................................................................................................................

**18.12.28** For the data of Table 18.A find:

   **a** The regression coefficient
(see 18.4.3g) ...................................................................

   **b** The regression equation in
terms of $\hat{Y}$ and $X$ (see
18.4.3h) ...................................................................

   **c** The residual sum of
squares (see 18.4.3l) ...................................................................

**18.12.29** For a sample of 27 pairs of $X$- and $Y$-values, the sum of squares of the deviations of the $Y$-values from $\overline{Y}$ is 2,700, and the sum of the squares of the differences between actual and regressed $Y$-values is 600. Find:

   **a** $r_{XY}$ ...................................................................

   **b** $\tilde{\sigma}_{y \cdot x}$ ...................................................................

# 19

# Sampling-Error Theory for Simple Linear Regression

**19.1.1** The regression model described in Section 19.1 of the text involves two types of specifications, namely, those pertaining to the population sampled and those pertaining to the method of sampling. Table 18.A (exercise 18.2.1) contains 20 pairs of scores (independent variable $X$ and dependent variable $Y$) for each of 20 individuals selected at random from a population of such individuals. Suppose this population conforms to those specifications of the regression model that pertain to the population.

**a** What is the *form* of the distribution of $Y$-scores for those members of the population whose $X$-scores are 4?

**b** Does the *form* of the distribution of $Y$-scores for members of the population who make the same $X$-score depend on the value of the $X$-score? That is, is the *form* of the distribution of $Y$-scores for members of the population whose $X$-scores are 4 different from that for members of the population whose $X$-scores are, say, 2? If so, how do the distributions differ?

**c** Suppose it is known that the variance of the distribution of $Y$-scores for those members of the population whose $X$-scores are 4 is 1.21. What is the variance of the $Y$-scores for members of the population whose $X$-scores are 9? Explain.

**d** In addition to specifications regarding *form* and *variability*, what further specification does this model impose upon the various distributions of $Y$-scores for members of the population making the same $X$-score?

**19.1.2** Again consider the situation of 19.1.1. Suppose that the sampling experiment that gave rise to the data of Table 18.A is repeated a second time in accordance with the rules of the regression model that pertain to or govern such repetition.

**a** Would this second sample, like the first (see Table 18.A), contain exactly five individuals whose $X$-scores are 4?

**b** Would it be possible for this second sample to contain any individuals whose $X$-scores are 3?

**c** The value of $\overline{X}$ for the data of Table 18.A is 5. On the basis of this information, is it possible to say precisely what the value of $\overline{X}$ would be in the case of the second sample? Explain.

**d** The value of $\overline{Y}$ for the data of Table 18.A is 7. On the basis of this information, is it possible to say precisely what the value of $\overline{Y}$ would be in the case of this second sample? Explain.

**e** In this second sample what is the value of the following?

$$k$$

$$\sum_{j=1}^{k} n_j$$

**f** In this second sample what is the value of $n_j$, where $j$ identifies the subsample of individuals whose $X$-scores are as follows?

9

8

7

**g** Now suppose the sampling experiment is repeated indefinitely in accordance with the rules of the regression model. Suppose that the following statistical indexes are computed for each sample. Indicate by placing check marks in the appropriate blanks those indexes that would vary in value—that is, have sampling distributions.

$\overline{X}$........................................................    $\overline{Y}$........................................................

$S_X$........................................................    $S_Y$........................................................

$b$........................................................    $c$........................................................

$r$........................................................    $\tilde{\sigma}_{y \cdot x}$........................................................

**19.2.3** Assume the data of Table 18.A (exercise 18.2.1) have been randomly selected from a bivariate population that meets the requirements of the regression model with $Y$ as the dependent variable. The following values have been previously determined for these data:

$$\begin{array}{ccc} \overline{Y} = 7 & \overline{X} = 5 & r = .91 \\ \sum y^2 = 126 & \sum x^2 = 96 & \tilde{\sigma}_{y \cdot x} = 1.1 \\ S_Y = \sqrt{6.3} & S_X = \sqrt{4.8} & N = 20 \end{array}$$

Also, the least-squares prediction line is

$$\hat{Y} = 1.04x + 7$$

That is, $b = 1.04$, $X$ is in deviation form, and the intercept is $\overline{Y} = 7$.

**a** Using equation (19.6), find $\tilde{\sigma}_b$.

........................................................

**b** The value of $\tilde{\sigma}_b$ in part **a** is approximately .11. Sketch in the space provided for the figure for 19.2.3b the *approximate* sampling distribution of the regression coefficient $b$. On the scale of values of $b$, indicate the value of the mean of this approximate sampling distribution, and also the values of the points that are 1, 2, and 3 standard errors above and below this mean.

**c** Which of the following characteristics of the sampling distribution called for in part **b** are exactly correct and which are approximately correct? Answer by writing *exact* or *approximate* in the given blank.

   **1** The value of the mean   ........................................................

   **2** The value of the standard error  ........................................................

   **3** The normality of the form  ........................................................

**d** Again using the information contained in this sample, sketch in the space provided for the figure for 19.2.3d the *approximate* sampling distribution of $\overline{Y}$. On the scale of values of $\overline{Y}$, indicate the value of the mean of this approximate sampling distribution, and also the values of the points that are 1, 2, and 3 standard errors above and below this mean. [*Note:* Use (19.10) to obtain $\tilde{\sigma}_{\overline{Y}}$.]

**19.3.4** Consider again the situation of the previous exercise.

**a** Suppose it is desired to test the hypothesis that the population value of the regression coefficient ($\beta$) is zero against the alternative that it is greater than zero. If .01 is adopted as the level of significance, specify the appropriate critical region for this test in terms of the scale of values of the test statistic $t$.

...............................................................................

**b** What is the value of the test statistic $t$ for the sample data?

...............................................................................

**c** What is the outcome of this statistical test?

...............................................................................

**d** Assume this hypothesis ($\beta = 0$) to be true. If this test were repeated indefinitely, each repetition being based on a sample selected independently and according to the stipulations of the regression model, what is the probability of a Type I error?

..................................................................

**e** Is the probability value called for in part **d** exactly or only approximately correct?

..................................................................

**19.4.5** Given the data of Table 18.C (exercise 18.5.4) and considering $Y$ as the dependent variable, establish the 99 percent confidence intervals for the population values of the slope ($\beta$) and the $Y$-intercept ($\mu_Y$) of the regression line in deviation form. (*Notes:* For these data $\tilde{\sigma}_{y \cdot x} = 3.0$. Use $t$ for $df = \infty$.)

$$\underline{\beta}_1, \bar{\beta}_1 = \text{..................................................}$$

$$\underline{\mu}_{Y_1}, \bar{\mu}_{Y_1} = \text{..................................................}$$

**19.5.6** Assume the data of Table 18.A (exercise 18.2.1) have been randomly selected from a bivariate population that meets the requirements of the regression model with $Y$ as the dependent variable.

**a** Estimate $\tilde{\sigma}_{\hat{Y}}$ for the subpopulation of individuals whose $X$-scores are 4 [use (19.19)]. (*Note:* Values for $\tilde{\sigma}_{y \cdot x}$ and $\sum x^2$ are given in 19.2.3.)

................................................................

**b** The value of $\tilde{\sigma}_{\hat{Y}}$ for part **a** is approximately .27. Sketch in the space provided for the figure for 19.5.6 the *approximate* sampling distribution of the estimated value ($\hat{Y}$) of the mean ($\mu_{y \cdot x}$) of the subpopulation of individuals whose $X$-scores are 4. (*Note:* $\hat{Y} = 1.04X + 1.8$.) On the scale of this statistic, indicate the value of the mean of this approximate sampling distribution, and also the values of the points that are 1, 2, and 3 standard errors above and below this mean.

**c** Suppose you were to sketch the sampling distribution of $\hat{Y}$ for the subpopulation of individuals whose $X$-scores are 5. How would this sketch compare with that for the sampling distribution of $\overline{Y}$ called for in 19.2.3**d**.

................................................................

**d** There are no individuals in the sample of Table 18.A representing the subpopulation of individuals whose $X$-scores are 7. Would it be possible, nevertheless, to sketch the *approximate* sampling distribution of $\hat{Y}$ for this subpopulation on the basis of the information contained in the data of Table 18.A? If you believe it to be possible, give the values of the mean and standard deviation of this approximate sampling distribution.

..................................................................................................................................

..................................................................................................................................

..................................................................................................................................

**19.6.7** Table 19.A gives the limits of the 95 percent confidence intervals for the $Y$-means ($\mu_{y \cdot x}$-values) of certain subpopulations of individuals making the same $X$-score. These subpopulations are the ones involved in the data of Table 18.A (exercise 18.2.1).

**a** Fill in the values missing from Table 19.A. (*Note:* When $X = 8$, $\tilde{\sigma}_{\hat{Y}} = .42$; when $X = 3$, $\tilde{\sigma}_{\hat{Y}} = .33$.)

**b** On the grid provided for this exercise, draw the line for predicting $Y$, given $X$ ($\hat{Y} = 1.04X + 1.8$).

**c** On this same grid, plot the $\mu_{y \cdot x}$- and $\bar{\mu}_{y \cdot x}$-values corresponding to each $X$-value. Using the $\mu_{y \cdot x}$-points as guides, sketch the curve representing the $\mu_{y \cdot x}$ locus. Similarly sketch the curve representing the $\bar{\mu}_{y \cdot x}$ locus.

**d** What do these two curves locate or determine?

..................................................................................................................................

..................................................................................................................................

..................................................................................................................................

**Table 19.A**

| $X$ | $\hat{Y}$ | $\underline{\mu}_{y \cdot x}$ | $\bar{\mu}_{y \cdot x}$ |
|---|---|---|---|
| 9 | 11.2 | 10.1 | 12.2 |
| 8 | | | |
| 7 | 9.1 | 8.4 | 9.8 |
| 6 | 8.0 | 7.5 | 8.6 |
| 5 | 7.0 | 6.5 | 7.5 |
| 4 | 6.0 | 5.4 | 6.5 |
| 3 | | | |
| 2 | 3.9 | 3.0 | 4.8 |
| 1 | 2.8 | 1.8 | 3.9 |

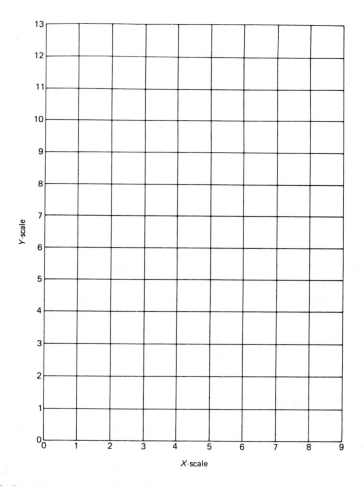

X-scale

**19.7.8** Consider the situation of 18.5.4.

**a** Find (to the nearest tenth) the estimated standard error of the distribution of errors in individual estimates (i.e., the distribution of values of $Y - \hat{Y}$) for members of the subpopulation of individuals whose $X$-scores are 70. Use (19.23). (*Note:* For these data $\tilde{\sigma}_{y \cdot x} = 3.0$.)

...................................................................

**b** What $\hat{Y}$-value (to the nearest tenth) is used as the predicted score for $Y$ for all members of this subpopulation? (See 18.5.4b for the prediction equation.)

...................................................................

**c** Now suppose the $\hat{Y}$-value called for in part **b** above is added to each of the error values referred to in part **a**. In the space provided for the figure for 19.7.8, sketch the resulting distribution. On the scale, indicate the mean of this distribution and the values of the points 1, 2, and 3 standard deviations above and below the mean.

**d** A randomly selected student has an $X$-score of 70. What is the *approximate* probability that his actual $Y$-score is above 27? (Use the table for the normally distributed $z$ in making this approximation.)

................................................................

**e** Establish the 95 percent confidence interval for the actual $Y$-score of an individual whose $X$-score is 70. (Use $t$ for $df = \infty$.)

................................................................

**19.8.9** A certain professor of psychology developed the notion that intelligence is a function of the speed of the transmission of the nerve impulse. Using 20 of his students as subjects, he first measured their intelligence ($X$-variate). He then measured the time ($Y$-variate) between stimulus and response in the knee jerk of each of these subjects. The measurements of the knee-jerk reaction times, which were made with knowledge of each subject's intelligence score at hand, were obtained by means of a rather crude method that involved some subjective error in observation. The correlation between the two variates for the 20 subjects was $-.50$.

**a** State the statistical hypothesis that when tested with these data would provide a check of the possible validity of the professor's notion.

................................................................

**b** What is (are) the alternative possibility(ies) to this hypothesis?

................................................................

**c** The professor tests this statistical hypothesis using .05 as the level of significance. Specify the critical region in terms of the scale of values of the test statistic $t$.

...........................................................................................................................

**d** What is the particular value of $t$ for the sample data at hand?

...........................................................................................

**e** Because this value of $t$ falls in the critical region, rejection of the hypothesis is indicated. The professor published his results with the conclusion that intelligence is largely dependent on speed of transmission of nerve impulse. Should the professor have held up publication until additional subjects could be tested? Do you think his conclusion is unwarranted simply because of the small number of cases investigated? (Assume the requirements of the regression model to be fully satisfied.) Justify your position.

...........................................................................................................................

...........................................................................................................................

...........................................................................................................................

...........................................................................................................................

...........................................................................................................................

...........................................................................................................................

...........................................................................................................................

...........................................................................................................................

**f** Cite two possible explanations of the outcome of this statistical test that are different from the one adopted by the professor.

...........................................................................................................................

...........................................................................................................................

...........................................................................................................................

...........................................................................................................................

...........................................................................................................................

...........................................................................................................................

...........................................................................................................................

**g** The professor's theory is not one that is generally accepted by psychologists. Comment on the level of significance adopted by the professor in view of the controversial nature of his notion.

..........................................................................................................................................

..........................................................................................................................................

..........................................................................................................................................

..........................................................................................................................................

..........................................................................................................................................

..........................................................................................................................................

..........................................................................................................................................

..........................................................................................................................................

..........................................................................................................................................

**19.8.10** It is desired to test the hypothesis that the correlation ($\rho$) between variates $X$ and $Y$ is zero for a certain population. The alternatives are $\rho < 0$ and $\rho > 0$, and it is desired that $\alpha = .01$. What is the smallest absolute value of the sample correlation ($r$) that will lead to the decision to reject the hypothesis if:

    **a** $N = 10$? ...............................................................

    **b** $N = 122$? ...............................................................